Supermac

SUPERMAC

Phillip McCallen

with Phil Woods

Aureus

First Published in hardback 2000
This paperback edition published 2021
©2000 ©2021 Phillip McCallen and Phil Woods
©2000 ©2021 Aureus Publishing Limited

Cover photograph © James Wright - Double Red

A catalogue record for this book is available from the British Library.

ISBN 978 1 899750 50 4

Aureus Publishing Limited
Castle Court
Castle-upon-Alun
St Brides Major
Vale of Glamorgan
CF32 0TN

Tel : 01656 880033
Int. tel : +44 1656 880033

www.aureus.co.uk
sales@aureus.co.uk

Contents

Acknowledgements

My thanks go first to Phillip's mother Betty and Brian Overend for their diligence in producing a superb set of scrap books that made my normal sources of research redundant. Brian's diligence as statistician and archivist provided invaluable assistance and I'd like to thank Simon Brown too, for helping out a stranger.

I'm very grateful to Phillip's wife Manda for the important contribution she has made to the book, her frankness, friendship, help and hospitality too. I'd also like to thank all the other people who have contributed to this book with their anecdotes, information, memories and pictures.

Finally, I'd like to extend my congratulations and thanks to all the race team members, timekeepers, sponsors, medical personnel, unpaid helpers and unsung heroes who have contributed so much to Phillip's racing career; I know they all feel as privileged as I do to have shared such wonderful times together.

Phil Woods

This book is dedicated to my Dad, Eric McCallen,
so we can share my success.

1

I knew it was going to be a big accident long before I hit the wall. I was on the absolute limit, riding a kitted 750 Honda RC30 in the 1990 Isle of Man Senior TT. It had slipped out of gear and hit neutral around eighty miles an hour, coming into a dangerous corner called The Nook.

I remember carrying on straight across the road and hitting the high grass bank on the left hand side there. I realised for the first time it was actually a stone wall covered in grass and thought this wasn't the ideal way to find that out.

The bike exploded on impact, I let go and we rocketed up the bank - eyewitnesses in the crowd couldn't believe how high we both went up in the air. "That's that," I thought to myself, "job over!" before I smashed into the middle of the road. I didn't feel any pain, nothing except a terrible, deafening noise in my ears. I couldn't believe there was no pain at all, nothing except blackness and a weightless, kind of detached, floating feeling, that is very hard to describe.

Vision of a sort started to come back and the floating sensation increased. I couldn't work out what the little white dots underneath me were and it took some time to realise they were white houses next to the road. I realised I was looking down at the track getting smaller and smaller and there, suddenly set out below me, sitting in all their majestic beauty lay the fields, mountain, hills and villages which are scattered across the Isle of Man, getting smaller all the time. "This is it!" I thought. "At least I'm going in the right direction!"

The previous few days flashed through my mind. It'd been an altogether unlucky week for me, really disappointing because I'd swept everything before me on my first visit to the island in the 1988 Manx meeting, winning two races, the first 'newcomer' ever to do so. I'd raced motorcycles at just about every track and road meeting at home in Ireland and of course had heard all about how tough the TT course was. But the first time I rode it I couldn't believe how wide the place was - as big as a motorway compared to most of the tracks I was used to risking my neck at.

I'd graduated to the TT in 1989, leaving Kawasaki for support from Honda in what I regarded as my 'learning year' on the island. Now in 1990 I'd come to the TT to prove how good I was. The Lightweight (250cc) race was bittersweet really as I had a new RS250 Honda and finished in the top six, but I could have done so much better if the bike hadn't developed carburation problems early on in the race, which never cleared.

The whole week had started really badly because I'd had to pull out of the opening Formula 1 event when the linkage broke on my RC30's twelve thousand pounds worth of carburettors. It had started to run on only two of the four cylinders so I pulled off the course at Kirk Michael, borrowed some tools from a spectator who had his road bike there and whipped the RC30's fuel tank off. It was a simple break to fix so I ripped some wire off a fence, lashed the broken parts together, fired the bike up and restarted the race a lap down.

I so wanted to do well because I knew I could get up there with the top boys, but realised I needed as much practice as possible, so I kept going, learning the course all the time. The bad luck was desperately frustrating, but just made me even more determined to do well in TT fortnight's final race, the Senior.

I'd qualified way down the field over a week earlier in practice, somewhere past twentieth place, as I was still learning so much with every near forty mile lap. The weather was showery, wet then dry then wet again. I'd started well, going like a bat out of hell and soon found myself getting great time and place signals from around the course and suddenly I was in contention. I was flat out, fighting with Trevor Nation on his rotary engined Norton, swapping second and third places with him all the time on my RC30 and staying in touch with my team mate Carl Fogarty, who was in the lead a few seconds ahead of us.

It'd been an unlucky week but finally I knew this was my big chance to make my mark at the TT and I was determined to get a result. The roads were very wet in places - it'd been raining hard earlier in the day, but by the first pit stop I took a bit of a gamble and changed to cut slick tyres.

I'd spotted Trevor Nation still had wet tyres on his super quick Wankel engined Norton and by the fourth lap a dry line was starting to appear. I knew this would force the Norton team to change to cut slicks too, or intermediates - far more time consuming than on my endurance style single sided swinging arm RC30 - all I had to do was refuel and pull out all the stops on the last two laps.

Brilliant! The tyre gamble had paid off and the strategy was working, my time signals around the course showed second place was mine for the taking - Fogarty had drawn further away in the lead and was uncatchable by now unless he had a problem, but I was still flat out with Trevor Nation hot on my heels.

We'd had trouble with the RC30 jumping out of gear all year (it wasn't until later that we traced the problem to a little spring linkage on the gearbox selector drum). I was really flying at the end of the fourth lap and came screaming into The Nook, which is just before the start / finish straight on the Glencrutchery Road, changing down from third to second, when the same thing happened and it jumped second gear and went straight into neutral.

If I hadn't been on the limit maybe I could've saved it, but when you're flat out like that you need everything to help stop the bike. In gear, with the throttle shut off, the engine is slowing down the rear wheel, but it's also loading the front of the bike, giving you front end grip for the extreme braking I needed.

It seemed like the bike took a lifetime to cross the road, I was fighting it all the way but knew it was useless. There was an almighty bang on impact, total blackness and then as I said, I was just floating, higher and higher. The little white houses got smaller and smaller and I was thinking to myself "This is definitely it - I'm on my way to Heaven!" The feeling wasn't bad at all, my mind was quite peaceful, except for the terrible noise which wouldn't stop.

A girl's face floated into my vision and spoke to me. "Everything's fine, don't worry Phillip, don't worry, you're OK now with us. You're in the helicopter and we're taking you to the hospital - you've only been out a few minutes." "Heaven will have to wait a bit longer for me then!" I thought - and that was the end of my TT for the year.

Crashing a bike is one of my earliest memories. The first is a big tin bath at my family's house in Ballalisk - Betty, my Mum, has still got it today - it's full of plants, but I can remember getting in it for a bath as if it were yesterday. We didn't have a proper bath in our house, which we were only living in temporarily. My Dad was going to build a new one for us as he was a good bricklayer and builder, but he got multiple sclerosis around that time, so he never did build it.

One of my earliest memories of him is watching him take the stabiliser wheels off a little blue bicycle which I had inherited from my older brother Ronald. Taking those wheels off was significant, I remember really wanting them off because that meant I was a big boy and could ride without them. Everyday I just wanted to ride along the lane outside the house, which went down quite a hill with right and left hand corners at the bottom. We weren't allowed to do it of course, it was a really dangerous thing to do apart from the traffic and I got beaten whenever I was caught doing it.

Nevertheless, I used to race flat out down the hill with a crowd of lads from the local park all the time. There was kind of a dump on a bit of wasteland off to the left at the bottom - someone always crashed there, including me. My Aunt Gwen was looking after Noel, my younger brother, Ronald and I one day while my Mum was away visiting Dad in hospital. I'd fallen off the bike at the bottom of the hill and come back to the house with my teeth sticking through my lip and a bust up face.

I came in the house screaming and going mad with no idea Aunt Gwen was terrified of blood. All she did was start screaming too and threw me outside onto the grass with a towel over my head and the blood pouring out onto the grass. The only nursing I got was from our Lakeland terrier Furry and the chickens (we had one each in our hen house at the bottom of the garden). I can't remember what happened to the blue bike - I expect I wrote it off but I lived to tell the tale.

In three years the disease went straight through my Dad before it finally overcame him in 1973 when I was nine. It's a terrible illness that affects people in different ways - my Mum still sees patients today that she met at the same time my Dad was ill. He got one of those blue AC three wheeler invalid carriages and was well enough then to build me a little seat inside so I could ride around with him. I was starting in primary school around then but always went with him if I had the chance. I was his runner - we'd stop at all sorts of places and I'd take messages in for him or dash into the shops to pick something up.

Of course, I'd egg him on to go as fast as possible in the little three wheeler and remember the thing heeled right over and trailing the ground with the Villiers two stroke engine screaming, it's a wonder we never turned the thing over - Mum would have had a fit if she'd known what was going on. Dad could walk with crutches but as the MS progressed he needed callipers and finally a wheelchair - more wheels!

I'd take him out in the chair and we'd wait for a downhill section when I'd sprint behind him to get the speed built up, then jump on the back and we'd go careering down the hill together with Dad controlling the steering with the brakes. Mum was with us one day when I fired us down a hill and leapt on the back a bit too heavy sending the chair, me and my Dad flying over backwards; I nearly killed him but we ended up all over the road laughing our heads off, with Mum going berserk behind us.

Me and my brothers had no idea how sick he was, Mum kept it from us while she never stopped working. She seldom speaks of those times and we tend to avoid the subject, because I know it causes pain to this day, getting on for thirty years later. One time she used his name strongly I remember, was when I got my second moped at sixteen. "If your Dad was alive you wouldn't be having that!" she said. He'd had a motorbike, there's a black and white picture of Mum and him on a 250 BSA and I think he had a bad accident on it before they were married and was unconscious for a day and in hospital for a week. I expect that was the reason the motorbike went and he bought an Austin A30 before they got married.

Her father was a farmer in Ballyknock who had opened a general shop with a Post Office and a butchery in Laurelvale and Mum and Aunt Gwen worked on that side of the business. The milk from the family farm went to the local Creamline Dairy for pasteurising and bottling and we had three or four milk delivery runs. Once we were old enough to walk we were taught to carry milk bottles and it was our job in school holidays and at the weekends to go out with the vans and deliver the bottles. I was always keen to go because I was allowed to drive the van up and down the private lanes and the parks! I started off just in first gear for a while, but soon got the van into second on the straights and I was driving from a very early age.

We moved into a more modern house - with a bath! - in Ahorey about three miles from the family business. That was where I used to ride my cousin Pearl's bike. She was four or five years older than us and for some reason her ladies bike had been sitting in a shed out the back for ages. The tyres on it were flat and rotten, but I used to ride it around the yard at the back of the shop on its rims, making a terrible racket when I was five or six and get whipped for it.

And that was where I got my first ride on a motorbike. Cousin John had a 50cc Ariel Pixie with a four speed box - really advanced stuff in its day! My big brother and I waited for him to go to work on one of the milk runs and Ronald got the thing started somehow, just pulling and pushing everything to work out what they did, until we were off into the fields and away on my first ride on a motorbike.

Dad was spending more and more time in hospital during the final year of his life, only coming home at weekends to see us. Then he stopped coming home completely and we weren't even allowed to go and see him. The family had a sort of rota, one would go and visit Daddy, while another would look after us - I didn't realise what was wrong - when you're that young you just accept it. I just knew that Dad was sick, but expected him back next week because being sick was something you got better from; people went to hospital sick, got better, then came home.

Mum came home crying on a couple of occasions towards the end when it must have been obvious to her. My Dad's sister Aunt Nora was looking after us one Thursday night; next morning Mum was there when we got up and told us Daddy had died, on 15th March 1973.

The father figure in the house became my Mum's brother Ivan. If Ivan told you to do something you did it and Mum's big threat was always "I'll have to speak to Uncle Ivan about that." and if she did, you were definitely in trouble.

I was starting to earn pocket money on the milk runs or by working in the shop weighing potatoes. The business was good but not good enough for anyone to live for nothing, everyone had to do their bit. Mum always taught us that you only get what you work for. My Grandad worked until he died, we all worked hard, a habit that's never left me to this day. Uncle Ivan was taken sick in 1994, the second year I raced in England. By coincidence he was taken into hospital the same week he'd sold the business and died three weeks later.

The Embassy cigarette representative who called at the shop was Davy Wood, (Joey Dunlop's manager) who was a well known motorbike racer in the late 1960's and early 70's.

Tandragee was only a couple of miles down the road and my Mum's brother Joe had a house on the Tandragee 100 course itself. We'd watch the famous Tandragee 100 motorbike road race, sitting on Uncle Joe's garden wall and we'd look out for Davy Wood in his trademark chequered leathers, flashing past on his Yamaha 250 and I loved it. Davy was quite a famous racer but he realised managing other riders was easier than doing it himself and he's done a great job for Joey and many other motorcycle racers since.

I wasn't of much interest to Davy Wood back then because the only riding I was doing was on my push bike. But to tell you the truth looking back now, I can't ever remember when I wasn't racing it on the roads and footpaths in the parks around Ballalisk. The 'course' around the church was especially good, with a downhill section for speed ending in a big bank which, if you hit it fast enough, launched you into the air over the graveyard. The winner out of us neighbourhood lads would be the one to jump the highest and leap the furthest.

One day, I must have been ten or eleven years old, it got down to me and my childhood friend Paul in a final play off. Paul's jump was the longest anyone had ever seen to date, which I was determined to beat. I pedalled my bike as hard as I could down the hill, hit the bank at a crazy rate of knots and took off like a rocket, flying through the air, before smashing into the electric fence which kept the cows out of the churchyard.

I'd won by a country mile - the judges' decision was unanimous but me and my bike were tangled up in the fence jerking away, being zapped by jolts of electricity every second or so. None of them would help me get out of it for fear of being electrocuted themselves. I must have dug myself out eventually and carried the bike home with two buckled wheels, and that's how I started to learn about mechanicing.

The broken bikes would only go to Billy Hazeley's bike shop in Tandragee if they were seriously damaged. Dad was gone, my uncle did his best to help me, but was busy in the family business of course. So I'd set about trying to fix them myself and learnt to do everything I could, even relacing the wheels with new spokes and all - I thought I was a real whizz kid.

My cousin's boyfriend stopped by one day, he was going to the North West 200 road race. With no Dad around we appreciated opportunities like that for a day out. It was the year the Suzuki works rider Tom Herron was killed on the big 750 two stroke; the bike seemed so fast to me, all exhausts and power, just unreal, screaming past like a banshee. Little was I to know I'd be doing the same thing and winning - only a few short years later.

I started to race my bicycle seriously about fifteen or sixteen years of age, doing a lot of riding around the Tandragee 100 motorcycle race course to get myself fit, I was training hard on my push bike on the roads doing ten miles a day, then fifteen, twenty five and fifty miles on the weekends, very hard training. Around this time, I started taking the train up to Coleraine for the weekend's partying at the North West, sleeping in a tent in a field and having a great time. I was really into going fast on my push bike and a local man called Tom Fletcher asked me to join his club, the Craigavon Veloes and I did a couple of races and began really training like mad. Then the worst thing ever happened when I was about fifteen and a half - a Suzuki AP50 came up for sale for a hundred and eighty pounds - I emptied my bank account and scrounged everything I could and that was the end of push bikes. Tom was so mad, I must've been his big hope.

I was too young to have a licence of course and was becoming a bit of a Jack the lad with no Dad to control me. Mum would have gone mad if she'd found out I had a motorcycle, so I hid it up at the local graveyard and walked home and into the house holding my crash helmet, with Mum thinking my friend Paul had given me a lift back. I'd discovered how much faster I could go on a motorbike than my push bike with none of that pedalling, just a twist of the right hand. "Brilliant, this is the thing to do!" I thought, so I sold all my racing push bikes which I'd hand built with all the best parts - Italian Campagnola chainsets and Weinmann side pull brakes.

From the moment I got it, I rode my little Suzuki from morning till night. I was getting six pounds a week doing the milk run and every penny went on petrol and two stroke oil - I was still only fifteen and a half and of course the police were going to catch up with me sooner or later. I'd given them a run for their money and the slip several times because I knew the local back roads and shortcuts very well from so many years working on the milk runs, knowledge which eventually added 'failing to stop' to the charges.

You've always got an advantage on a bike against a car of course, with alleyways and narrow paths, but one night I was two up on the little 50cc Suzuki coming home from a nightclub with my girlfriend on the back which gained the interest of a police Land Rover. I turned off the lights and tried to lose them around the back roads in a place called Horseshoe Lane, but forgot about the brake light shining out like a beacon for them to follow whenever I dabbed on the anchors. There was a steep climb ahead - I knew if I could get to the top I'd be away and They'd never get me - so the race was on between my little moped, heavily handicapped two up and the police Land Rover.

The flashing blue light was lighting up the whole lane helping me to see and I raced down the other side. They went straight on into a farmyard at the corner at the bottom of the hill and I thought I was away, forgetting the uphill climb on the other side of the lane which widens out there towards the top, so I couldn't keep them back by holding the middle of the road. They got alongside us in the end and forced us sideways into a ditch. Mum found out and that was it.

I was terribly ashamed having to go to Court. The bike had caused so much trouble I was forced to sell it, but it wasn't long before I spotted a 50cc Yamaha FS1-E parked in a customer's garage on my milk run. It was a good looking one in yellow, with black speed blocks, Kenny Roberts style, an immaculate unrestricted 1978 model with only 200 miles on the clock and I had to have it. I was sixteen on September 22nd and got my full licence within the month. By the time the Suzuki case came up in the Juvenile Court I was road legal, being a good boy and lucky to get away with a one pound fine for each charge and a four week ban on each count, to run concurrently. So, I couldn't ride my new bike over Christmas and got a severe bollocking from Uncle Ivan, but I was road legal and away at last.

My friend Paul was always a bit of a lunatic - he got hold of a Suzuki GT250 when he was about sixteen and then moved up to the 380 triple. We'd been out to a nightclub on it one night and were on the way back with a girl sandwiched between us, three up and only two of us with a helmet. The policemen in the squad car we passed obviously felt three was a crowd on the Suzuki, caught us up and tried to pull us over with the sirens. Paul grabbed a big handful of throttle which threw me straight off the back of the bike, but as luck would have it my feet taught under the girl's arms. She held on real tight, if she hadn't I would have been in serious trouble - luckily I was sixteen or seventeen and pretty fit, playing a lot of rugby at the time and I somehow managed to hang on as we screamed off down the road on the 'stroker'. The police never caught up with us, they must have had a heart attack watching what was going on.

We went back to the girl's house. Eventually I got to sleep behind the couch because I had a milk run the next morning and had to be up early. I presume Paul ended up having hanky panky with the girl on the floor of the sitting room because when the door opened, waking me up, a voice said, "Lucy (which isn't her real name) are you not going to bed?" a gruesome face then appeared around the door, looked at me, then saw what was going on in the middle of the room and gasped "Lucy! - you are in bed!"

She started beating the hell out of Paul while I crept out of hiding, got out of the house and fired up the Suzuki; as soon as Paul heard that, he rushed outside, leapt on the back and we made our second escape of the night on the GT380. Having that huge violent woman in her horrible nylon nightie after you was a lot more frightening than being chased by those cops in their squad car I can tell you.

Tandragee Junior High School hadn't held much attraction for me, I never did any more than enough to pass my exams there and was happy to leave with my friend Davy Hamilton, both of us starting at Portadown Technical College on an engineering course. We weren't particularly interested in the academic aspects of education, much preferring practical work to theory. Today, I'd like to take a year out and spend the time in education, especially in computers and technology. I know I'd really enjoy mastering it.

I'd always loved working on my bicycles and now motorbikes, so I decided I was going to be a mechanic and got all the City & Guilds credits and passes at the Technical College. Strangely, I never wrote anything down, just remembered it all. In fact I was accused of cheating at the exams, they couldn't believe I was doing it all from memory but I was. I met a young fellow on that course called Woolsey Coulter. He had a Yamaha 'fizzy' too - a purple one, which had the edge on speed over mine for some reason. We'd head off at lunchtime - in fact at every opportunity we could get to race each other till we fell off, crashing all the time, nothing serious really, just slide offs. We'd meet up in the morning for a scrap on the roads before school, I was always on the limit because his bike was faster and we were always experimenting with jets and removing baffles, trying expansion chambers, anything for more power. Mine had a little nose cone and a racing seat hump all in the Kenny Roberts colours, a beautiful little thing.

Woolsey and I came full circle in the 1999 season when, as reigning British 250 Champion, he rode my Yamaha R6 in the British Supersport Championship whilst I was injured, smashing the lap record at Oulton Park by nearly a second - that takes some doing - before falling off! Nothing changes! He was wearing a set of my leathers at the time, which made a change from destroying our school trousers falling off motorbikes.

I got all the exams at college but couldn't get a job as an apprentice mechanic anywhere and got knocked off the 'fizzy' when I was hit by a car close to home on the Ahorey Road, cracking my spine and fracturing my pelvis, with internal bleeding. I remember walking the two or three hundred yards to my house before collapsing. I'd been for an interview at a fabrication engineers called Food Engineering some weeks before and a letter arrived from the bosses Sam Forbes and Jim Falloon asking me to come in again to see them while I was in hospital recovering from the crash.

They'd hired an apprentice who'd enabled them to get some sort of grant which gave him the advantage over me, but he hadn't lasted, which was why they got in touch again. My Mum rang up and they asked if I could come in to see them again, "No problem." she said, "I'm just going to get him from the hospital." I remember the car Mum fetched - - in getting as close to the door as possible and I hobbled in for the interview on crutches, got the job and funnily enough left the job on crutches twelve years later after a big crash at Daytona!

The works was basically a shed in the middle of an old linen factory that had been converted into a variety of uses, including a livestock market. In fact on Fridays you couldn't get in or out of our place because it was surrounded by a sea of pigs. We were a bit of a sideshow for the farmer who used to peer in at us, but business went well and we soon moved.

I was just about the first employee Sam and Jim had and as the business grew, so did my part in it and my wages. The extra money meant I could save enough for a bigger bike. My flat rate was twenty eight pounds - one week I earned a hundred pounds with a huge amount of overtime and bought a Kawasaki KE175 trail bike. It only lasted a couple of months because it just wasn't quick enough for me and I traded it in for a 250 Suzuki K7 which was a refined replacement for the GT250. I partied a lot in those days, but kept working hard, there was just no stopping me. The Yamaha LC's came in around then, but were giving a lot of trouble. My Suzuki had never let me down once so I traded it in with Ross Raymonds in Portadown, paying cash for a brand new one in 1982.

Frustratingly, the new bike didn't perform anything like the old one, it wouldn't go right for two or three months after I bought it. It would only reach a few thousand revs and then start to splutter, so I was having to change up really early until one night it suddenly cleared and I couldn't believe how it went. I'd been working quite late that night and the Suzuki cleared coming home, revving out full and all of a sudden going like a bomb, unknowingly I flew past a police car which chased me for three or four miles before I was stopped at a routine police check point.

I tried explaining to the police officer what had happened, which was the truth, but he didn't seem too impressed with me or the story, so I was back in trouble for speeding.

By this time I felt I could travel the world on a bike so one day I got started, taking my girlfriend of the time, Mandy, who I'd first met at technical college, down to catch the ferry out of Rosslare into Cherbourg, heading for South of France on the X7. Mandy was moaning about a sore back all the way down to the Mediterranean and it wasn't until some time later I realised that the back pack I'd forced Mandy to carry, which was full of everything we had, (I didn't want to put any luggage on the bike and scratch it!), was terribly heavy - poor girl, perched on the back of the little 250 for a thousand miles or so with half a hundredweight on her back.

It was amazing we ever reached the beaches in the south of France. To start with we stopped for petrol in France and with no language skills whatsoever managed to fill the bike up with paraffin, which made it smoke like a chimney and run like a camel for a long time. We stopped in Bordeaux and couldn't believe how hot it was, but we went off sightseeing anyway. It was my first time on the continent and we liked how there was a bar on every corner. This was thirsty work and we stopped at every one to have a beer, just to quench our thirst.

We got back on the bike that evening to travel back to the campsite and everything was really hazy and wavy - Mandy was feeling the same too and the conclusion we came to was that we had sunstroke - so stupid!

It wasn't until our massive headaches the next day that we realised we'd got drunk. Every lesson I've ever learned in my whole life I seem to have learnt the hard way. I bought an air bed the same morning and we went far too far out to sea, diving into the water to cool off, then sunbathing until I got too hot and diving in again. Mandy got in the shade after a while but I carried on for hours having a whale of a time. The next morning I woke up in so much pain and looked down to find I was covered in blisters the size of tennis balls - very romantic. I was a tough guy by then though, so I decided to burst them with a pin, sitting outside the tent. It wasn't long before a kindly French family took pity on me and got me to hospital where they patched me up as best they could, a bit like trying to cover a huge raw meatball with Elastoplast.

So I got back to Ireland older and wiser, having learnt about beer, French fuel, women's carrying capacity and exposure to sunshine. At least my shoulders were too sore to carry the rucksack and Mandy had to carry on with it, but by this time I knew I could ride a bike and a significant thing happened on the way home.

There were boys on the same ferry with some serious bikes, I remember one was a big water cooled Z1300 Kawasaki and there was a KH400 two stroke triple too, which I thought was some bike at the time. We raced them to Dublin - about a hundred miles or so over those very technical roads there in southern Ireland and completely whipped them, Mandy on the pillion with the huge rucksack on her back and all. In fact we got so far ahead of the pack, we'd been stopped at a little cafe for some time before the rest of the 'field' even showed up - they just couldn't believe it.

I hammered that X7 everywhere, especially going to work. There was a fast, blind, tight left hander on my way there, about a mile or so from the house on the Market Hill Road that's been straightened out a bit now; at the time I could take it about eighty miles an hour on the 250. I knew one of the local dairy farmers had his cows down this bit of road and into the field by eight o'clock, which left it clear for me and my crazy antics.

One morning the milk man had held up the farmer with a chat and he was late taking his cows down the road. At eight fifteen on the dot I came flat out round the corner straight into the herd, locking the bike up sideways and losing it on its side, skittling the legs of thirty to forty cows out from underneath them.

The farmer was rooted to the spot in total shock and couldn't move or speak. Somehow I'd ended up on top of a hedge next to the road, but after I clambered down I picked the smashed bike up, helped the herd of cows back on their feet and got them into the field all by myself. The shit had hit a lot more the fan that morning I can tell you, but luckily, none of the animals had broken legs, some were badly bruised and needed walking for a few weeks, although I'd cut teats off a couple of them, which I did feel bad about. I spent the next few weeks worrying that the farmer was going to sue me - he was doing the same too apparently, worrying I was going to sue him.

I'd spoken before about just such a scenario and it's become a scary thing with me. It seems that when I say, "I wonder what would happen if...", the very same thing happens, so much so, I've learnt not to say it anymore. That was one of the occasions it had happened. At the time you laugh it off but looking back it was a dangerous accident and a dangerous corner too - I'd had moments there before. As I said it's been straightened out a bit now.

I was on the back of my older brother Ronald's Honda CB200 going round there one day, when the school bus pulled out of a side turning right in front of us and I really thought we were gonners. I remember the row of young terrified faces looking out of the windows at us, as Ronald went grass tracking onto the verge, into and out of a ditch and back on the road, keeping going as if nothing had happened. He was a very talented rider, but didn't keep it up.

My younger brother Noel and I were starting to buy and sell some classics as a hobby by then; we had a James Cadet, a Triumph Tiger Cub and a Speed Twin amongst others. Noel had got a Yamaha 350LC, followed by the bees knees of the time, a Honda VFR500F2 which I messed about on. That was when I decided I needed more power.

So I bought a Suzuki GS1000S which cost me so much money to keep running it was unreal. I was leaving long, long black lines up the road everywhere and spending all my wages every week on chains and sprockets and tyres - my record was three hundred miles on a rear tyre. After the early two strokes I'd been used to riding, there was so much power and torque from that big Suzuki four stroke. I'd be passing cars, looking in their windows, while the bike was sideways in fourth gear, coming out of turns in the wet. I just loved playing with it and making her dance. If I didn't make a 140 mph on my way to work - there was only two places you could get up to that sort of speed - then it was a bad day and there was something wrong. This was serious stuff to me.

It had a Dunstall four into one high rise pipe on it, which I'd have trailing the ground around the bend following 'cow' corner on Markethill Road, at a hundred miles an hour, incredibly dangerous. In retrospect it was just natural talent; I didn't realise it then, but it wasn't long before I started to find out. There was a second set of cows I had to watch out for down that way, but they stopped using that bit of road for some reason, which made that section much safer, so I could go faster still.

Work was going well and I started to concentrate on installing Food Engineering's stainless steel fabrications in customers' food and canning factories. One factory in Limerick was a particular favourite as it was packed wall to wall with five or six hundred female workers, from teenage girls upwards.

I disappeared from the job once with a very flimsy excuse, to ask one of the girls for a date and came running back to work through the factory, taking a flying leap at an overhead pole, from which I was going to vault onto the gantry we were working on. I screwed up my takeoff a bit though and only got one hand on the pole, grabbing the live terminal of an arc welder with the other. Holding on to that real tight and being nicely earthed on the metal pole with the other hand turned me into the world's only living firework, the crackling noises only being drowned out by the gales of laughter from above and below. Another lesson learnt.

Well, I may have been a failure at gymnastics, but I always knew where I was on my bike and so did everyone else in my neighbourhood, even down to what time I'd be coming. That didn't include strangers to the area of course, including a new postman I met one morning coming in the opposite direction in his van. I was at a hump on a road at a place called Burke's, which was a ninety mile an hour jump on the Suzuki, which sent the bike straight up in the air on its back wheel after landing, just before a corner which sweeps round to the left. All the postman saw on his first morning was this bike coming at him, straight up in the air at ninety miles an hour; he wasn't to know I was always about a foot from the middle of the road about then, completely in control, ready to bank it on its side and take the corner on the back wheel. I remember thinking that the strange postman's face was white, with an expression looking like someone had put a death wish on him as I screamed past.

It wasn't until after work when I'd gone back to Uncle Ivan's house for my tea (because my Mum was still working), that I found the postman had arrived at my family's Post Office still white and shaking, saying how he'd met this motorbike coming the other way out of control and couldn't believe how the rider had survived what he'd seen.

He'd wrecked the side of his van going off through the hedge and down a steep bank. Of course they asked him what time it was and knew it was me - what a doing I got from Uncle Ivan that night. It became obvious to everyone and eventually to me too that the GS was going to get me sooner or later; 140 miles an hour everywhere. It was just far too fast for the road and so was I, a fatal accident waiting to happen.

I'd got hold of a Honda CR250, a nice competition off-roader sometime before and it was improving my riding immensely, all the lessons I was learning riding it on dirt, I was putting to good use on the road. Some people think I'm really stupid, but I'm quite sensible really. I know when the odds are against me and that's why I started racing, to stop myself getting hurt on the big Suzuki - that really is the truth of it.

I'd always thought only famous people went racing but knew Woolsey Coulter had started competing and another lad I'd been with at Technical College Mark Farmer. And then I had a chance encounter with a racetrack on my CR250 and that was really the start of it all.

2

Racing takes place on Saturdays and Sundays, but I was always too busy earning overtime installing Food Engineering's fabricated equipment in factories at the weekends, while they were closed. My best friend from school (and best man at my wedding) Davy Hamilton was heavily into cars but had a moto-crosser too, so we started to go moto-crossing together.

One day quite by chance we came across a moto-cross track all laid out near Craigavon Lakes for a meeting organised by a guy called John Lynne. There were a lot of moto-cross riders there - I didn't know who they were, I didn't know anyone in motor sport at all and I just joined in on the track and thought that this was a bit of fun. My first impression was I seemed to be sort of beating them really - not whipping them - but definitely giving them a hard time and I was really having brilliant fun just messing about.

Davy had been spectating with John Lynne. They knew one another through the motor trade. On the way home Davy mentioned that John had asked him about me saying, "Who's that lad there, is he a serious rider?" Davy had told him I was just his friend Phillip and that we only went riding together for fun. "See that fellow there your friend's beating Davy?" John had said, pointing to a rider I'd passed and was getting away from, "Well he's in contention for the Irish Championship."

This encounter had given me a bit of a taste for competition. Sunday was the only day I could get off work and we went to a few 'black' meetings, which were races you weren't allowed to ride in, if you were a race licence holder.

Davy had sold his bike but was happy to trailer mine down to the track behind his car for me and spectate while I competed for fun, paying two quid to be able to race all day on a proper track. These were fairly long races, half or three quarters of an hour and pretty tough when you'd been up all night partying, and I learnt a lot of lessons. There was one track with a section on it called the 'Washboard'. The crowd was waving at me and cheering me on as I was leading by a good bit, having come through the field from the back. The trouble was I was starting to feel completely knackered, with my arms feeling like they were about to give way coming down the rutted 'Washboard' section with the ends of the handlebars beating me on the chest.

So I pulled in to the side and the officials rushed over to see what was wrong. "I'm knackered" I said. They just couldn't believe it as I was whipping some good riders, but I really didn't mind, I was still doing it for fun and still am to this day I'm pleased to say.

I didn't realise I was losing out because of the amount of wheel spin I was getting in the races. I just thought that was usual and had no idea how much time it was costing me nor that it was simply down to my tyres. I thought a tyre was worn out when the knobbles had gone. One day someone told me to try reversing the rear, so Davy and me did half way through one meeting and lo and behold, I couldn't believe the grip when I went back out. I was used to coming over the jumps, holding the throttle flat to the stop, I just thought that was what you did. Having turned the tyre round I went out and immediately flipped the bike right over the top of me, I held on for grim death and pulled both my thumbs out of place, it felt like I'd broken both my scaphoids.

That was racing over with for the day, but another enormous lesson learnt. I started to win a few races and earned some prize money, maybe five pounds for a win, but was now learning fast at every meeting. The luck couldn't go on forever of course and I crashed quite heavily in one of Billy Nutt's (the promoter) beach races one day. You could hire the bikes for an hour at a time and race around the sand dunes which was really good fun, a bit like our own mini Paris-Dakar! It teaches you a lot, racing on sand, particularly to keep the throttle wide open to make sure the front stays light because as soon as it's not, it'll start to dig in and then it's only a matter of time before it tips you off.

I'd come off when I'd landed after a jump and was OK, lying on the deck when another bike smashed straight into the middle of my back. Everyone was laughing at me of course and nobody believed I was really hurting quite badly.

We were on the beach later that evening with two young ladies and a few beers when Davy's RS2000 Escort got stuck in the soft sand with the tide coming in. I told him I couldn't push anything because I was in so much pain with my back, but he wasn't having it at all and made me do the shoving which just tipped me over the edge.

I'd been coming in to work Monday mornings a bit beaten up and tired which the boss was starting to notice, but I was in agony on this particular occasion and they sent me off to hospital. The x-rays revealed a cracked and displaced vertebra and I didn't go back for weeks, but there was another wreck soon to come, this time at a meeting near Castletown, where I finally put an end to it. It was the last race, a handicap and nothing had been going right for us all day.

I think I'd arrived still tired from the clubbing the night before and had made some silly mistakes earlier in the day and was trying to make up for it, starting to come through the field until I'd reached the good guys at the front. One was giving me lot of hassle and kept coming back at me, so I decided to get rid of him, took a third gear uphill section in fourth and the bike fired into the air like a spaceship. I was jumping all over the front trying to get the nose down because I didn't want to land on my back again, having already cracked my spine. It nose dived into the ground and I heard a big snap when I hit the deck and I thought my neck was broken.

The first thing you do after an accident like that is see if your neck moves and I was delighted when it did. But I could hear bikes screaming up the hill towards me, went to crawl off the track and it was then the pain hit me and I realised my shoulder was broken. I went to work the next day - I was terrified of losing a day's work and upsetting the boss, so I carried sheets of metal around tucked up under my armpit for days in absolute agony. I'd worked my way up to foreman by then and was sort of running the workers the best way I could. It was unofficial Company policy that, anyone turning up with a hangover would be put inside a steel tank to do some welding - a horrible job even when you were feeling OK. I'd won that award a few times with the rest of the lads hammering on the outside to help me along with the headache of course. I don't think Jim was very impressed and he gave me a serious warning about all the injuries I was getting and the time off work I was having because of them. Quite right too of course, he was trying to build the business and here was this little menace messing around with motorbikes and limping - or worse - into work every Monday morning.

Business was going good, Sam and Jim bought themselves new Cortinas and I was given the privilege of using Sam's old Citroen GS Club. A week later it broke in half for some strange reason and my first company car had become my last.

I did a lot of growing up there and learnt some important lessons filming that job. Mum's always said I inherited my Dad's determination. I'd always keep going at work and finish the job, no matter what the problems were and how long it took, particularly doing the installations and Food Engineering got to rely on me and give me more and more responsibility which was good. On the few occasions we ever had a problem, I became the Company's troubleshooter, dealing with the client and resolving the problem too, which developed my customer relations and PR skills as well!

Sam taught me that nothing is impossible and if a job looks too big to handle, then just think of it as a series of little jobs. Good advice I tell you. I think Jim got through to me at the time too, because I starting to realise the beating I was getting from moto-crossing was getting it much, so I decided to go road racing, thinking it would be much safer! (There's one born every minute you know.)

I rode bikes on the road a lot more than Woolsey Coulter and Mark Farmer did and thought to myself if they could do it, so could I, and I bought a duff 1979 Yamaha TZ125. I had to spend a lot of money on it before my first race in August 1984, in a round of a tough series called me John Player 125 Trophy, which was being held at a short circuit called Aghadowey.

We lost our way going to the track and got stuck behind a herd of cows for miles, arriving very late. Davy Wood got me out in the final practice session so I could have a look at the track and ride the bike for the first time. I qualified sixth or seventh out of my group of thirty, even though I didn't know where I was going. It was really wet in the final, I was braking later and later all the time and was in the top ten before I dumped it. People watching said it was only a matter time before I crashed, other people were congratulating me for doing so well on my first time out.

It wasn't until later when I met up with some boys from TZ Motorcycles in Banbridge, David Beattie and John Giffen, that I realised what the problem was. These boys knew what they were talking about and were involved with Trevor Steele, who'd won at the Ulster Grand Prix. It was through talking to them I found out I'd been racing on hard compound Dunlop TT100 tyres. I'd just raced on the tyres that were on the bike - it was a miracle I'd survived as long as I did. With soft compound tyres, now I could go faster still and I was really hooked, riding in six more short circuit meetings that year, but having a lot of trouble with the bike.

Not only was the little TZ troublesome but a bit of a toy compared to my big Suzuki road bike and I decided to go for more power, already knowing I could handle everything the GS1000 could come up with. That winter I sold the little 125, buying the ex-Trevor Steele Ulster Grand Prix winning Yamaha TZ350 from TZ Motorcycles, a bike that was reputedly well sorted.

I worked my butt off that winter doing all the overtime I could get and building myself a trailer in my spare time after work, so I could transport my race bike next season. I enjoyed my work there very much, there was a great atmosphere and some larking about. Lunchboxes would get nailed down, your boots would get painted odd colours if you stood in one spot with a welding mask on for too long and on one memorable occasion a work mate called Tommy got a condom in his ham sandwich.

He was probably the worst timekeeper Food Engineering had ever had, always late or not showing up at all. He got a good talking to about it one day and an official warning. When he was asked if he had anything to say he said, "Yes boss. Could I take next week off to get up to the North West 200?"

Davy Hamilton and I raced everywhere together, me on my Suzuki and him in his RS2000 - totally reckless behaviour looking back on it. We'd come up behind a car at a rate of knots one day, Davy took it on the outside in a bit of a wild move, so not to be outdone I went up the inside, on the pavement at about 70mph. It took the plain clothes police some time to catch up with us and it's safe to say they were suffering from a severe sense of humour failure by then and gave us a good dressing down.

I talked Sam into giving me a character reference in Court one day "It's only speeding Sam." I'd said, and he agreed to come and stand up for me. I remember him going white when the charge was read out in Court, "Travelling at 87mph in a 40mph limit". But luck was with me again because it was a Court local to the North West 200 course, it was practice week and there had been worse cases than mine, so I got off lightly.

20

In my heart though, I knew the Suzuki GS had to go, because by now even I was convinced it was going to kill me. So I sold it and bought a Ford Fiesta that very nearly did. I'd started to train like mad. I was already pretty fit but I wanted to get fitter and stronger for more stamina and endurance in the races and I cut out drinking alcohol and going with the boys. On Thursday January 24th, 1985 I went to the pub meet my mate Davy Hamilton for a few games of pool and a lemonade, to find he'd got one of the first new XR2 Fords in the country.

A mutual friend called Percy wanted a lift home mid-evening but I'd arranged to go back to work to help the boss's son work on his 250 Suzuki trail bike. Mercifully, Percy went with Davy. I woke up a few days later in Belfast City hospital in real trouble with my left foot smashed into a thousand pieces, chest, wrist and stomach injuries. Naturally, I was quite interested in what was going on and asked the staff what I was doing there. They told me I'd been in a car crash - I said that was impossible as I didn't have a car - I only rode bikes!

Davy and I had been racing each other back from the pub, flat out down a hill not far from the Tandragee course as it happens; apparently I was on the outside, Davy on the inside when the tarmac surface changed and we hit pure black ice entering the corner at the bottom of hill. We both went straight on, Davy shooting between two huge gateposts and up a driveway to a doctor's house, which turned out be quite handy, managing to stop somehow.

They thought I'd managed to veer up a lane going off to the right hand side there and got the shock of their lives when They'd turned around and found me and the Ford buried into the big old fashioned solid stone wall outside. So much for selling the Suzuki for safety. The little Fiesta's engine had finished up in the passenger seat right where Percy would have been sitting, having crushed my left foot between the floor and the pedals on its way. It was impossible to tell it was a foot from the x-rays and the surgeon did an amazing job putting the jigsaw back together, holding the thing together with several pins.

It took a year for me to walk properly on it again. Unfortunately, if you race motorcycles for a living, you have to put up with a lot of pain, it's just part of the job, but the agony that went on for week after week as the swelling in the foot went down and the pins started to burst through from the inside out lives with me to this day. Sleep was a stranger to me for many weeks.

It's still pretty mangled today and it wasn't long before I mashed my right foot in a crash at the North West 200, so now I've got a matching pair of twisted tootsies. The Ford was written off of course, all I had was third party insurance and the TZ350 had to go before I'd even turned a wheel on it. My boss was going mad as I was off work again, this time for six weeks up to Easter, with the whole situation being detrimental to my racing career, to say the least.

I'd been running, training, racing, doing anything I wanted before waking up in hospital. The day I left I cried, not only because of the intense pain, but because I thought the active, physical part of my life was over for good and I'd never walk properly again. Colleagues of the doctor who'd operated said the surgeon had performed a miracle rebuilding the foot - a year later I was walking normally.

I've always tried to fix things that are broken and I began reading a lot of books on painkillers - it was getting ridiculous the amount of pills I was swallowing. I started taking cod liver oil in the September and three months later I was starting to walk again. I really believe it works and recommend it to anyone - your joints need lubrication just like an engine needs its oil.

I didn't seem to have much luck with Ford Fiestas, going to sleep in one at the wheel a couple of years later, shooting off the road and down a twenty foot drop into a field. It rolled a few times and I ended up upside down but wriggled out OK and even managed to get the thing upright on my own. Davy Hamilton had been following me and found me in the end and we got the car going and took it straight to his workshop, which had burnt down a short while before. Davy is a bit of a wizard with motor cars and grafted a new roof onto the little Ford for me. He'd just about finished the work a couple of weeks later and I popped in to have a look and was really impressed at the job he'd done to fix it. I was so pleased I got stuck in to one of the upright wooden beams that had remained after the fire and needed removing, using a big hatchet which suddenly flew out of my hands up in the air, before dropping straight through the Fiesta's brand new roof. That was it for me and that car.

So the whole of 1985 was written off and I never rode my first 350. I missed racing terribly - I'd really started to love it and genuinely felt road racing was a safe way to go - cars hadn't done much for my safety record had they? The thrill of that first race at Aghadowey never left me - a whole wide open road I was allowed to use, with nothing coming the other way - and you were allowed to cut the corners! That was half of the buzz of it; all my life I'd been taking big risks doing just that on the road.

Returning to near full mobility I thought, let's have another go at it. I'd scraped a little bit of money together by now and bought another Yamaha TZ125, about four years old and that was me, off again, to prove another point. I'd got a race licence when I'd started competing which was only good for circuit racing, you had to complete so many races before you were allowed to compete on the road, which I felt was real racing, not this track stuff, just going round and round. I wanted to be doing the same thing as the real Irishmen, Tom Herron, Joey Dunlop, Roman Brown - they were the proper racers in my opinion.

I did four short circuits at the beginning of the year, enough to qualify for a road race licence and learnt quite a bit more about tyres. Then the Tandragee 100 came, which was my local road race, my Mum's house only half a mile from the track. In those days every road race was heavily oversubscribed, and I was just an unknown nutter who was going to be overlooked and excluded as the officials could take their pick from the queue of riders wanting to race.

I pulled as many strings as I could with friends, and friends of friends in the local North Armagh Club, persuaded and begged until I was given a reserve entry. Because of the size of the field there were separate groups those days; someone didn't turn up so I was race number 34 on the back row of the 'B' group in pouring rain, having somehow managed to scrounge a set of wet tyres. That was it. Time to race round the same roads I'd travelled to school for so many years, flashing past the bus stop at Parks Corner where I'd waited for the bus in my school uniform.

I came right through my group and by halfway round the first lap I was into the back of the 'A' group and started picking those boys off too, eventually finishing fourth on the road overall - I'd done good - wiping the floor with these so called top riders on brand new 1986 Hondas, a far better bike than my ageing Yamaha.

Who was this unknown local lunatic the papers asked? Being local and knowing the roads obviously helps through familiarity, but the advantage is limited really because racing lines are totally different, and you have to learn them from scratch. I had no one to help me either, until a local building contractor offered to. I was working off the back of a trailer when Tom Heatrick, who was from Tandragee, stepped in with an offer of transport in the back of his van. He'd sponsored a young rider called Sean McStay the year before, who was the same age as me, and showed a lot of promise by winning the Manx Newcomers race in 1985 I think, riding the ex-Norman Brown 250 EMC.

Heatrick was also sponsoring a well respected road racer called Courtney Junk who'd been Irish 125, 250 and 350 Champion. I'd met him before, helping the team out at a few of their races in return for the support. I was doing a lot of homework learning the courses I was racing on and Courtney started to give me some significant help. I'd fill the car up with petrol, pick him up after work, drive to the course where the next meeting was going to be held, Cookstown, Killinchy, Carrowdore, all of them and drive round and round until I'd got it right. We'd keep going until there was only enough petrol to make it back, often into the early hours of the morning.

If you got caught doing that a week or so before the event, going around at ridiculous speeds, you'd be banned outright for bringing the sport into disrepute, so we'd go a couple of weeks prior to the course being marked out. We got on alright, I think he liked me and saw how keen I was to get on and learn. This went on all year, so that when I was arriving at a new course it felt like I'd already been there. I also believe Courtney was doing it for the love of the sport too, he was a genuine road racer, the real thing and I'll forever be in his debt.

I became a threatening presence at all the meetings that year, really only being beaten by lack of speed, and was quickly promoted from the 'B' to the 'A' rider groups. This was important because it meant you were away with the fast boys, a much better place to start from because I was learning so much more dicing with the quality riders. Before that I was having to make up thirty seconds just to catch them. I was pleased to finish the season eighth in the Ulster 125 Road Race Championship.

One of the Smiths boys was killed that season, one of his bikes came up for sale and I bought it, a 1986 125 Honda. I can't remember how we got all the money for it. "This is what I need to make me a winner, now", I thought to myself and we, (my younger brother Noel and I, with the backing of the whole family by now), took it down to the final race of the season, the road race at Killalane, which is adjacent to the Skerries, the two courses overlap by a few yards in fact.

There used to be a tree right in the middle of a junction on the course. I'd qualified on the front row in Saturday's race and I was ready to prove what I was capable of. I was right behind Robert Dunlop who was leading the race and at last I had the speed of the others - this was it - there was no way I was going to let Robert get away! We both broke the lap record more than once, pushing everything to the limit until Robert crashed, leaving me comfortably in the lead and I knew the race was mine. I was just so keen, so carried away by the thrill of it all, I kept up the frantic pace and crashed disastrously just two corners later, throwing away my first race win on a competitive bike.

Everyone went mad, telling me what a fool I was crashing in the lead with only a couple of laps to go. I'd learnt another lesson the hard way. It's a strange thing but you have to learn how to win a race, how to control things from the front while keeping up a winning pace - much, much harder than anyone thinks. I was just too keen, still experimenting. I walked away unscathed, (I'd invested in the right protective gear) ashamed and humiliated at throwing away the race win but totally hooked, because now I knew what I was capable of on a bike with speed.

That winter I talked to a few tuning people who reckoned they could make my 1986 machine as quick as the revolutionary new aluminium framed RS model Honda were bringing out in 1987, the talk being that this new bike would take a while to sort out. However, the first race of the year proved that there was a vast difference between new and old and I didn't do at all well at the Aghadowey event on Easter Saturday or at Kirkistown on the following Monday. Back to square one - we'd found out our bike just wasn't good enough.

Matt Lavery, a joiner from Tandragee and a builder, John Wilson from Richill were in to racing, and were sponsoring a rider called Raymond Hannah. They'd known our family well through the years and had been watching me, this new kid on the block performing well on uncompetitive machinery. Matt Lavery offered me his 1985 Rotax 250 to ride in 1987 - I'd had a brief ride on it at the end of the previous season and Matt and John joined forces to sponsor me after They'd seen how slow my 125 was at the Easter meetings.

We located the last 1987 model RS Honda in the UK, somewhere in England which arrived on the Wednesday before the Tandragee 100. The trouble was we couldn't get it to run right while I was running it in, trying everything we could, changing all the settings, literally everything on the bike until we were grasping at straws, eventually borrowing a rotor from another rider who'd just broken his leg, so couldn't ride at the Tandragee. It was the very last thing we could have changed and at about midnight on the eve of the race we found the original part hadn't been located properly on its spline at the factory.

I fought for the lead with Robert Dunlop until he got by me on the last corner, and I was beaten by half a bike. But now I knew I had a bike capable of doing the job and it was only going to be a matter of time before I won my first race on it. I couldn't have been more wrong because at the Cookstown meeting a couple of weeks later I won the 250 race on my Rotax. I was lucky in that Brian Reid and a couple of the other top men had left for the Isle of Man TT, leaving an opportunity for someone else which I was determined to take.

It wasn't plain sailing though by any means, a very tough race on a bumpy course. Setting up my suspension was still largely experimentation and guesswork for me and the back wheel was on its full stroke during the race, rubbing through the seat and burning my backside! That wasn't all, with two laps to go a footrest fell off meaning I couldn't get up off the saddle for the bumps and jumps making it desperately difficult to keep control at speed. By now the rear tyre had burnt right through the seat and the bottom of my leathers. I'd passed a lot of good people to lead that race and there was no way now I was going to give it up. By the time I took the chequered flag the bike was beaten to death and so was I, featuring a world record skid mark on a very delicate part of my anatomy.

It was around the same time I started winning some races that I was given the race number nine a couple of times. I'm not superstitious about much else in life or racing, but ever since those very early wins, I've always tried to have number nine on my bike where possible. Earlier that day, Robert Dunlop and I had been fighting it out for the 125 race after I'd squeezed past Leslie McMaster on his MBA. I'd been tracking Robert a lot by this time and thought I'd got him sussed out. I was ready to pass him coming out of the last corner as I was carrying more corner speed but he started weaving all over the track - really knowing what he was doing, preventing me from coming past. He won by half a wheel length again and things started to get a bit hot and tense between us and this continued all year.

Everyone was starting to tell me to go to the Isle of Man for my first Manx Grand Prix but I resisted, knowing deep down I wasn't ready for it. I've always been the same; I never attempt to do something before I'm ready and I just didn't have the knowledge for it - apart from anything else, although I'd won on it, I knew the Rotax wasn't competitive enough anyway.

The next race was the Killinchy 150 and finally I'd got it wrapped up, leading the 125 race on the last lap, ahead of Robert Dunlop in second place by two or three seconds. The corner half way round the Ulster Pond Prix course, 'Windmills' is the most important to get right, because you need maximum drive for the steep climb going up the back straight of the course. Right in the middle of the corner a back marker blocked me and I lost all drive, Robert came flying past on the straight having carried all his speed around the corner and I lost by just half a heel again. He had more experience than me at the time, a couple of seasons, and he was using it. But a week later I got my first win over him and finished consistently enough over the season to win the 125 Irish Road Race Championship and the 250 title for good measure on my good old Rotax.

I had really upset Noel Hudson, the ex-Irish Champion in a 250 race at the Carrowdore 100 on the Rotax, which was slower than everything in the field; wherever the opposition started braking I'd have to brake later and muscle them out, which was the only way I had to make for the lack of power. Riding like that I'd accidentally run into people a couple of times, but on this occasion Noel's bike was at least twenty miles an hour faster than mine. I was holding the Rotax flat out over the jumps and bumpy sections in an effort to stay in touch, ridiculously wild riding looking back on it.

I finished second to Steven Cull on his Honda, who had won at the North West and the TT in 1987. I remember being in the top four, all of us in the air together coming over a jump, including Noel Hudson who got ahead of me on pure power, leading by about fifty yards going into the last corner. Somehow I cut him up and out-braked him to get second, which felt as good as a win, I can tell you. Hudson was a devout Christian who then astonished everyone by giving me the bollocking of my life in the paddock, screaming at everyone including Matt Lavery.

He'd also shouted at Matt that if I had been on his Honda during the race, the rest of the field wouldn't have seen me, which funnily enough contributed to me getting the 250 of my dreams the following year. By now, media attention and prize money was starting to mount up, a hundred, or a hundred and fifty pounds for a win which was a lot of money to me in those days. We'd started selling space on promotional wall calendar planners to local businesses for thirty pounds a square - anything we could think of to raise cash, which went straight back into the bikes of course, which are always a bottomless pit. People say a boat is a hole in the water in to which you shovel your money and racing effort is just the same - the budget is never big enough. I had a team of genuine helpers building up now including Robert Gillis, Trevor Toal, Ian McKinney and Roy Alexander; we all worked together and there was a terrific spirit.

Because I'd been winning both road races and short circuits at home, I raced in one round of the British Championship at Brands Hatch, towards the end of 1987. In those days I never put the same effort into short circuits, I would if I really wanted to, but road racing was where my heart was. You'd be wanting to put your money on me in a road race, not on a short circuit, so I didn't set the world alight at Brands, finishing a respectable fifth in the 125 race. I liked the circuit a lot, but it was a big effort with vans, boats, travelling, time off work and of course the expense of it all. My first win outside Northern Ireland had been on the 250 Rotax at Scotland's Knockhill, quite a technical track where I'd arrived wanting to win as usual and had set the fastest lap on my 125.

The 125 event was actually the most important race of the day and I remember coming smoking through and opening up quite a lead on the first lap before I dumped it, because of cold tyres. What a fool - pure inexperience. I came back to win on the 250 Rotax later that day as I've said, so I salvaged some pride for the journey back home. Knockhill's quite easy to get to from Northern Ireland with just a two hour ferry crossing from Larne to Stranraer, followed by about the same on the road and it's a popular trip for the fans from home.

What I desperately needed now was a decent 250 for 1988, so that winter we all worked hard with a common goal. Matt Lavery and John Wilson teamed together again and bought me a brand new Honda RS250 - a dream machine, I just couldn't believe it. Bobby Cambell a local car dealer from Lurgan sponsored me with a Yamaha TZ350 a 1982 'H' model, which I think was the last year they were made, brought up to date with a Spondon frame and everything else needed to make it fast.

I'd saved up some money of my own and with some help from a friend, bought a brand new Honda RS125. I maintained and ran it, Bobby Cambell looked after the 350, the team and I worked on the 250 and with quite a bit of money we'd raised through sponsorship that winter, I bought a Renault van and had my sponsors credits put on the side - the big time! I was working day and night by then, going into work on Sundays when I could, to make up for taking Saturdays off. Things were starting to get a little bit strained with the boss, but I just couldn't help it, I was addicted and went at it hell for leather in 1988.

The first road race of the year was now the Cookstown 100 which was moved to the last Saturday in April because a lot of riders were missing it for the TT. I was really still just doing it for fun then and using the short circuit stuff as a warm up for the real thing, the road races. I went out on the 125 and smoked everyone in the race, before riding like a man possessed in the 250. I whipped TT winners Brian Reid and Noel Hudson in that race, in fact every established 250 star of the time and did it again in the 350, smashing Raymond McCullough's five or six year old lap record. I'd broken the 125 and 250 lap records too, beating everyone first time out and that was it, I'd done everything - I was king of the pile!

I kept training hard that season, watching what I was eating and getting even more determined, still upsetting a lot of riders with my aggressive style. I followed my Cookstown clean sweep with 125 and 250 wins at Tandragee (the 350 had a problem) and entered my first international race, the North West 200 and - disaster. There was no 125 class, so I started on my 250 and qualified sixth or seventh, pretty good really for my first ride at the place.

Still psyched up and raring to go faster I leapt on the 350 and crashed it. The 250 had 17 inch wheels with the latest radials, whereas the 350 had eighteen inch wearing crossplys and I hadn't allowed for the difference - really hard to adapt from one to the other and it was pure inexperience. I loved the course, easy to ride and the fastest circuit I'd ever been on, but the crash tore off the whole right hand side of my right foot and broke it in two across the middle, giving me the aforementioned matching pair! That was the end of that. So, gutted not to be riding, I stayed and watched the 250 race, which featured an English guy with a growing reputation called Carl Fogarty, who, unknown to me at the time was soon to become my friend and team mate.

Steve Cull, who I'd whipped at the Tandragee 100, won three races in one day on his 500, 350 and 250. Not long after that, he set fire to the old record (and his bike incidentally) with a new 119mph lap at the TT a few days later, winning the 250 race too. I knew I had his measure by then and was desperately frustrated.

I'd stayed to watch the racing at the North West and missed an appointment at the hospital and was in trouble again with a serious insection which got into the bones of the damaged foot. Two weeks in hospital, with my lower leg in plaster dangling from the ceiling and my boss was really starting to have a sense of humour failure. I sneaked out of there, begging a flight to get me over to the Isle of Man with Matt

Lavery, John Wilson, Wilfie Herron, and Willy Neill, a great bull of a man who piggy backed me around all week, while we trekked around the island. I couldn't walk, I should still have been in the hospital.

The first thing that struck me was that the course was more like a Grand Prix road race, with wide, smooth roads, nothing like our bumpy tracks in Ireland. I got a few laps round there with some boys in a car and all I wanted to do then was come back and win. There's only a few months between the TT and the Manx, so I planned to come back one weekend and learn the course.

The first weekend in July was the Skerries and by then I was in serious trouble. We'd spent a lot going to the TT, I hadn't worked for six weeks and we had a broken bike to fix from the North West. I just had to win to get the money we needed. I'd been laid up for six weeks and had got smashed up on my last outing which is never far from the front of your mind when you're back in the saddle for the first time; I had lost a lot of money, but hadn't lost any sharpness thankfully as I got the victory we desperately needed in the 125 race, without too much trouble in the end.

There was great excitement for the 250 race because it had been announced that for the first time ever, there was to be five hundred pounds prize money for a combined win and lap record. Five hundred quid! We needed this money so badly because we were severely ripped. Steve Cull was just back from the TT a hero of course and it turned into a very tough race indeed. He'd been up against me a few times by then and knew I was a trier. I stuck myself to the back of his bike and he knew full well what I was up to. Wherever he went I was going and whatever he did on the last lap I was going to do more. We smashed the lap record seven times in the first ten laps, five in succession - real serious racing; and to make sure I didn't forget the prize money on offer, brother Noel's pit board signal was saying +500 or -500 every time I went past, depending on whether or not I'd got the lap record on the previous lap!

Towards the end of the race we'd developed a big lead, thirty seconds or more and halfway round the last lap he sat up and virtually stopped, looking round at me, but I knew what he wanted, so I sat up and slowed right down too, calling his bluff until we were in danger of being passed by the third place man. The Skerries is probably the hardest road race course in the South. There's a long tunnel section where you weave left to right coming uphill through a canopy of trees, ending in a left hand kink.

Before the kink there's a 150mph jump where you have to knock off round the throttle to get your bike down, left and up the hill to the finish where the cricket pitch is turned into the temporary paddock. I decided from the very first lap that what I was going to have to do on the last lap was take the jump flat out in sixth gear, reckoning it could be really risky, but that it was possible to do it. Steve hadn't done it in the race so I knocked the Honda off the throttle and on again about a quarter of a mile before the jump, which let him get about twenty yards ahead.

He knocked his throttle off at the jump as usual while I was still flat out, by this time I was carrying so much speed I appeared right beside or him. He tried to force me out onto the grass and mud at the side of the course, assuming I would back off but I needed this win too badly for that and, carrying that bit more speed I got him by half a bike's length at the line and the gamble had paid off.

I had I earned a thousand pounds for the team that weekend which meant new tyres, new pistons and with new parts by now I knew I could win. The season continued well and I was looking forward to my first Ulster Grand Prix where I competed in two 350 races, both crackers, but I was a little down on power against first class opposition. In race one Carl Fogarty went off like a bat out of hell but Brian Reid got past him at the end of the lap being chased by the group just in front of me, consisting of Eddie Laycock, Steve Williams, Steve Hislop and Woolsey Coulter. I spent the race concentrating on fighting off former Suzuki works rider Chris Martin and was really pleased to get a sixth place.

The second race was even fiercer with a big battle being fought between Foggy, Woolsey, Joey and Eddie Laycock, with me tucked in behind Brian Reid who'd got off poorly. Woolsey and Joey crossed the line together with Joey getting the decision while I came in not far back for another sixth place, which I was happy enough to go home with.

I made history shortly afterwards at the Mid-Antrim 150 road races with the first ever hat trick of wins ever recorded there and a third place too. The weather was atrocious at the six mile circuit, with the senior race reduced in length which only seemed to make the fight fiercer from the off. Using my Honda 250, I swapped first place with Johnny Rea (who was on a 500 Suzuki) and Chris Dowd's 350 Yamaha, with Sam McClements pushing us hard on a big 998 Suzuki. Chris got a bit of a lead and suddenly Brian Reid was on my tail in clouds of spray but I stopped him getting past, using the conditions to my advantage, finally nailing Dowd around half distance

He came storming back past me but crashed out at the final corner and I went through for a hard fought win in a brilliant race. In the Junior race I got ahead of Leslie McMaster early on who clipped a telegraph pole while he was chasing me which I didn't realise, keeping up a frantic pace to win by thirty seconds or so. I won the lightweight too and was third in the combined 350 / Formula Two race behind a hard charging Brian Reid and Chris Dowd.

So by the time the Manx Grand Prix came round, which is really just a more laid back, relaxed version of the TT, my spirits were high and I was looking forward to making my mark at the road racing capital of the world. The 125 stayed at home, while my 250 and 350 machines went to the island.

An Irish Championship round at the Carrowdore circuit clashed with the Manx meeting so I'd arranged to fly home in between practice sessions and raced on borrowed bikes which is a desperately hard thing to do, to keep my Championship points up. These were so important to me and the team, we actually nearly skipped the Manx altogether. I'd been back for a weekend after the TT with a few of the boys, for them to party and for me to do some learning.

The petrol stations don't stay open late at night on the island, so I'd fill up the rented car in the evening, go to bed and get up at four or five in the morning - the police weren't around that early - and keep driving round and round the course until the car was out of petrol, going back to bed when the tank was empty. A lot of the course didn't have any speed limits then either. The agency's next customer wouldn't have been too pleased to get the rental car I'd been using the day before I can tell you - the thing was completely hammered, brakes shot, tyres shredded to ribbons, the lot.

I've never really liked learning circuits on bikes. For me the best way to do it is in a car, because you can concentrate more without having to worry so much about the surface, drain covers, obstacles and all. That comes later. To learn the TT course you have to associate yourself with it, really familiarise yourself with it. You can only pick certain things up with every lap, landmarks like a telephone box leading to a tight corner for example. The important thing of course is to remember what's coming next. My advice to anyone starting out is learn the course first, then start to worry about the racing lines.

My decision not to go in 1987, which everyone wanted me to do, to start the learning process was right in retrospect. Even great riders have got their corners mixed up on the TT course and paid the price through injury or worse. Since I'd started learning with him in 1986, my mentor Courtney Junk had been beating it into me that you can't go fast on the road if you don't know where you're going. It sounds simplistic but it was another vital lesson to me at the time. I took a few risks experimenting with apexes though, particularly at night when you can pick up the lights of oncoming traffic at a safe distance.

I had a bit of a reputation as a nutter, a real risk taker, but everything I did was calculated and worked out in advance, I was a safe learner putting in more work than anyone else possibly could. I'd tried following so-called experts at other tracks and nearly got myself killed on more than one occasion and dumped that plan, even when I got to the TT. Anyone really good is going too quick for a learner to latch on to and follow - there's a lot of stories about people learning like that but take it from me, that's all they are.

I'm still a slow, careful learner today. My wife Manda can whip me on those PlayStation games so I guess I'll never change now, I have to know the course before I'll open it up, even on the TV screen! I started to get to grips with the countless number of corners on the TT course, some of which catch me out there occasionally, even today. It's no wonder some riders got killed there when the TT was still a Grand Prix round. So many just didn't know where they were going, with blind corners and worse of all, corners that look the same but are totally different. The Black Dub used to scare me the most - I had a massive slide and a great 'save' there in 1997 on my RC45, leaving a huge black line up the road. The next two lefts after that are extremely difficult, at the first you're accelerating flat out in fifth gear but then you're hard on the brakes for the next. Those two lefts really used to confuse me. They are where Rob Holden was killed and if you get them mixed up you're in real trouble. I just knew the more I practised, the better my chances of winning, common sense that I was proving to myself time and time again at home.

You used to have to do a Manx race before you were allowed to ride at the TT. That rule was lifted the same year, but entries for the Manx were still heavily oversubscribed. I was leading the 125, 250 and 350 Irish Championships at the time, had beaten TT winners Brian Reid and Steve Cull that year, so a few good words were put in for me by Irish officials with connections, while I started shamelessly begging for places. You were lucky to get a Newcomers' slot on your first visit to the island and had really hit the jackpot if you got a second entry, but I ended up with starts in the Newcomers' event, the Junior, (which was the 350 race at the time) and the Lightweight 250 event too, which was simply unheard of. I decided to win all three! This was my stepping stone to the TT next year - learn the mountain course at a slow pace, but quick enough to go for the win.

The team consisted of Noel, Roy Alexander, Trevor Toal, Rab Gillis, who has been a friend for years and my girlfriend Christine, who was doing all the secretarial work, race entries, while being cook, tea maker and more. The team would take off the fairings and wheels and do all the cleaning for me, while I did everything else myself, including all the mechanic work.

I'd learnt everything myself, self trained - put in a piston wrong and the bike would seize - and you'd just have more work to do because you hadn't done it right in the first place. It was a desperately hard schedule, doing all the work stripping the bikes after practice before rebuilding them and then back out on the course again in a car for more laps in the evening. I missed one Saturday practice session flying back to Ireland to keep my Irish Championship hopes alive, having set up a team to get everything ready for me to fly in to the Carrowdore. I got a couple of good results and dashed back to the island to rebuild the bikes on Sunday, after Friday afternoon's practice to be ready for Monday's first race, the 250, madness!

I'd had a real fright flat out on the 250 in practice, flying into a section of sweeping corners called Quarry Bends, when I went for the front brake and it wasn't there! I couldn't believe it at first and groped around for the lever but it had definitely gone - just fallen off. "My God!" I thought, "I'm dead, what do I do?" I was so, so lucky it happened there. Quarry Bends aren't that sharp, in those days I was taking it in sixth gear, but with caution, not like I do it these days. I got the back brake on and thought about putting my legs down but by then I'd recognised where I was, threw the bike into the corners instead and came out the other side.

I took a really stupid decision then, thinking I'd ride it back to the paddock and get my 350 out in the next session, desperate for every single possible chance for a lap. (Newcomers and Classics used to go out together, then 350, 250 'regulars' and big bikes). I remember coming down the end of the straight going into Sulby Bridge, out-braking other riders with just the back brake, reckoning the back was OK, I'd just use that and I completed the lap at over 100mph. Recording that sort of speed, no one believed me when I'd told them what had happened! The big problem was we couldn't afford luxuries like spare levers.

I'd rung home to get the lever taken off my 125 and flown over, but also put an appeal out on Manx Radio that Wednesday night, asking if anyone had found it. Lo and behold a man did find it while he was out walking his dog and handed it in to Ramsey Police station; by Thursday morning we had two levers and an enhanced team programme of safety checks, with every team member double checking other team mate's tasks. I wasn't going to let that happen again.

By this time I was getting on top of suspension and had fitted a softer spring on the 250, making it work better with the Dunlop intermediates I was using at the time. I've always had my bikes 'soft' for the roads, too hard and the bumps send the things crazy. Race day came quickly and now this was it, on the fabulous mountain course, in anger, for the first time and I was loving it, knowing roughly where I was going by now and thinking how easy it was on this big wide road, before the fork seals burst which slowed me quite a bit.

I kept up what I thought felt like a moderate pace, still trying to win, the team were learning how to give me signals out on the course, (there were four radio points in those days) and I got some, but was really surprised to find I'd smashed the Newcomers' lap record by over seven miles an hour at 107.01 mph on the last lap, with fork oil pumping out all over the place.

I was told by friends at home, who'd been listening to the Manx Radio race on the radio, that suddenly the commentators announced I was in the lead by so much time, but then said "No, that can't be right." and there was a bit of confusion for a while. The timekeepers were bang on though and later confirmed that I'd completed the 154 mile four lapper at an average of 103.53mph, winning by six minutes, even after adjusting my own chain and changing my helmet at the first pit stop! Boy, was I a happy man, I couldn't get the grin off my face for a long time.

Paul Wright worked on my Yamaha 350, which was owned by Lurgan car dealer and sponsor Bobby Cambell. They'd usually prepare the machine at home for me and I'd take it to the races, but they were on the island with me and in trouble because the bike hadn't been running right all week. We worked on it all day Tuesday, until I was totally exhausted, really finished I tell you and I just had to go to bed. The (new) clutch started slipping badly by the second lap of the race, one exhaust was trailing the ground at every right hander but I settled down to ride through the problems and started pulling back places until I was in third place on the fourth lap. It was then the clutch started completely giving up the ghost which was an interesting experience in those days because as the plates broke up, the pieces would fly out like shrapnel from a land mine and pepper your leathers. I was really sick with disappointment, I'd set my heart on winning every race there, but kept my head down, determined to do better in Friday's Lightweight, when I'd be back on the 250.

Honda's London headquarters got some fork seals over to us for Friday morning, all arranged by an efficient young parts lad called Martin Marshall, who was really helpful back in those days. Mum taught me good manners and I've always tried to be pleasant to everyone, a philosophy that has stood me in good stead time and again. Some riders can be rather demanding and ill-tempered at times - it's a dangerous, high pressure sport after all, but at the end of the day it gets you nowhere. Martin has since worked his way up to a position of some clout at Yamaha and was only too pleased to help again when I began developing the manufacturer's R series, starting to race them in 1999.

Back at the Manx we got special dispensation for delayed scrutineering while we fitted the fork seals in the nick of time to start the race. Two laps into the battle they started to leak again, so I just cruised the last lap, afraid to go too fast and fall off with the oil pumping out everywhere, but I won again, the only newcomer ever to have won two races in one week and for good measure, I burst the lap record for the 250 race this time, raising it to 107.45mph, averaging 105.68mph for the whole race, winning by over three minutes, but knowing I could have gone much faster if the bike hadn't let me down.

I remember the talk amongst the regular racers in the riders' briefing about which one of them was going to win, my name wasn't in the equation while I was thinking to myself, "Well boys, I'm going to whip you all." My chances were rated so poorly that I'd been a fifty to one outsider before the first race and the team had scraped about a hundred quid together to back me as the Lightweight winner. The boys gave the money to me to for the course bookie one morning as I was going down to the paddock on a few errands. I got sidetracked and completely forgot about it.

It wasn't until the team started talking about the party we were going to have with the five thousand one hundred pounds we'd won that I remembered the stake was still in my pocket. We'd spent over two thousand pounds of our own money to compete, with no prize money available as the Manx races are amateur. We really could have done with that money, so it wasn't the perfect fairy tale ending to the meeting, but afterwards I thought about it and decided it was probably a good thing because if I had put the money on, with the leaking forks and all, I might have pushed hard enough to crash.

Those victories tasted so sweet, with the promise of greater things to come. Unknown to me, Honda UK boss Bob McMillan was at the Manx that year, and followed my progress with interest.

So Phillip McCallen went home on the crest of a wave and everyone, all my friends, family and sponsors were hiding out in my garage, lights out when I got home. They'd had to move some bikes outside to make room and stitched me up nicely. "What are my bikes doing outside?" I asked before the lights went on and I got the surprise of my life - and a brilliant party that went on late into the night. Feeling like a hero lasted less than a week, as I was straight back to work at my job, feeling really embarrassed at all the time I'd been having off. The firm continued being really good to me and I tried to repay them by working as hard as I could.

In 1988 I won seven Irish and Ulster Road Race and short circuit Championships in the 125, 250 and 350 classes. The work schedule was unreal, racing every weekend with three bikes to keep in tip top condition, while still working really hard at Food Engineering, albeit only five days a week now. Towards the end of the year Johnny Rea tried to get me on his beast of a Yamaha TZ750, the one Joey Dunlop had won the Jubilee TT on. I was actually a bit scared of it, thinking it would be too powerful even for me and that I wanted to live long enough to ride my own bikes, so I avoided throwing a leg over the thing. Then Winston Macadoo gave me a ride on his Honda RC30 and that was it, a beautiful, strong machine for the class that was really coming into its own by then and I knew I had to have a big four stroke.

3

I liked the RC30 to ride and Davy Wood, through his connections with Honda managing Joey Dunlop since the early eighties, helped me to approach them towards the end of the year, but we were far too late by then. They had already cut deals with Carl Fogarty, Steve Hislop, Brian Morrison and many others, so boss man Bob McMillan said he was very sorry, but just couldn't help me. I'd started to realise by now that I was making a bit of a name for myself, because former racer turned manager Mick Grant contacted me, to see if I would be interested in a 600 Suzuki ride. Mick was running a young kid called Jamie Whitham on a Suzuki at the time, a rider I was to come up against later on, in a titanic battle at the Ulster Grand Prix.

Kawasaki's Alex Wright contacted me too, wanting me to be the Irish equivalent of the official Kawasaki UK team, also on a 600. They wanted to promote their new bike in Ireland, basing their effort through Norman Watt, a Northern Ireland dealer; having tried the RC30 by now though, I wanted a factory 750 for the TT as well and told them so. They offered me a ZXR750 road bike, with tuning parts to follow, a 600, a KR1-S 250 road bike, a mechanic and wages plus the greatest temptation of all, a factory 750 - magic! We knew Honda couldn't help by then so I signed my contract as a professional rider at a major press launch in a big Belfast hotel, all organised by Kawasaki UK. A window system manufacturer based in Portadown called Turkington's offered sponsored transport in the form of a brand new Mercedes van, a deal organised by Fleming

Keery and the faithful old Renault was pensioned off so I was all set. I reckoned I'd really cracked it now in my conversion to four strokes. The feeling was short lived.

My first win came pretty quickly on the new 600 in the Seniorstock short circuit race at Aghadowey, but the bike had been totally outclassed for power at Kirkistown in the first round of the season's Regal series. What Kawasaki had come up with was basically a road bike, which immediately proved uncompetitive against Brian Reid's fully tuned Yamaha in that first outing and I started crashing the thing regularly in an effort to stay in touch with the faster machinery.

That 600 was completely destroyed when I was in a fight for second place with Sam McClements during the first serious road race of the season, the Cookstown 100. It was being held on the Sherrygroom circuit between Cookstown and Stewartstown and was another important Regal round. Brian Reid was way ahead on his Budweiser sponsored Yamaha and I was giving it everything I'd got and some more just to stay in touch with McClements.

Somehow Sam and I dragged each other up right behind Reid and I thought I was in with a chance if I could hang on, but I was having to ride the bike way beyond its limits and the engine blew up after a con rod burst out of the bottom of the crankcase, pumping oil all over the place. The throttle was stuck wide open because one of the pistons broke up and some big pieces stuck in a butterfly on the carbs jamming the others wide open, meaning the other three kept filling with live fuel.

I couldn't work out why the thing wouldn't shut down, with me flicking switches all over the place out of control at 150mph. I decided to part company with it at that point, breaking a foot in the process, while the bike fired itself flat out into a field and there was nothing left of it, wheels, frame, forks, engine of course, all totally destroyed. I was disappointed as usual not to have won the race, but I can't say I was sorry to see the thing atomise into a thousand pieces. "It was me or him", as they say in the movies.

We went over to Scotland's Knockhill track, which is just north of Edinburgh shortly after that for some testing with Kawasaki UK, taking what was left of the 600, literally in boxes. That didn't go down too well as you can imagine, but then I did get hold of one that had been race prepared in England, as opposed to the stock road bike I'd been racing. They were two totally different bikes.

All of a sudden I was fighting for the lead, instead of riding on the absolute limit just trying to stay in touch with the leaders back in fourth or fifth place - this was a far superior machine to my first 600 Kawasaki. Now I had the extra speed I needed I started competing at the front of the field, winning at Aghadowey and only just being beaten into second by Dave Leach at Kirkistown.

I got a great start at the Tandragee 100, fighting Brian Reid all the way, each of us leading for three laps until he just beat me to the line. I'd been advised against going with Kawasaki on their new, unproven machine, particularly as I was lacking in four stroke experience. But the prospect of a full time mechanic, a fellow called Jim McMahon and wages, had been too tempting to turn down. I'd keep working at my own job and do the lot I thought, that's me!

Jim Falloon, the boss at Food Engineering called me into the office one day in the spring of 1989, to discuss what had been building up for some time. After the big crash on the 600 smashing myself up for the umpteenth time, Jim was quite blunt and said give up motorbikes and work full time or leave. I knew they didn't really want me to go, yet I understood they needed commitment, so we ended up agreeing I'd work part time, concentrating on site work for three days a week. I still never worked less than forty hours a week even then.

I now had the speed I needed with the 600, but was still lacking reliability and back up. Norman Watts had a motorcycle business to run and had no choice other than to restrict the time the mechanic, Jim McMahon could work on the race bikes, which were based at his Temple Crossroads dealership.

That meant Jim was struggling to prepare the bikes the way he and I wanted, compounding the fact that there never seemed to be enough spares available. Kawasaki UK genuinely believed this was the ultimate deal we'd all agreed and everyone was trying their hardest to make it work. Crucially though, the factory 750 hadn't arrived, nor did the tuning kit for the ZXR750, which was one of the most demanding bikes I've ever ridden.

I was so frustrated at not getting enough competition they gave me a production kit for the KR1-S and I took that out in quite a few races, often managing to fight it out in the top six on a road bike which was very good. The ZXR750 was quite a handful in practice for the Production race at the North West 200, I was weaving going into Portrush at 150mph, really struggling to get the machine handling the way I wanted. Kawasaki tried to help but they were having similar problems with the bike on circuits in England and all over Europe too. As it was a totally new bike still under development, no one had yet perfected the ideal race settings. I couldn't get comfortable with it at all on the very fast North West 200 course, so withdrew from the superbike events and then my 600 broke down too, the end of a very unhappy 1989 North West 200.

On the way home I'd stopped at Joey Dunlop's pub to console myself a bit and he told me I should have been riding his bikes at the meeting. (Joey had been smashed up at Brands Hatch in one of the first races of the season, when Fred Merkel and he had touched, ending in a pretty bad crash, which cost him an arm and a leg in both senses of the word). I got the impression from Joey that he believed I'd have been better off riding more proven machinery than the new Kawasaki models of the time.

He'd had some spares problems just before the 1988 TT and I'd lent him what he'd needed for his 250, so we'd already developed a good relationship. I beat him a couple of times in 1988 too and there weren't many people doing that. I really don't know if it was him or Davy Wood - or both - who put in a good word for me at Honda, but whatever, it produced results. I rang Kawasaki the following Monday looking to get out of the deal but of course I'd signed the contract and they had an option on me for the second year.

My girlfriend Christine worked for a solicitor who was a superb legal eagle with a great mind, Christine was her right hand girl and we discussed the situation with her. It was no-ones' fault but Kawasaki were obviously struggling to provide me with competitive machinery and the support that had originally been agreed, while the number of days were ticking away to the TT.

Just in the nick of time, Davy Wood got a definitive answer from Honda and rang me to let me know that if I did not have a deal with Kawasaki, they would supply me with bikes. Kawasaki made a statement saying there had been delays in the development of the factory ZXR-750, they didn't want to hold me back and had agreed to release me. I really appreciated their attitude and we parted on good terms.

Honda immediately arranged for me to collect a CBR600 from a dealer in Belfast and I also got the use of Joey Dunlop's 125 and 250, plus Steve Hislop's spare RC30, as Steve was going to be getting a new bike at the TT, all of this happening in the week before practice for the Isle of Man was due to kick off. Jim McMahon stayed with me, moonlighting in his spare time and we worked round the clock to get as prepared as we could.

So my first ever ride on a competitive 750 was on the RC30 at the TT. In practice, coming down Bray Hill, which is a steep downhill section at the very beginning of the lap, I was wondering how on earth I was going to get through the right kink at the bottom on the missile I was sitting on. You start off on the right hand side of the road at the top of the hill and you need to be running the bike down the left hand side by the time you're at the bottom, ready for the next right which leads up to Ago's leap, but usually you're still way out on the right fighting the thing over.

On a 250, you'd be holding it flat out down there - it's very fast and pretty hairy on something that small, let alone an unfamiliar RC30. A 250 is probably the most manageable bike for me around the TT course and the least demanding, with a good 600 a close second. The difference with a big 750 is the extra speed and weight, meaning you've got to line it all up really carefully when you're travelling at 180mph.

Those first laps on the RC30 were really scary; when I got to Ballacraine I thought how on earth am I going to stop at this speed and turn the thing right? It was a really tough time getting used to the power, weight and speed of the RC30, which was the most lethal machine of its time. That revolutionary V4 kicked out massive brake horsepower and the chassis took no prisoners in the handling department. To be honest there were times when a bit of self doubt crept in here and there and not a few frights.

We struggled to get the 125 running right and I finished seventh in the Ultra-Lightweight TT on the 125, having a bit of a battle with fellow Irishman Michael McGarrity, Robert Dunlop taking the win up front. However, the Junior TT was the one I really wanted to prove myself in as I'd been getting up to the front on the uncompetitive Kawasaki at home, but never really succeeding in showing I could make the transition from pure two stroke race bike to the four stroke production racers.

In the race I was getting into the bends as tight as I could - every inch saved in this way makes up time - and I caught my right shoulder on a stone wall bordering the final corner at Quarry bends, coming out onto the straight in fifth gear at well over 130mph. I hit the solid rock so hard I honestly thought I'd ripped my shoulder right off, the pain was unbelievable, so unbearable. All the power went out of my right arm, I couldn't hold up the bike any longer, or operate the front brake lever so I just had to stop.

It sounds stupid but I wasn't at all sure if my shoulder was still there, thinking if it had survived and was still attached, it must have been completely smashed by such an impact. I pulled over at the Sulby Glen Hotel and stopped. "Excuse me, but can you look and see if my shoulder's still there please?" is an unusual question for a lunchtime drinker to say the least, but I'm pleased to say I got a positive answer - the fans at the TT are a wonderful crowd and cheered me up a lot. I joined them for a cool drink and a bit of a recovery, watching the race go past for a while. It didn't take long to find out I was still in one piece and when the pain went off a little bit, I remounted for the run back to the paddock, because I didn't want to end up being stuck out there.

Half way through the week I went down with the 'flu too, so with wrecked shoulder, thumping headache and streaming nose, I started the Senior race some way from top form. I can't remember if I caught Phil Nicholls, an experienced TT rider, or he caught me, but we spent most of the race locked in a titanic battle, bashing fairings all the way round the course. The pace in the 750 class was up around the 119mph average then, compared to my limited 250 experience of around 108mph and that's a big difference on a much heavier production based four stroke.

Apart from that, Phil knew his way round much better than me as it was my first TT, having only ridden the Manx before and we fought it out from the first lap. I was sticking my bike under him, over him, any where I could see an opportunity to pass and he'd get me back, until I lost it in the middle of Rhencullen's 'one and two' corners. Instead of sweeping around to the right, I went across the road, heading straight for the wall of the house which lies in the middle of that section. Talking to Phil afterwards he felt I'd had a lucky escape because if I'd crashed I could have been badly injured, because that's the nature of the TT, the toughest race in the world by a long way where, if you make a mistake, you're going to get hurt.

Popular TT hero Phil Mellor and Steve Henshaw were killed in the Production TT that week, an accident that cast a shadow across the whole event. Honda had brought a CBR1000 road bike across for me to use in the Production Race, but I didn't fancy the idea of man handling such a big bike around the course.

I watched the race at Cronk-y-Voddy and saw Brian Morrison fighting a CBR1000 there, with the thing bending in the middle and bucking around making me so pleased I wasn't out there myself. Production machinery has come such a long way since then. Steve Henshaw was trag-ically killed at Quarry Bends and Phil Mellor crashed his GSXR1100 three corners before Black Dub, losing his life in the same race, both des-perately sad events.

Apart from sheer exhaustion, I was badly weakened, suffering heavily from the 'flu while carrying the injury from trying to rip my shoulder off in the Junior. It was a tough, tough battle in the Senior with a hard, experienced rider who knew where he was going, while I was still really groping my way round some sections. Idiotic of course, but I was caught up in the adrenalin of the race, the sheer exhilaration of the battle with the other rider.

With Joey Dunlop's arm and leg injuries sidelining him and Steve Hislop's new 750 surprising him with its power, he led the race from the word go. He'd already set light to Steve Cull's 119.08mph record of 1988, with a practice lap of 121.99mph, completed in 18m 33.4 which was some going. Earlier in the week, his first lap from a standing start had broken the Formula One race lap record at 121.34mph and his over all average speed of 119.36mph was higher than the old lap record he'd broken. He'd won the Junior, in which I'd collected my injury at record pace too, with a record 113.58mph second lap.

The course has been consistently improved over the years which obviously helps with lap record breaking, every year it's getting better and better. A lot of work has been done on smoothing out the really rough sections, which makes corners faster. There's an argument that says this makes the racing a lot safer, but opponents say it also encourages you to go a lot faster as the bike's not getting as out of shape as before. I don't really believe the latter - if the bike's calmer then that's got to be a good thing and it's up to the rider to control the speed. It also shows that you must never stop learning the course and its surface. These are public roads after all, and there's a lot of them; white lines are renewed and added in the winter too and burnt off the most crucial sections before the TT, which can cause their own unique little problems.

I eventually finished seventeenth in the Senior, two places down on my performance in the Formula One, where I'd scored my first ever F1 world championship point. It wasn't bad for a first attempt, but nothing like I'd been hoping for. Honda chief Bob McMillan had told me at the beginning of the week that I wasn't under any pressure because he had Carl Fogarty and Steve Hislop as his top riders who were both expected to do well. When it was all over he took me to one side and said "You've got your 600 to take home with you, take the RC30 too and practice."

So that was it, I had a tenuous grip on becoming full time with Honda who agreed to support me with bikes and spares until the end of the year. Hislop had set another lap record at 120.15mph in the Senior, once again from a standing start. Talking afterwards, he said that he'd wished Joey had been riding because "It could have been good!". Joey agreed, saying it was a lot worse spectating than riding and he was look ing forward to taking Steve on in 1990. So was I, and Joey too.

Honda were still celebrating their 40th anniversary and three time TT winner Luigi Taveri was let loose on the six cylinder ex-Mike Hailwood Honda 250 for a parade lap, filling the roads with the glorious sound of that unsilenced six. There's nothing like it in the world. Grand Prix racing is all the poorer since the self imposed decibel limits were introduced - a poor decision in my opinion at long last (slightly) reversed in 2000.

There was no Honda Britain team in 1989, the official Barry Symmonds run Honda team had split up in 1987 and nothing had formally replaced it, just Honda UK supporting some riders via a pretty loose structure, really running by itself. Spares came from Martin Marshall and Bob McMillan was handing the bikes out until Neil Tuxworth took over in 1990. So I went home and now had a much more competitive 600 and started to really enjoy the class, immediately up there in the races, fighting for the lead.

New bikes meant new leathers and helmets to match, which got me into trouble at the Killinchy 150 which was my first race meeting after the TT. In the rush to get things ready I forgot to get my new Arai scrutineered and the officials reacted by banning me from riding in the final two races of the day and handing me a thirty day suspension. I was so disappointed with the officials handing out these rulings and made it quite plain how I felt. They were robbing the paying public who wanted to see top racing action on the track too, apart from costing me vital practice and set up miles, in preparation for the Ulster Grand Prix.

I had quite a few rides on the still-injured Joey Dunlop's 250. I was mastering the big RC30 too and my aim was to beat Sam McClements, who was the RC30 king at home at the time, definitely the most respected big bike rider around. At the Skerries road races in early July I was leading the big race for quite a way until Sam rode the backmarkers better that me and I finished second on the big Honda. I was leading him in the wet during the 750 race at August's Mid-Antrim meeting and I thought I'd finally cracked him before my bike started to misfire and I had to pull in, Sam flying past for the win.

What felt like a long, lean spell finally ended at the Castlepollard's road races in County Westmeath with a great win in the 250 after a race long wheel to wheel fight with Johnny Rea. I ran away with the 350 event, winning by over thirty seconds before a momentous encounter with Sam McClements on the 750 in the big race. I'd get past then Sam would come back at me, setting the fastest lap before his motor gave up the ghost on the fourth lap and I won, with Dave Leach in second. I followed those race wins up with another short circuit hat trick at Aghadowey a week later with McClements absent, but Sam and I were soon fighting each other for the lead again at the Munster 100 in Clonakilty, where he beat me on the 750 twice, while I picked up two race wins on my 250.

The Ulster Grand Prix that year was the sixth round of the Formula One World Championship where Foggy retained his title with second place in the big race, while I was delighted with eighth and the fifth fastest lap of the race, beating Sam into ninth place. I'd had a terrific scrap with quite a few riders including Charlie Corner, Nick Jeffries and a young Jamie Whitham on his Durex Suzuki, who got it all wrong at Flow Bog in the melee on lap eight, breaking his ankle in the crash. Jamie and I'd had a wonderful fight earlier with Dave Leach in the 600 race. What a race that was! Brian Reid was leading on his Yamaha which was the better bike at the time, having a definite edge over the Suzukis and Hondas.

Dave, Jamie and me fought it out throughout the race until Dave ran out of petrol with half a lap to go, leaving Jamie and me to tough it out to the finish. I was passing him on the quicker corners at the back of the circuit, some of which you take at about 150mph, while he was getting me back on the brakes in some of the other sections. We were alongside each other coming into the last corner before the start / finish straight and I stuck it up the inside of him - what a bang there was as our fairings clashed. Jamie went wide towards the hedge and I went through to take second place, it was that good a fight it should have been for the win but Brian was doing well on the Yamaha at the time and deserved the victory, although it felt like an outright win to me.

It was definitely safer for Jamie Whitham racing at the Ulster Grand Prix than getting a lift from a friend of my Mum's, whose husband had passed away, leaving behind his car amongst other things. I'd thought motorcycle racing was the most dangerous thing to do on the roads until Racey, as we nicknamed her, who'd never driven in her life, decided to take driving lessons. I don't know how many driving instructors took early retirement having encountered her driving but at least she was being kept under some sort of control with L plates on display as a warning.

It was obvious she was going to struggle to pass her test but one day, heaven knows how, she did. "Are you sure?" she asked the examiner who had given her the glad tidings, "Everyone will be so surprised, no one ever thought I'd pass!"

Travelling with her was always entertaining. One day I couldn't drive because my leg was in plaster, she agreed to give me a lift to my girl friend's house so I was giving her directions - "Take a right at the round about" I said and she did, straight into the oncoming traffic.

This wasn't the first time it had happened as she was still coming to terms with road sense at the time, driving anywhere she fancied, the wrong way up a fast dual carriageway one day on her way home back from Banbridge. She couldn't work out why everyone in all the cars coming the other way was frantically waving at her. "How does everyone know me all the way up here?" she asked her terrified passengers, who were speechless with fear. I knew the feeling myself!

My season long battle with Sam McClements came to a tragic conclusion at the Carrowdore 100, where I was in second behind Sam, pushing him all the way hard enough to shatter the lap record on lap four in what was turning out to be a really storming race. Sam was leading when he made contact with a back marker, whose engine it was reported had cut out, with the rider coasting his bike back to the pits.

Sam lost control and was killed at the right hander just before Bally-boley corner, on what was ironically one of his favourite tracks. It was a tragic loss of a genuine folk hero to everyone and the sport itself. It's a dangerous occupation of course, I can't think of many things that carry as high a risk as road racing motorcycles but we all know the dangers.

Photography doesn't come anywhere near on the scale of things but I know of one cameraman who had a very close shave, courtesy of yours truly. I was leading a 125 race at the Skerries on one occasion and lost control, coming round a really sharp corner and I ran into the bank and bounced right across to the other side of the road, but managed to stay on it, I don't know how and got caught in a sort of gully, which turned into quite a deep ditch which I got stuck in, still doing around 70 or 80mph.

Squatting in this ditch on the outside of the corner in front of me was a wee photographer called Billy Cambell, perfectly positioned for action shots on the apex of the corner opposite. There was no way I could have stopped, even if I'd wanted to throw the race win away, but Billy heard me coming and of course swung the lens towards me thinking he was about to get the action picture of his life, before realising he was actually about to get killed.

He leapt out of the ditch like a scalded cat, camera equipment flying everywhere and with nowhere else to go dived painfully through the thorny hedge as I screamed past with the track still at shoulder height. The ditch shallowed out a bit and I used my old moto-cross skills to keep the thing upright on its slicks and rejoined the race, taking it easy for a couple of laps to wipe the mud off the tyres and going on to win. You got paid by cheque, in Irish Punts, and of course the only place to cash the cheque for Sterling would be the pub.

The Skerries has a great reputation and attracts a lot of visitors from far and wide. The first time I turned up to race there I couldn't believe this was the track, it was so narrow and bumpy after the roads I was used to in the North. In places, some of the fastest sections too, it's impossible for two cars to pass and the obstacles range from mud, wet leaves, cow pats and even scattered potatoes I spotted one day.

The Skerries is like that, but it's hard riding keeping a bike under control there, with all the bumps, odd cambers, twists and turns. I set a lap record when I rode there on a fast and nimble 250 at around 103mph I think, but a good, fit man on a sorted 750 would be able to go quicker in the unlimited class. Someone told me recently that I still had the lap record there from the early 1990's. It's well worth the trip if you've never been, the crowd is terrific and knowledgeable and the friendliness and hospitality out of this world.

I had a similar incident in a ditch in 1990 at a road race at Clonakilty in Cork, leading once again, this time on the RC30, when it high-sided me right across the road. No one had expected me to turn up because I was off to race in a Formula One round in Finland the following week end and wouldn't want to risk anything, but you can't keep a keen racer away you know!

I remember hanging on for grim death, ending up in a ditch again, this time at around 100mph. It gave Dave Leach, who was right behind me, the fright of his life and he knocked it off straight away as my Honda turned into the fastest muck spreader of all time. Luckily, about a hundred yards up this ditch, there was an entrance to a field with the ditch sloping up towards it where the Honda and me came popping back out of the gully looking like the creature from the black lagoon.

With me dirt tracking and Dave Leach having given it up, Steven Hazlett had got by and thought he had the race won by this time and couldn't believe it when I came flying by, with just the whites of my eyes showing as the rest of me and the bike was covered in mud. He and Dave just gave it up on that occasion, thinking that if I was that determined to win, there was nothing they were going to be able to do to stop me!

For a couple of years it seemed like all the races were between Dave Leach and me, until he got seriously hurt at the Tandragee 100 in 1992. An Englishman from Halifax, he loved Ireland and the road racing scene, moving to live here and he was an honorary Irishmen, we adopted him really. He was a good rider, coming very close to being European 600 Champion one year. He wasn't averse to experimenting with tactics. At one meeting at the Fore down south, practice had finished with the two of us sharing just about all the pole positions before I had a row with my girlfriend.

I don't drink when I'm racing, if at all, but Dave offered to go out with me to help drown my sorrows, so off we went into the local town. I was drinking whisky and something, while Dave stuck to vodkas. This went on for a long time, round for round until I realised I was extremely drunk and Dave had disappeared. The fans party all night there and it wasn't until the next morning I remembered doing stunts on a C90 for a big crowd of fans in one of the fields.

One of my team had thrown open the back doors of the van where I'd fallen asleep, about an hour before warm up was due to start and the sunlight burnt into my brain like a welding rod. Dave of course was fine, because he'd been drinking water all night - not vodka - while I was so ill I had to stop half way round my first warm up lap and get a marshal to hold my bike while I was sick as a dog.

By sheer luck I ended up having the last laugh. I can't remember what happened in the 250 race, but our encounter in the 600 sticks in my mind to this day. It was our toughest fight ever, one of the biggest battles of my life with the lap record being smashed lap after lap. By the end of the race I was completely dead, totally drained of energy but in a final suicide attempt, got the front of my bike over the line ahead of Dave. I was so drained I couldn't even make the rostrum - really finished, but with the big race of the day, the unlimited event with the major prize money still to come. Dave could see I was finished and in his mind was already spending the prize money he was going to win on his Yamaha OW01, before the luckiest thing happened.

In the final race before the main event, a sidecar engine blew up at the end of the straight, spewing its oil and internals all over the road and into the dangerous 100mph corner which followed, putting an end to all further racing for the day. The organisers decided to hand out the prize money anyway, based upon grid positions and guess who'd got pole the day before? It's never over till the fat lady sings as they say and that was the easiest money I've ever won racing in my life.

By now I was starting to love racing the 750 and was having fun on it all over the place, including the Sunflower meeting which is held at the end of the season. It was a really important meeting for me, with some big name riders coming across from England to fight for the substantial prize money on offer and my last chance of the year to impress my Honda bosses to help build the case for another ride in the following year.

I was leading the big 750 race quite comfortably from Carl Fogarty when the RC30 popped out of gear again and I had a big, big moment only just getting the thing under control at the last second, but I kept charging hard, eventually finishing fifth instead of cruising to what had looked like a good win.

By then though, I'd made a big enough name for myself in 1989 to be invited to the traditional end of season jamboree event, the Macau Grand Prix. Kevin Schwantz had won there the year before on his Suzuki and I think it suited Kevin's style. I thought it was a great circuit, a good balance between power and riding skills, reminding me of some of the tracks in Ireland, so I immediately felt right at home.

The bike races supported the Formula Three GP round there and we challenged the F3 boys to a bit of go-kart racing. We were having a lot of fun, whipping them on times so badly that they wouldn't take us on head to head on the track. Of course we were charging about, knocking each other off at the corners whenever we could, really aggressive stuff, so they didn't want an on track battle like that.

I did a little bit of karting from time to time, smashing the 250 course record while I was out East in fact and I did really well at Nutts Corner a couple of times in kart races. I had a lot of fun on four wheels at Donington Park once too, at Honda's launch of their Integra R. I was a second a lap faster than Aaron Slight and Colin Edwards, even though I had three passengers in the car. I remember getting it completely sideways going through Craner Curves flat out in fourth and really struggling to hold it. The passengers I had in the car thought it was all part of a normal lap and didn't blink an eye, never cottoning on to how close we were to a very nasty roll.

Cars are so safe compared to bikes; you know every time I've fallen off I've got hurt - you've got to go to the limit without going past it or you're off, but with four wheels you can experiment more. Spin out, lose it, go off on to the grass and so what? Just get it back on the road and start again. Do it on a bike and you may not be getting up.

My old friend Davy Hamilton has moved in to karting and I'd like to have a little go at that at home soon - the 250 class with the Rotax engines are the business. Who knows where that may lead me?

At Macau I did really well from the off on my kitted RC30. I led the race for a while until Robert Dunlop got past me, so I just stayed right behind and had got him sussed out for a pass towards the end of the race, when my brakes started to fade dramatically, probably down to the extra heat and I had to settle for second in the end. It's a great place to compete, the scene of many superb races which often brings out the best in riders for some reason.

Maybe it's because the pressure of the season's gone, championships have either been won or lost by then. There's big prize money available, (cash, in Hong Kong dollars) and some fun to be had. Macau's an off-shore gambling mecca for the Chinese who love it of course. It was a Portuguese colony until the end of the nineties, when it was handed back to China. There's a new short circuit been built a bit further north there, called Zhu Hai, where I believe it's planned to host Grand Prix, probably bikes and F1 cars, so maybe the event will eventually disappear. After the week's racing at Macau, it's traditional for the whole field to travel to Pattaya, Bangkok's nearest beach resort for a bit of a party, which is another story. I hope the event survives Macau's transition to Chinese rule, because it's totally unique.

Jim McMahon, my mechanic put in a spectacular performance too, at one of the receptions put on for the teams and riders in a top Macau hotel. You arrive there on a Sunday, practice is on Wednesday and the parties start the next day when the buffet and drink is all free. "Free!" said Jim when he found out and started eating and drinking for Ireland.

By nine o'clock Jim was absolutely hammered, I mean completely dead on the floor and he got carried off to his hotel room to sleep it off. Three hours later, showered and changed he was back downstairs ready to go again as fresh as a daisy, drinking until five in the morning. By this time the other teams were wondering who was going to be getting my bike ready for the next morning, but I knew Jim well enough and there he was at seven in the morning before anyone else, bike fired up and on the line with my leathers hung up over a heater all ready for me. What a team!

I raced at Donington Park for the first time during the 1989 season, in a one-off event and loved the track, which was unusual for me at the time, being a short circuit. I was using the RC30 and had a real go in the last race with new tyres on the bike, but crashed out big time at Craner Curves. Sitting amidst the wreckage, licking my wounds, I realised how much I'd been enjoying it and decided there and then, that was it, I was going Formula One racing next year and no one was going to stop me!

Winning in those days, particularly on the 250, was starting to become a habit, so much so I started to accumulate Northern Ireland's very own champagne lake. When there wasn't enough room to park the car in the garage because of the boxes of bottles inside, we'd throw a champagne party and drink the stuff all night - no other drinks allowed! It's a tough job, but someone had to do it as the saying goes.

At the end of the 1988 season, I returned my 250 to John Wilson and Matt Lavery, who has it in his garage to this day. Next season, I'd really got an even more competitive 250, campaigning Joey Dunlop's while he was injured. (My sponsor, Turkingtons financed a brand new bike in 1990.) With sorted machinery like that, I was starting to win just about every event, to the extent that it was starting to look like a bit of a one-horse race. There was never enough money of course, the sponsorship was appreciated and really helped, but I desperately needed more cash and was happy to take it from any source. It's no excuse for what I did, but funds were short and the temptation for a bit of extra cash so high, that on a few occasions I accepted a 'consideration' to make a poor start.

There was never a direct request, just a wink when someone began wondering how far I could come through the field if I happened to make a really bad start. Of course, it was great entertainment for the crowd; any race, even a whole series can be boring if one rider is racing himself way out in front - look what happened when Mick Doohan was totally dominating Grand Prix in the late nineties. It could get boring on your own at the front too, I much preferred mixing it with the other guys - that's what racing's all about of course.

So, indirectly I was offered a couple of pounds for a bad start and indirectly I took it, but it was a dangerous thing to do, as easy as pie to plan getting away about tenth and then find yourself eighteenth or something, maybe worse, with someone good getting away at the front and then I was in trouble. I regretted doing it on more than one occasion and nearly lost races because of it, but the crowds just loved watching this brainless nutter carving his way to the front, coming right through the field. Some people said I made it all look easy in those days but make no mistake, there were some very good riders in those fields and I can't remember ever having an easy race. At least I wasn't as extreme as the old Spanish Grand Prix star Angel Nieto. He'd be leading a race by half a lap, then slow right down, letting the entire field past, before getting back up to speed and winning the race. Now there's crowd pleasing for you.

Nieto was world champion thirteen times in 50, 80 and 125cc classes and a great rider, really dominant. He was practising at Dundrod for the Ulster Grand Prix once, when GP photographer Volker Rauch had positioned himself track side to get a shot of the diminutive Nieto on his tiny Derbi. He came screaming into shot but lost control, disappearing through a hedge at a rapid rate of knots only to reappear through the hole a minute or so later with his leathers torn to shreds, carrying his bike under one arm! What a picture! He pedalled off down the road and restarted the bike, spraying bits of hedgerow all over the track.

Grand Prix riders in those days did everything of course, often competing in the 250, 350 and 500 classes on the same day, taking their bikes over some of the roughest courses too. I'm not comparing myself to them, but racing in Ireland is held over some tough, rough courses. Running the RC30, the 600 and the 250 in 1990, people would ask me if it was hard switching between the three in different races on the same day.

There'd be a warm-up lap to settle down with whichever bike it was and by half a lap into the fifty miles or more of the race, I'd be perfectly at one with the machine. I've started forgetting about riding a 250 in the last few years though, because it is a bike you really have to be racing every week for maximum performance. You can't just leap on one in May and expect to do well at the North West for example, as there are specialists now, as with industry and so many other things. Each class is becoming more and more specialised, with the effort of getting one bike to the line much greater and much more complicated, that's just the way things are going. Technicians are becoming more specialised too, with telemetry and software becoming critical parts of success, so it looks like the days of riders competing in three or four classes will soon be gone forever.

I wrapped up the 1989 season as the Ulster and Irish 1,000cc Tarmac Champion with a win on the 750 at Aghadowey and a final hat trick at the Killalane road races, with two wins on the RC30 and one on the 600 Honda for good measure, a race memorable only for the fact that Dave Leach crashed his Yamaha straight into an ambulance, breaking his collar bone in the process. At least he didn't have far to go for medical assistance.

I got a real nasty shock one morning when the tax man sent me a bill, which was something I'd never even thought about, let alone planned for. Of course, the Inland Revenue was counting up the prize money and thought it was about time to send me a bill. It was for thousands and thousands of pounds and left me a bit shocked to say the least. I'd been putting everything I had back into my bikes of course, every last penny, but luckily I had met my solicitor's husband by then, who was a chartered accountant and was quite friendly with him - and he helped me sort it all out.

Manager and ex-rider Davy Wood was keen to continue assisting me along with Leslie McMaster and the Dunlop brothers. I could see how it was difficult for one manager to fight for the benefit of four different riders, all in the same class. Any sponsorship deal would surely have to be split four ways? I couldn't afford that, if there was any sort of sponsorship on offer then I needed it all. The way I was storming through the fields by then, I don't think the other riders would have wanted me as part of the same team anyway, so with guidance from Davy Wood, I began working harder on my own behalf. I felt I was ready to smoke ahead and knew I was as competitive as anyone else out there. By 1990 I was starting to do a lot more for myself, approaching companies who had started to hear about my success, like Arai helmets who have supported me ever since, their superb products having saved my life more times than I care to think about.

Jim McMahon continued to come down to my house and work on the bikes in the evenings. The RC30's complex V4 four stroke engine was beyond my expertise at the time - I'd worked purely with two strokes up until then - and more often than not we wouldn't finish until late at night, just trying the bikes up and down the road in the pitch black, to make sure they were running right after the fettling.

The neighbours have probably got more stories to tell about it than I have; on summer evenings it had turned into a bit of an attraction with many of them inviting their friends round to stand outside the front of their houses (there was a long row of houses down our road) to watch me testing at speeds of up to 150mph. 'Neighbourhood Watch' has never been so much fun! Other residents obviously weren't too happy about these highly illegal antics and made complaints to the authorities about it.

We even had anonymous tip offs about that on more than one occasion and we wouldn't go out testing that night just in case. I think the neighbours and the powers that be were good enough to turn a bit of a blind eye to the goings on and by doing so contributed in their own way to our continuing success.

4

Honda Britain as it is today was formed towards the end of 1989, under the management of former rider Neil Tuxworth, The team relocated for the 1990 season from Honda's well named Power Road, London headquarters in Chiswick, to more cost effective workshops in the Lincolnshire town of Louth, just down the road from the Cadwell Park short circuit.

I was under contract to the world's biggest motorcycle manufacturer, Turkington Windows had renewed their support, I had new bikes, was part of a professional team and felt on top of the world. I had a dream start to the year too, at the lightweight short circuit meeting at Kirkistown. Eugene McManus led the 250 race for a while, followed by me, Alan Patterson, Brian Reid and Johnny Rea - the usual suspects - but I got past Eugene, taking Johnny Rea with me and held him off to take the win, followed by another on the RC30 in the 750 race.

I then scorched the field in the Stock Cup with a 'flag to flag win', lapping everybody up to fifth place and things were suddenly looking good for the year. But I was soon back down to earth at Northern Ireland's traditional Easter weekend race meetings which were pretty disastrous for me. I destroyed just about everything two or three times at Aghadowey's Enkalon Trophy meeting on the Saturday, although I did win on the 750 and hold on for a podium on the 600. The crashes continued back at Kirkistown on the Bank Holiday Monday. I was being over keen in trying to get my bike exactly how I wanted it and was experimenting with stiffer and stiffer steering damper settings to try and keep it under control. I went out on the RC30 and passed Mike Swann to lead the race early on, but Dave Leach got past me on lap four and I got into a massive slide at 120mph, trying to get back on terms with him. I couldn't correct the bike because the damper was set so stiff and the Honda threw me right over the top and beat me to bits. Another lesson learnt the hard way. Honda had heard about all the carnage through the grapevine and they called me on the Tuesday morning to find out what had been going wrong.

I'd signed a contract for bikes and spares, which always makes you feel happier getting your supply line secured, but I suppose they quite fancied having some parts available for their other riders. I'd salvaged some pride with a second in the Regal 600 race though, which had put me five points clear in the Championship.

The gremlins followed me to the Cookstown 100 where I got off to a flier in the 250 race with Joey Dunlop and Brian Reid hot on my heels. I was storming away, keeping Joey at bay, the two of us having got ahead of Brian Reid when the clutch gave up the ghost on lap three and I had to retire. It was a really popular win with the crowd for Joey, who had come back from the bad accident he'd had the year before to not only snatch victory but smash the lap record too. It was great to have him back to mix it with.

Finally things came good when I took the feature race of the day on the 750, with a hot second lap of over 104mph, holding off Dave Leach who then put in a 105mph lap record chasing me down, with Brian Reid in third. It had suddenly turned in to another big fight with Dave, real nail biting stuff for the crowd over the last two laps. I was fractionally ahead when Dave tried a suicidal move up the inside on the second to last comer, but I wasn't going to let this one go and didn't give him an inch, forcing him to back off and into second place at the line.

I picked up another two seconds on the RC30 behind a Honda 500 triple mounted Eddic Laycock at Mondello Park, plus a third on my 600 in the Seniorstock race. This set me up perfectly for my 'home' Tan dragee 100 in early May where I got a great start with Johnny Rea, who was on Eddie Laycock's RC30 (his first time on an RC30 since the North West 200 the year before) which had better kit fitted on it than mine. I wasn't sure how he was going to settle on the 750 after such a long break, but I soon found out as he came screaming past on the second lap, setting a new outright record of 99.74mph.

1, The fastest gun in the West! 1970, aged 7. (Unknown)

2. Here I am at fourteen with my Junior High rugby team. (Unknown)

3. Starting out - on my Yamaha 125 at the Carrowdore 100, 1986. (Unknown)

4. Beating Robert Dunlop for the first time on my 125, the Temple 100, 1987. (Unknown)

5. Lining up Steven Cull (1) on my 250 Rotax on the way to my first £1,000 pay day. The Skerries, 1988. (Unknown)

6. Fame at last! Pleased as punch after my 1988 Newcomers' win
at the Manx Grand Prix. (Eddie Beater)

7. On my Championship-winning 250 Rotax at the Carrowdore 100, 1987. Note the boot - I didn't have enough money for dinner in those days, let alone new footwear. (Roy Alexander)

8. Trying to be a hero, fighting my 600 Kawasaki at the Cookstown 100, 1989. (Brian Gordon)

9. A bit over enthusiastic at the new stop box. Lightweight TT, 1991. (Unknown)

10. Winning the 1990 Carrowdore 100 at record pace on my RC30, my first race back after a bad crash at the Temple 100. (Roy Harris)

11. On my RC30 - a competitive 750 at last - at the Ulster GP1989.
Trevor Nation (JPS helmet, just showing), Dave Leach (7) and Nick Jeffries (17) in pursuit. (Unknown)

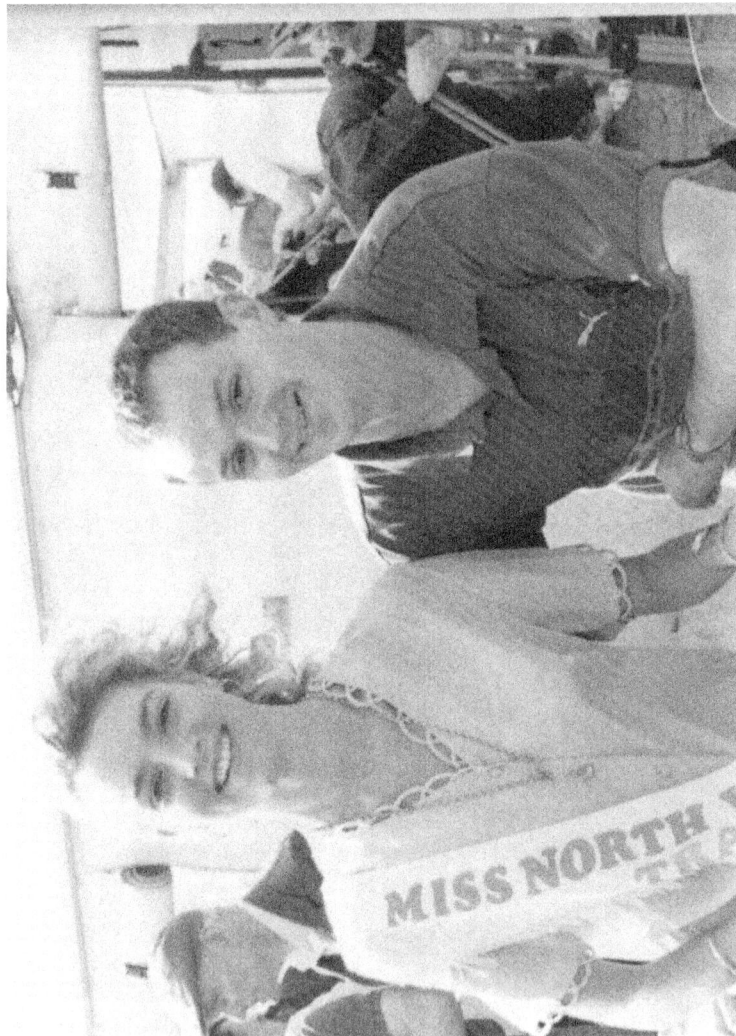

12. Meeting my wife Manda for the first time, North West 200, 1992. (Clifford Maclean)

13. And the winner is...
(Irene Sjodahl. Motorbuild)

14. Leading the 1993 Senior TT at Creg-ny-Baa, braking from about 150mph. (Island Photographic)

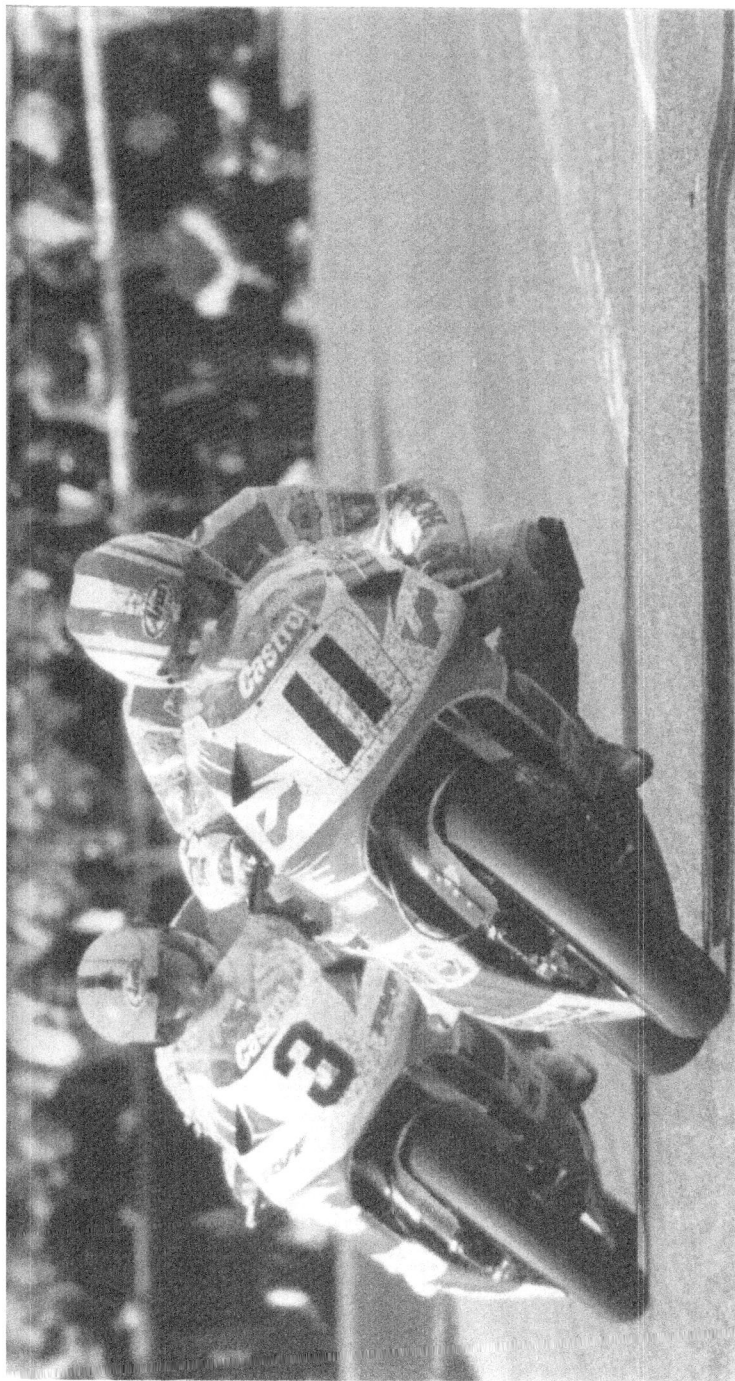

15. A fierce battle with Joey Dunlop during the 1994 Formula One TT, where I finished 2nd behind Steve Hislop. (Eric Whitehead)

16. The challenging Macau road circuit demands total concentration. V4 500 Yamaha, 1995. (Unknown)

The pace hotted up so much I felt sure that we'd finally broken the 100mph barrier, but in the end I think we were actually slowing ourselves up in the fight and I led for the final six laps to take the win, feeling on top form for the forthcoming North West 200. The Bell crossroads on the course is only half a mile from my Mum's house at Ahorey, so she'd come down and watch me do a few laps, but she's a nervous spectator and I don't think she ever stayed to the end.

I'd crashed at the North West in 1988 and 1989 had been the year of my nightmare on the Kawasakis, so the 1990 event was really important to me as it was basically my first meeting there with everything going right and a competitive 750 to use. The RC30 had arrived at the beginning of the season plain white, and we had to do a pretty complicated, time consuming red white and blue paint job on it, as specified by Honda. I was more than surprised when Fogarty and crew turned up with their bikes painted plain red, because they'd had a few crashes and found the striped job just too complicated to keep doing. No one had bothered to tell us of course.

I was determined to do well, really fired up to make that 750 count. Practice went pretty well for the North West with me sixth fastest in the superbike class and third in the 250. We'd been struggling all year against the new 600 Yamahas of Brian Reid, Johnny Rea, Dave Leach and others, because in comparison the Honda 600 was really finished. I knew we were on a hiding to nothing on such a fast track but went out anyway, coming home seventh, but really concentrating on riding hard in the 250 and the 750 races.

Barry Symmonds, who'd left Honda in 1987, had got a superb set up with his Norton team well sorted out for Robert Dunlop. They were good bikes, very fast, the quickest ones out there and Robert Dunlop was a good rider and very light, the ideal combination for a power circuit like that. It's a real sprinter of a track, do or die everywhere which is why the short circuit guys from England can come over and be competitive there, it's short circuit riding at high speed, all slip streaming and hard braking, with really only the coast road to learn. The wind can make a bit of a difference there, but two night's practice on Tuesday and Thursday and you've learnt the track. It's a tough day's racing but practice week gives you plenty of time to prepare.

Guinness had sponsored the meeting and there was good prize money to be had. In the first superbike race I was riding the RC30 as hard as I could in fifth place, right behind the second of the black John Player

Special sponsored Nortons ridden by Trevor Nation. He was trailing Joey Dunlop and Carl Fogarty, who'd got pole in practice and leader Robert Dunlop on the other Norton. I was right behind Nation's Norton at around 180mph going towards Coleraine when it started misfiring a bit. My RC30 was flat out on the rev limiter and I was using Nation's slip stream to stay there, when all of a sudden the Norton cut out right it front of me and I don't know how, it must have been God got me out of it as I pulled to one side and the Norton's exhaust can right up the side of my fairing and I caught Trevor's arm going past him at 180mph.

That was close, a real close one and I finished fourth after that, following a big scrap with Eddie Laycock who took third. So, so lucky. Trevor came up to me after the race and apologised for the incident, saying he'd got no idea how I'd managed to get past and he thanked me for it. It goes to show how fast the Nortons were though, I was flat out and only hanging on inside the slipstream of the Norton that wasn't even running properly! They used to gob great sheets of flame out of the back of them, so big you could have been roasted by them if you got too close.

The big race of the day with the serious prize money went a lot better. Fogarty, Robert Dunlop and Trevor Nation had got away again, with Eddic Laycock, Nick Jeffries, Joey and me in hot pursuit. Fogarty and Nation went out with problems at about midway making me second. Eddie Laycock had got past Joey by this time and was really having a go at me on his 500 Honda triple, which was a faster bike than the RC30, so I was very pleased to keep it all together and hold him off, coming home for my first 750 podium at the North West.

I'd been up the steps a little earlier in the day following the first of two really terrific 250 battles. The first was probably the better of the two, an absolute fight all the way between me and Woolsey Coulter, Kevin Mitchell, Eddie Laycock, Johnny Rea, Alan Irwin, Ian Lougher and Ian Newton. Woolsey got away nicely and I was right behind him with Ian Newton on my shoulder all the way. Kevin Mitchell got past both of us, while I stayed smooth and fast, just concentrating on quick laps and seeing what was going to happen.

Plenty did, both Kevin and Woolsey crashing out with Eddie Laycock getting past as I took avoiding action. It was anyone's race on the last two laps, with Ian Lougher joining in the fun at the front. I timed my charge to perfection and led the lot of them at the Roundabout and I got away a bit, but overcooked it at the Metropole only running wide enough to lose two places though and I salvaged third. A brilliant race, one of those that no one should have lost and the champagne was tasting sweet up there on the podium of the North West. I got a fifth in the second 250 battle of the day and was over the moon with the two podiums in one day.

The Killinchy 150 followed the North West and I was fifth in the 250 race, fifth on my 600 and second in the big race of day, so we really couldn't have asked for a better build up to the 1990 TT and the team arrived in confident mood. Practice went well enough, particularly on the 250 and I ended up third fastest.

I've got a bit of a reputation for not practising as much as I should which really all began when I was starting out. I just didn't have enough stuff to go out and practice much because if I burnt it all out I wouldn't have had anything left to race with. Early on I thought that the idea was just to get out on the track and go round and round in practice and start going quick in the race itself. It took me a wee while to work out that the right thing to do was practice at racing speeds!

But my thinking was still that if we only had two sets of tyres, then what was the point in burning them up during practice? Getting work I couldn't do myself done on engines, plus the spare parts was expensive too, not to mention the petrol - every penny counted and we saved everything we could for the race. The results at the North West were our biggest payday ever by a long way, which of course helped us in so many ways.

Looking back, I can see now how lucky I was not to have needed to practice because of the natural talent I'd been born with, particularly on the roads. Later on, especially short circuit racing at the highest level, I learnt that you couldn't afford to qualify badly, because then you were always playing catch up from midfield or worse. Don't give anything away to help the opposition is a golden rule and I've always included cameras mounted on the bike in that. I was forced into it at the TT in 1992 as this promotional work was part of my contract, but luckily the camera only worked intermittently and most of my secrets remained safe.

I've never seen the point of showing the opposition your lines on film and giving everyone else the benefit of years of hard work and experience. It's hard enough to do without showing everyone else how, and smart people would have watched it for sure.

There's nothing you can do about other riders on the track learning from you but you can limit it. I used number twelve on my bike one time at the TT, (they don't issue number thirteen) and I couldn't get eleven for some reason and I didn't want people starting behind me, because you just put a big target on your back. If they do get on the back of you, you're finished. The danger is of course that they're going to be riding way beyond their ability, just to catch you. You can't start right at the back with seventy riders in front, including some slow ones, so ideally you want to be starting at the front, with a clear track ahead of you. Being first on the road has it's own problems though; time and place signals are slowed, the amount of insects you pick up is extraordinary and you can quickly run out of (visor) tear offs because of it. You'll be the one to clear any stray cats and dogs out of the way too and it's so boring with no one else up front to scrap with. Hopefully no one gets on the back of you if you're a good rider and it's still great fun, but I much prefer racing in company to being up front on my own. I very nearly won on my 250 from the front at the TT once, having led from the start for a long way when I hadn't seen another competitor for the whole race, except while I was in pit lane. It was a strange experience, not like being in a race at all and Robert Dunlop beat me by a fraction of a second, which was a great victory for him as I'd had a big lead at one stage.

I started the 1990 Formula One TT race thinking I had a real chance, until I had to fix the carburettor linkage at the side of the road and that put paid to my chances. I've never worried about things like that though, machines break - you can limit that a lot with proper preparation - but you just have to put it behind you, learn from the experience and carry on, which I did, pleasing myself by putting in a leader pace lap of 118mph. I finished a lowly thirty ninth, but had two hundred and twenty six more TT racing miles under my belt.

I treated it as vital further practice for Monday's Junior where I had more frustration from the carburation problems on the little 250, eventually finishing sixth behind Ian Lougher, Steve Hislop, Eddie Laycock, Foggy and Johnny Rea.

The 600 Yamahas had been dominant so I didn't expect to do well on my Honda at all. It turned in to a race of contrition with Foggy and Hislop going out early on, while Dave Leach and Brian Reid fought it out up front. Steven Hazlett went out, followed by Leach and Rob Holden, which I guess improved my position to a final fourteenth, only the third Honda home, Yamaha took ten of the first fourteen places with Brian Reid taking a solid win, followed by Dave Leach and Johnny Rea.

The weather was particularly bad for Friday's Senior but gave me the chance to really go for it and I was in third place behind Trevor Nation and Carl Fogarty at Ballacraine on the first lap. Hislop and Suzuki Durex man Roger Burnett pulled out saying there was no point continuing because of the road conditions and blinding spray but I was keeping up a good pace, the conditions not worrying me at all as I was so determined by now. I watched Nick Jeffries crash in front of me just past Sarah's Cottage, but turned it up even more, feeling this was my real chance and by the end of lap two I was second, forty seconds behind Fogarty going in to the pit stops.

I switched to a cut slick in the pits, which clears the water a bit and gives you better grip and the signals I was getting back out on the road showed Nation had got ahead of me by nine seconds at the end of lap three, but by then I knew he'd have to switch tyres on his second stop because of the weather and that meant I'd got time in hand. I hadn't got a good signal team in those days, just one or two people out on the course, so I was actually getting most of my information from the public.

I've never gone past The Nook since without that fall in the final stages of the fourth lap - and helicopter ride to hospital - being somewhere in my mind, but its never slowed me down at all. You just can't start treating parts of the course differently, they have to remain all the same in your mind. Start to like or dislike sections and you start slowing down here, going faster there and you're soon in trouble, particularly somewhere like the TT. It's so important to get all the comers right, you've got to get them all together in one go and it's only then, when you've got all those thirty seven and three quarter miles perfect, that you get a fast lap. I very rarely use the clutch on the island, apart from starting and only when I'm really, really on it, I use it to get the bike on the slide going in to some of the first gear comers, which shaves more vital fractions off your lap time.

I was totally gutted after the Senior to say the least. My crash meant Nation got second, who lost about seventeen seconds to third place man Dave Leach during the tyre stop I'd been banking on. So near yet so far.

I've always believed in God, I didn't know where I was when I woke up after the accident, but I did know I was floating, so where else could I be? Mum always made sure we were regular church people. We'd go three times on Sundays, once to the church service, plus Sunday school in the morning and the afternoon, so I knew all about Heaven and genuinely thought that was where I was off to. I'd been unconscious for quite a while after the crash, but once the helicopter team had got me to the hospital I checked out OK, just slight concussion and I got out of there and back to the paddock in time for the podium celebrations.

I was disappointed of course, kicking myself for not being up there with Fogarty, Nation and the champagne, but pleased to know I'd been at the front fighting it out with them. I decided I was ready to go Formula One World Championship racing there and then and went home to make my plans. My RC30 was now in Honda Britain's all new, all red colours and I brought it home second in the Killinchy 150's big race just behind Johnny Rea and in front of a hard charging Joey Dunlop, smoking a Honda GP500 triple round the course.

Johnny won again in the 750 race at Aghadowey and I was third behind Dave Leach, with my excitement mounting at the trip ahead of me.

Finally I left Ireland as the Honda Britain team went to the southern European track of Vila Real, for the Portuguese round of the Formula One World Championship, my first really big international race. I didn't have a factory lump of course, just an ordinary kitted engine, while Joey Dunlop and Carl Fogarty had the real thing. New team manager Neil Tuxworth persuaded me to drive my truck the whole way down there from Ireland, via the team's English headquarters in Louth, Lincolnshire, where I picked up Fogarty's bike for good measure, all for half the diesel and ferry costs.

Fogarty and his crew flew in to the local airport, after we'd ground our way down there overland and got the awnings and everything else up in the paddock, ready for their arrival. What a deal! But the truth of it is, I was pleased just to be there.

Apart from Joey and Carl, Robert Dunlop was there campaigning the rotary engined Norton, which was dramatically faster than our bikes with its weight as light as the F1 rules allowed and its alleged near 1200cc capacity. (The Norton factory insisted the bike's twin rotor Wankel engine had a capacity of 588cc, while the FIM, the sport's governing body disagreed, ruling it was twice that size.)

This was the time I began working with Fogarty's chief technician of the time, Dennis Willey, who has since become a life long friend. He'd started by helping me sort my spares out before the start of the season, which I'd collected in my truck from the new workshops near Cadwell. He was an experienced guy, having worked on race bikes since he could ride a bicycle, travelling all over the world on the Formula Two circuit and he was good to me, making sure I got the right stuff and wasn't given any parts that didn't benefit the machinery. He started helping me more and more in fact and I'd let him have some trick little bits I was having made at home.

I had some quick release wheel balancers designed and made for the RC30 in late 1989 and got one for Dennis. No one else had them for the RC30 then, there were some horrible screw up things about that took twenty minutes to get on and off, but mine were beautiful, Dennis appreciated it and no one's ever bettered the mechanism to this day. So that helped improve the parts and information flow and the team got tighter because of it.

Fogarty wasn't the best at setting his bike up for a new track in those days, he was a good rider but struggled to make the connection between suspension settings and the behaviour of the bike, so Dennis would just wait until after practice when I'd got the RC30 as I wanted it, check my settings and put some of the ideas into Foggy's bike. Easy!

My engineering knowledge has stood me in good stead with manufacturers and aftermarket firms to this day and the team's contributed to the development of many of today's aftermarket parts manufacturers.

I hadn't qualified that well in Portugal, because I'd been learning the four or five mile track and the race was very tough for me, not being used to riding in what felt like about 100 degree heat. But as the race progressed I settled well and got stronger and quicker and could have finished on the rostrum I think, but for a strange bit of marshalling. Fogarty was in the lead with Robert second on the Norton when I started getting glimpses of Joey in third ahead of me which spurred me on, until I finally caught him going into the last lap. I think Joey was fading a bit by then when a marshal, who'd been watching this lunatic (me) coming through the field very fast, suddenly leapt out in front of Joey, frantically waving a blue flag.

This woke Joey up straight away, so instead of me surprising him with a nice clean pass and getting away after his brother and Foggy up ahead, he got all fired up and on the gas to defend his rostrum position. I got past him on the brakes, but the surprise element had gone and the power of the factory engine sent him flying past me on the straights and that was that, fourth place in my first Formula One race Overseas - not bad I suppose, with the consolation of the Irish contingent, Robert, Joey and me taking three of the top four places.

A few days later we went on to Finland for the next round and had a bit of a bizarre incident in the truck on the way over. I was at the wheel of the Mercedes, driving through Sweden at night on the way to the circuit when a huge animal, which turned out to be a moose, suddenly dashed out of some trees and across the road right in front of the truck. I hit the brakes and there was a bang from the back of the truck, which turned out to be one of the mechanics being catapulted out of the top bunk and into a steel partition. I managed to swerve just in time to miss the beast, only to run into a second one and there was an even bigger bang.

There was screaming and moaning coming from inside the truck and the poor animal wasn't too happy outside either. The rudely awakened mechanic had stumbled outside in a bit of a daze and was nearly trampled to death by the first moose. He ended up on the tarmac nose to nose with the second one, the freezing night air turning their breath into clouds of vapour, making the aftermath of the crash look like something out of a horror movie.

The police were quickly on the scene and tried to shoot the animal in the head with a handgun, but the bullet just ricocheted off it's skull; they really are massive creatures. They're beautiful animals and a protected species in Sweden and I was a bit upset at causing the death of such a wonderful creature. We spent hours in the police station filling out forms, where the staff said the bigger animal was sure to get killed too, as it would be wandering the roads looking for its companion (which had been humanely put down at the roadside). I hope it survived.

The accident delayed us for a long time, so we arrived at the track at four or five in the morning instead of the evening before as planned. Not a good way to start practice at all. I qualified OK on the kitted RC30 but the power of the other riders' factory engines didn't turn out be such an important factor this time, as it was a very wet race. Foggy was leading by about five seconds and I was closing on him in second, superb stuff, well pleased with my performance, thinking I had the potential to pull him right back.

Maybe I could have, maybe not, but I didn't have the chance to find out as a back marker, who'd been off the racing line when I came across him towards the end of the longest and fastest straight on the track, suddenly pulled in front of me onto the drier racing line, getting ready to take the corner.

I was in sixth gear, flat out at about 170 mph approaching the five hundred metre marker board with nowhere to go except straight into standing water at the edge of the track. The bike aquaplaned, we parted company and I hit the deck at well over 150mph, hurtling up the road on my back for about five hundred metres, steering myself quite nicely with my elbows. Another chance of a rostrum position and a fight for the lead with Foggy had slid away with the bike.

I was very disappointed because I like the wet - in fact I like everything, I just love riding bikes and I sincerely believe I would have had a serious chance there for a Formula One win, in my second ever race in the Championship. People said I was trying too hard, but it wasn't that, just an inexperienced guy swerving in front of me, leaving me without any options except heading for a lake.

Foggy and I were on very different machinery of course and his background gave him some big advantages. He was moto-crossing from a very young age, which gives you all the instinctive bike control you need to succeed on the track in later life. He also had a few seasons' start on me, apart from the advantage his exotic factory kit was giving him. His Dad George had competed with some success I think, so coming from a racing family, Carl had obviously been around the scene for a lot longer, with a knowledgeable father giving invaluable advice based on experience. I was giving myself advice based on experiment and guesswork.

True, I had an engineering background which really helped in lots of ways, including helping with the setup of our bikes. Such was his level of skill, he seemed to be able to ride and win even when his bike's handling was way off, the mark of a true champion. Oh well! I just had to try harder and found out on the few occasions we mixed it in close company, that Carl definitely had the pedigree of a World Champion.

There were never any team orders in those days, I think it was assumed that the factory boys would be way out in front anyway. My greatest challenge was not having any professional guidance, ideally from someone who'd 'been there and done it' at this level before, who was also capable of alleviating some of my other worries - bikes, transport, sponsors, spares - the endless list of things that need organising to run a professional and successful race team.

It would have let me concentrate more on racing and I think my career would have been very different. If I'd met the right person I believe we both would have benefitted handsomely, but there you go. I'll always be indebted and so very grateful to my helpers and sponsors in those early days, who were doing it out of pure friendship and love of the sport, which is part of the magic of it all of course.

This situation became much more noticeable when short circuit racing in England, particularly at international meetings, where everything was happening so much faster, meaning I had much less time to prepare properly.

When I was injured for a year and managed riders in 1998, I knew from my experience that you need to give people the maximum if you want them to do the maximum job for you. Ian Simpson, Michael Rutter and Jim Moodie got the very best I could possibly give and the team worked even harder to provide them with what they wanted. And those boys won, at the highest level.

Jim was really keen to stay with the team and he's one of the most discerning riders around, who demands the highest standards of bike preparation. We'd only one full time mechanic and a couple of part timers working for the love of the sport, (including Dennis Willey), but Jim was winning and getting British 600 Supersport podiums time and again in the most competitive championship of the time, the year John Crawford won on the Suzuki GSXR.

Our team would work all night to get the bike perfect, consistently, week after week which gives the rider great confidence and belief in the machine and the team. That's when things get better and faster and championships get won. In a hundred starts under manager Paul Butler's control, the legendary Grand Prix Team (King Kenny) Roberts recorded eighty eight podium finishes.

That's why I never talk about 'I' when I'm discussing my racing, it's always what 'we' the team has achieved, because I know from bitter experience that the rider is only one part of the winning equation. A team is only successful when it's being run by a complete professional and behind every champion is a figure like that, with a dedicated team focussing on just one thing.

I've thought about going into team management myself - we were successful and earned the riders' respect in 1998, but I'd want a team and a rider with the same commitment as me and that's difficult to put in place, as the top riders and technicians are already committed.

Back home I had a wonderful result at the Skerries, winning all four races I started in, two each on the 250 and 750 Hondas, the first rider ever to do so. Johnny Rea went off like a rocket in the first race and I'd got a poor start with quite a bit to do, but once I got in front I eased away for a convincing win in the end and followed it up with a start to finish win in the second 250 event.

This was the meeting where I really started to turn the tables on Johnny Rea in the 750 class that season with a double win, but it wasn't easy as Johnny got his nose in front on lap two in the first superbike clash and fought hard until I eventually won by four seconds. Dave Leach brought his OW01 Yamaha home in third. The second race was practically a carbon copy of the first, with Johnny Rea once again leading and the two of us keeping a good sized crowd on its feet, until I drew away in the closing stages to increase my lead in the 750 Irish Road Race Championship to twenty three points.

I didn't even bother starting in the 600 event as we'd been struggling for speed on the Honda all year, which was basically a standard road bike that Jim McMahon had tuned to the best of his ability. I had never had the benefit of a tuned motor, but Foggy had blown his engine good and proper in the Junior TT and we'd got hold of it. We put the cylinder head and a lot of other parts we salvaged off it onto my bike and suddenly I had the quickest 600 I'd ever had. "I'm going to win everything on this!" I thought the first time I'd got it out. I couldn't have been more wrong.

The next race I was entered for was a Regal Championship round, the Temple 100, which is a really fast course with 150mph jumps. It's a very tough course indeed with every section full of challenging jumps and tums and I was fighting it out for second place, with Steven Cull and Dave Leach, while Brian Reid was leading, all of them on the quick Yamahas, so this was the stir among the pile.

Just before a bridge the bike took off sideways at over a hundred miles an hour in a spectacular crash, firing me straight into an electricity pole, which I bounced off back onto the track unconscious, a very serious crash with every witness convinced I couldn't have survived.

But I had, Fred McSorley, the doctor on the scene had helped with that and he scraped me off the road into the ambulance to be rushed off to hospital with a broken foot and shoulder, suspected fractured skull, and bad haemorrhaging inside my head and eyes, which meant I was blind when I came out of the coma. I was to give Fred quite a bit more business after that.

When I finally came round in hospital, the pain was very bad and I couldn't see a thing, thinking I'd got something stuck in my eyes. I was lying in bed calling out "Get me Rab!" because my friend Rab Gillis has a gift with healing eyes, something his father has passed down to him. People go to see him from all over the country and he helps patients who've been in hospital with serious problems for days or weeks with his method, it's a brilliant charm he has.

I was cursing my luck because someone told me Foggy had won the Formula One Championship by then and Honda had promised me his factory engine for the Ulster Grand Prix.

I knew that it was going to be difficult getting a result there without the use of my eyes and I resigned myself to having to wait to see if my sight was going to come back. Either way I knew I'd have to wait yet another year to prove myself there on a 750. Without my eyesight, my ears had picked up a lot of my visitors' reactions when they'd seen me for the first time. My bed was right by the nurses' station and I was in plain view of all arrivals to the ward. Yet everyone coming to see was stopping and asking the nurses which bed I was in, while they were standing right next to me. Worryingly, when the nurse on duty pointed me out, there had been a lot of gasps and sharp intakes of breath.

Dim, blurred images gradually started to appear until some sort of vision started to come back. I wanted to see the damage for myself. All mirrors had been carefully removed and I was refused one when I asked, so I resorted to blackmail. I'd seen a nurse doing something rather wrong one morning when she obviously thought I was still blind - I won't say what because she came up with a mirror in return for my solemn promise that I'd never tell a living soul what she'd done - sorry about that - it's a great story too, but a promise is a promise!

I plucked up courage and looked in the mirror and it did scare me. I twisted it and turned it because it obviously wasn't me; a big, bloated, jet black face was staring back at me and it was then they told me about the haemorrhaging and massive bruising and that I should have seen it a week ago...

To add insult to injury, Fogarty's factory engine went to Steven Cull for the Ulster Grand Prix. Bike racing is a tough sport and there's little room for sentimentality and the best equipment has to go to the rider most likely to succeed. It was still desperately frustrating though, lying in my hospital bed with opportunities like that passing me by.

Against all the odds, my comeback race was at August's Carrowdore 100, only five weeks after my horrific crash in the Temple 100. Unsurprisingly I had a real job passing the medical, hobbling onto the 250 to break the lap record during a big race long fight with Brian Reid, who beat me on the last comer, leaving me fuming and determined to win the 750 race. I did and took the 750 Irish Road Race Championship for the first time with a close second behind Dave Leach at Killalane a couple of weeks later, with two wins on my 250 for good measure. A third on my 250 at Nutts Comer was enough to sneak the Irish 250 Short Circuit Championship from Woolsey Coulter, who only needed to finish in the top fifteen to win it. Woolsey crashed out of the race though and my podium was enough to take the title by just one point.

Macau is really something to look forward to at the end of the season, a true road racing track which really suits my style of riding; I'd done well getting second the year before and I fancied going one better this time. I only managed two fifths in both races though, ending up sixth on aggregate in the hot sunshine. Steve Hislop, a superb rider, won a very tough race from top German superbiker Peter Rubatto in second, with Dave Leach third, Robert Dunlop fourth, an American rider Donald Jacks fifth riding a big 1100 Suzuki which had been bored out to over 1300cc and developed about 200bhp. That monster was leaving us all for dead on the straights I can tell you.

Hislop had the full factory spec. Honda which he'd been winning on all year and Rubatto's Yamaha was semi-factory too, the two of them sharing the wins in the two legs, Hizzy edging the overall first by 0.9 secs. Dunlop's Norton was a rocketship compared to Dave Leach and my bikes. He did exceptionally well to be fighting it out at the front. I hung on at the back of the top group on my kitted RC30, cursing the lack of power. Well, you've got to blame something.

A good 500 Grand Prix bike was always the best machine to take out there in those early days, but now superbikes and Grand Prix machines are getting to be on a par on most circuits. It's much easier to get a world superbike spec. bike than a GP machine, which have become hard to get hold of recently. The only ones around are at least five years old, where as year old WSB kit can be bought quite easily. A modern GP bike versus a modern superbike round there would be a very evenly matched contest I think and the result would be down to the rider more than anything else.

What a season! I'd had quite a few crashes at the start of the year, a 600 which was uncompetitive until I turned it into a rocketship on which I then got seriously injured and a 250 which I seemed to either win or crash on! Thankfully, I kept pumping in the wins on the 750 though - the most important because it meant Honda stayed interested in supporting me and I could really focus on performing in the big international road races the following year.

5

We worked really hard on the bikes over that winter, still using the garage at my Mum's house that's there to this day. The building of it was organised by my Dad, who wanted a big garage when we moved to Ahorey, but he was sick by then and two of my uncles put it all together. It's big enough to keep a dozen bikes in and work on them.

Honda had got new backing for our machinery in 1991 and I took my Mercedes van over to England in January to collect the new bikes and some spares, including the new model CBR600 which caused us - and everyone else - big problems with carburation. We literally spent two months trying to get the thing to run right, testing up and down the road outside the house - and it'd be no good - so back in the garage, needles up, jets up, jets down, in, out, just non-stop for weeks on end. I don't think many of the neighbours got much sleep at all that winter, until we finally cracked it.

It was such a hard bike to ride for the first couple of races until I got used to its weird behaviour. You'd be flat on your side coming out of a corner, put the gas on and nothing would happen, until all of a sudden the thing would burst into life spinning sideways trying to fire you off. I didn't have the brains to shut it off, just kept the throttle wide open, fighting the thing up the track. I wanted to win everything that season so bad, I really did.

We were using Michelins at the time and their production tyres weren't the best available, but you couldn't get the free slicks if you didn't use the proddy rubber, which didn't make the 600 any easier to ride I can tell you. I was a winner of course and Michelin made me do it, but in those early days I had the toughest job because they were only road tyres and Dunlop, Pirelli, Metzeler and Avon were all developing soft compound production tyres purely for racing.

As I'd been 'up there' at the 1990 TT following my Manx success two years earlier, Michelin and quite a few others had recognised my potential and started to give me some support, thinking it was only a matter of time before some big wins came. The new Honda did just have the edge on power over the Yamaha though, which had been around for two years by that time, but that also meant it was better sorted too of course.

The important thing was support from such a major player like Michelin, another vital piece in the jigsaw that makes up a successful team. It doesn't matter how talented a rider you are, you can do absolutely nothing by yourself; you need the right bikes, the right parts, enough money to run it all, the strongest possible team around you, everything.

This is even more important in short circuit racing than on the roads, where talent and courage count for so much. It looked a bit like I was a one man band back then, but it was a hard working, tough little team which never stopped until things were finished and night. As our success was building, my older brother Ronald was getting more involved too. He was a mechanic by trade and technically minded. He could do a good job when he wanted to and the team was getting a lot more professional, whereas before we'd really been doing everything for fun.

We'd get started as early as we could after work as I was still 'keeping up the day job' before Jim McMahon would arrive from his, when Mum would have the tea ready and we'd all stop for a bit to watch Coronation Street - that was the only break we got really, with Mum keeping the snacks and drinks coming to the garage outside all night after that. With my two brothers and me all living at home with my Mum, the house was a crazy place, lots of fun, just full of people all the time.

If we loaded the bikes into the van by midnight on the Friday night before Saturday's race meeting, when Mum would be making up the sandwiches we'd be taking with us, we'd done well, even though we always aimed for nine o'clock on Friday. That meant we got a few hours sleep before leaving, which we all really needed as we would have been working until two or three in the morning every day since the last race.

Mum would often come in to the garage if it was that late in the morning and tell us to switch the light off and get to bed and more often than not we would. Mum knows best. Testing a race bike up and down the road at that time of the morning in the pitch black, sometimes on ice or frost in January or February was a bit of an experience too, not a particularly enjoyable one for the neighbours either, unless they happened to be ardent fans.

I'd heard all about the famous Daytona International race, held on the East Florida coast in March and was so desperate to get torn in to the season, I decided to try and ride there that year, as I really wanted to get into this big time stuff.

Then Niall Mackenzie joined Honda in 1991, in order to partner Carl Fogarty in the World Superbike Championship with the full Honda Britain line up being launched at London's Alexander Palace road race and superbike show early in the year. British 250 champion Alan Carter, Nick Jeffries, Steve Hislop, Foggy, Niall and I were all present for the media launch when it was announced Foggy and Mackenzie would clash for the first time at Daytona on 1990 RC30's, as the new bikes were yet to arrive.

Daytona rules prevented the use of factory engines at the races there and of course I was the only person who had been racing the year before using a kitted engine, tuned by Tony Scott. So, I had to hand mine over for Mackenzie to use at Daytona and my chance for that year was gone. Niall left the team quite quickly after that, I don't think he was too impressed with the bikes or their potential.

Road racing was my absolute passion and when the Formula One World (road racing) Championship was disbanded and the chance of international racing on the long five or ten mile tracks gone, I wasn't really interested in going into World Superbikes. It was the walls, ramps, posts, gates, fast corners, slow corners, humps, bumps and trees that made me feel at home.

All the World Superbike rounds were to be held on short circuits and I felt I still had so much to prove on the roads and especially at the TT. The capacity limits in F1 had been brought down to 750 in an attempt to limit the power and speeds of bikes on the grounds of safety and the trouble was, Honda hadn't really got a 750 that was competitive under the production based World Superbike rules. The RC30 was basically out of date by then and they were experimenting with variations of it; the E7D appeared at the time and Fogarty rode that for a bit.

He left the following year, feeling the equipment just wasn't competitive, so under the circumstances I was happy to stay in the UK and concentrate on what I wanted to do - have the success of being an Isle of Man winner, rather than travelling round the world racing on short circuits.

I did get on a long distance flight later in the season though, except in the opposite direction to Daytona, flying to Japan with Joey Dunlop for the Suzuka eight hour. We'd been invited by a Japanese dealer, who Fogey had ridden for the year before, scoring quite high, and I leapt at the chance because obviously it's an important international race.

The other important reason was it was being held on the same weekend as the Temple 100. I had bad memories of that course, where I'd got hurt so badly in my accident there the year before. So I was pleased to have a good excuse not to go back there as I wasn't ready to race there in my mind. I couldn't live with the gremlins it left with me though and decided a bit later that I'd go back next season and lay the fear to rest.

It turned out that Joey was a huge hero in Japan, like a God, with fans mobbing us everywhere we went, chanting "Joey, Joey!" The Isle of Man TT races are rightly revered in Japan as the ultimate challenge in bike racing and winners are held in very high regard - it was unbelievable how big a star he was there.

From the press reports I've seen, my popularity has now risen there too after my TT wins, but during that trip I was a nobody, standing for hours and hours in the hot sun, while Joey signed thousands of autographs. And that was about as successful as it got, we had nothing but mechanical troubles, really frustrating because I'd offered to bring my engine with me from home, but they'd insisted they had everything we needed.

We had old RC30s with a mixture of parts on them and it was a real disaster. We were using Bridgestone tyres which were still in development stages then and a big handful, the things spinning everywhere giving us a constant battle for grip. One of the qualifying sessions was damp and sticky when riding ability started to count and Joey and me got up to about tenth or eleventh I think, with me just a few tenths of a second quicker than Joey - we were really pulling out all the stops. It was a great experience racing with Joey instead of against him and I loved every thing, great track and superb facilities but with no power and no grip, everything was passing us on the straights and the corners.

In the race Fogarty and Hislop were way ahead of us on their official HRC (Honda Racing Corporation) machinery and finished third, while the race was won by Wayne Gardner and Mick Doohan We were nowhere. I would have liked to do more endurance racing, F1 style bikes with plenty of power and long, long races would have suited me well, because of my high level of fitness. I've had quite a few offers over the years, but never took advantage of them because the dates always seemed to clash with important stuff elsewhere.

Earlier on that year, I'd got the season off to a flying start by winning the big Easter Saturday race on my 750 at Aghadowey, my first Enkalon Trophy win along with seven hundred and sixty quid, that was some prize money at the time - just what I needed to get things going. I worked very hard in the 600 race, starting to get things together on the new bike with a second place and it was off to Kirkistown on Easter Monday where I went one better with a hat trick of wins on the 750, including the King of Kirkistown event.

The 600 was still not quite right though, only running well enough to get me a fourth in the important Regal Championship race, but it was starting to show the potential that I'd need if I was to take the tide for the first time that year,

Next up, I led the big 750 race at Nutts Corner from start to finish and managed to get the 600 into third place with the bike definitely feeling a lot better, just in time for the first road race of the year, the Cookstown 100 the following weekend. I'd got the new bike pretty much dialled in by then and it only needed some fine tuning to get ready for the real thing, my road racing. Sometimes we'd alter the cam timing or play with the ignition settings to get a bit more torque or better top speed in preparation for particular races, but broadly speaking I wanted everything all the time and settled for a happy medium.

Our English engine tuner Tony Scott was very strict about 'his' engines at the time; he really didn't like you messing about with them too much, so we were careful to respect his wishes. Tony had prepared all the engines at the beginning of the season for us but by now trusted us enough to allow Jim McMahon to maintain them - it would be some time before our budget allowed the luxury of Tony's personal attention throughout the season.

He is a superb engine builder and tuner, one of the best there is. We got on from the moment we first met, both having high engineering standards. I've always admired Tony's meticulous attention to detail and workmanship and I think he saw how serious I was to learn everything I could and do the best possible job in my races. His engines have won countless TTs and he actually relocates his workshop to the island for TT fortnight now, to support the teams and riders using his equipment.

As I said, Tony allowed us to experiment and play with the engine settings and quickly started to trust the feedback we were giving him, for better or worse. It's been a superb relationship that's developed over ten years. Micron Exhausts started supporting me in 1989 and I began to allow them to use my race bikes for development work on their dynos a couple of years later. Dave Hunter is their technical head and we'd get the bikes over to Micron's English base whenever we had the opportunity to do so.

They really trusted my knowledge of bikes and of course competition at the highest level on the roads is the greatest laboratory there is. I'd give them feedback over the phone every week, modified parts would arrive on a regular basis, we'd fit them and the process would continue. Every cloud really does have a silver lining, because the problems with the carburation on the CBR600 led to the start of my relationship with the two main men at Dynojet.

When we did dyno work with Micron in England, they'd got involved and saw that I really knew what I was talking about, beginning to feed me with special parts from their base in America. No one knew a thing about the new 600 at that time and we put a lot of work into getting it right before constantly improving it, which was expensive and time consuming with all the travelling to England and back.

It was much better when I could get there to physically work on the dyno with Dave Hunter and he preferred it too because I'd be bringing my own combinations of settings and ideas to the party. We'd work for hours and days on end in structured sessions to make it work and I was able to give him direct, realistic feedback on what would work, by physically checking throttle response and power characteristics as we worked towards the ideal combination of settings.

I remember one occasion when we'd had a long, long session one day in the middle of 1998 and were a bit frustrated because we hadn't made a great deal of progress. Everybody had had enough really and wanted to get on with the long drive home but my subconscious had been working away and I suddenly wondered if a particular combination of settings could be a way to go.

I persuaded everyone concerned to do one last run, which was difficult because we were tired, it was late, the idea was a bit off the wall, really extreme in fact and it was a boring chore changing the same things around time and time again. I wasn't under quite so much pressure as usual, as I wasn't riding at the time through injury and I dug my heels in enough for them to realise Phillip wasn't going home until this had been done.

As soon as the engine hit its top end on that final dyno run, the power curve went sky high and my stand-in Jim Moodie won the bike's very next race for us, a British 600 Supersport Championship round at Knockhill. Not riding made it so much more difficult; you can get a bit of feedback from other riders but it's obviously not the same and we definitely suffered when I wasn't in the saddle myself. The hard work's all worth it in the end you see, but endless - you can never stop the constant search for improvements.

The next meeting was the Cookstown 100 and we won the race of the day on the 750 and got a third on the fast improving 600 in the Regal round before the Tandragee 100 the following weekend. Of course I was desperate to win there in front of my home crowd but got a terrible start in the 250 event.

I'd crashed in the same race the year before, so I was particularly determined to do well this time but had to fight my way through the whole field before I could get on terms with Joey Dunlop at the front. Joey and I'd had a few battles before that but what followed was probably the hardest race I've ever had with him, literally wheel to wheel the whole way, pushing each other so hard that I was the first rider there to break the 100mph barrier. I won the princely sum of a hundred quid for my trouble, which had been put up years and years before when no one thought it possible. What a superb, naturally talented rider Joey is and such a wonderful opponent on the track or the roads.

I got the lap record in the 750 race which I won, to add to the outright course record I got earlier and just lost out to Brian Reid in the 600 Regal race, finishing second but what a great weekend's racing! We left the Tandragee happy and confident going into the North West with no injuries or Crashes to worry about and I had to prove a point. My first year there didn't really exist in my mind because of all the breakdowns, but in 1990 I'd fired some warning shots and now I was in top form and ready to go.

Practice went really good with the 600 finally running beautifully, just how I wanted it and I was quickest. I was down the field a little bit in 250 qualifying, but well pleased with third quickest on my 750 just behind Fogarty, with Joey fastest, all of us on Hondas and in front of the super quick Nortons. The RC30 had new suspension, springs and forks and I was still experimenting with it, a slower process for me in those days, but it had all come together in practice and we'd got it right.

The 250 race was a superb scrap all the way between Ian Lougher, Brian Reid, Steven Hazlett, Robert Dunlop and James Courtney, with Robert beating me fair and square by just half a bike over the line so I couldn't moan and was delighted with second, one better than my finish the previous year.

I was out again next in the superbike race, determined to prove myself in the big event after qualifying so well, knowing this was my big chance to finally show them who was going to be king at the North West. There's nowhere like the North West 200 in the world, over 100,000 genuine fans there on Saturday's race day; if you've never been, then get to Portrush on Northern Ireland's north coast next May, you won't regret it, I guarantee you. You don't even have to pay to get in! It's free to watch, but remember to buy a programme as that's the way the organisers raise the revenue to run the event. See you there.

The noise from a crowd of that size is something else, there's not many sportsmen anywhere in the world who have the opportunity to perform in front of so many people, let alone a home crowd of that size. It can be a huge lift when the fans get behind you, waving the programmes and cheering you on, making you want to win it even more. And winning there is so very special; more prize money, more recognition, the chance of better equipment and a better job; second place is no good to anyone, in second place you're just the first loser.

The partying goes on into the night, riders, teams and fans together, whether you've had a good time, or a bad time like we did there on the RC30 in 1991. It wasn't until some time after the North West I found out that I was being used as a test pilot. Racing is all about development and an oil company was developing a lot of products working with our Honda team, with the RC30 engine a real challenge.

The contract and partnership between the two companies meant we had to be part of the experimentation process. I didn't realise I was the only rider involved at this stage, draining oil out of my engines and handing it over as test samples for development analysis, after every race.

The problem was the test lubricant I was using in my superbike was still some way from handling the stresses of the RC30 engine and there was trouble as I came round on the warm up lap for the first superbike race. I was storming into Portrush at 150mph at least, dropping down to the Metropole, (before the chicane was put in there) and the engine started faltering badly, feeling like fuel starvation.

The bike had been giving occasional trouble with a blocked breather pipe and thinking that was the problem, I flicked up the fuel filler cap on the tank to try and get rid of the airlock. I was hanging on to the filler cap of course to stop it flying off, but the engine was still making the same horrible noises, with big waves of power loss coming and going.

Suddenly I realised it was trying to seize, snapped the filler cap shut and just as I grabbed at the handlebars and got hold of the clutch lever at about 130mph, the motor locked up solid. But I'd saved it at the very last moment, got the bike over to the side of the road and parked it.

I was absolutely furious, just boiling over with anger and frustration which was why I was so fired up for the 600 event which was the race of the day, a fantastic battle between seven riders. Mike 'Spike' Edwards, Steve Ives from up Stockport way, Jim Moodie, Johnny Rea from home, all the top riders. I got away really well to lead from the start going into the Metropole for the first time but Steve Ives and Leslie McMaster got past me before the end of the lap and less than three seconds covered us three, with Mark Farmer, Dave Leach, Bob Jackson and Johnny Rea behind us.

McMaster took advantage of Ives at the Roundabout on lap three and I tagged along behind him in the same move but then Bob Jackson got past both of us, with Jim Moodie joining in the fray just behind. Pure adrenalin and anger got me up front and I led for the last two furious laps to take my first North West 200 win. It had been a tough fight all the way, one of the hardest I've ever had in my life and particularly sweet after the frustration with the superbike.

It was an important win in so many ways, for Honda's new CBR600 at such an important event for sales in the showroom, for me to win my first major international race, for my sponsors who'd been faithfully supporting me, especially Turkingtons and the added bonus of it being my first road race win in the Regal Championship too. Superb stuff. Steve Ives was second on his Yamaha, a top English rider of the time, with Bob Jackson bringing another Honda home third.

My original deal with Honda had just been for a 750 and a 600, but they'd seen how well I was going, particularly on the 250 which was my 1990 bike and they promised me a new 125 and 250 for the Isle of Man which was very good news. We needed some by then because we'd taken the blown RC30 engine apart and found it had seized on all four cylinders; the faulty oil had destroyed everything, the crankshaft, the big ends, the only thing left in one piece was the cylinder head and the gearbox.

If it had gone one second earlier, riding one handed at 130mph on that section with the petrol cap open, I would have been injured without a doubt. The problem then was, with the TT only two weeks away, no spares were available, there weren't any new crankcases in the country so we had no alternative than to rebuild the wrecked engine. Tuning mae-stro Tony Scott had to heat and cool the twisted crankcases to get them back into some sort of shape, but the pistons were so loose and slappy, it was unreal.

Having to go to the TT with an engine like that was bad enough, but then two new Honda 750 RVF's arrived out of the blue and I was upset, because I knew I'd be at a huge disadvantage on the Isle of Man against the experienced Fogarty and Hislop aboard Honda's 750 works of art.

These were priceless pieces of kit, the only two in the world at the time, absolute jewels which were going to be impossible to beat, hand built to the weight limit of Formula One rules, something like 130 kilos, whereas my production based RC30 would have been around 170 kilos. I remember works riders Mick Doohan and Wayne Gardner saying at the time that if their Grand Prix 500 Hondas handled like the RVF, then nothing could have touched them. Their power to weight ratio was unbe-lievable and they handled on the road like a 250, but had 750 power, that's how good they were.

Fogarty hadn't been expected on the island but a superbike round (the Formula One championship had been disbanded by then and the TT no longer had world championship status) had been unexpectedly cancelled and he'd been asked to compete on the hand built rocket ships from Japan, which had been flown in, in secrecy and popped out of their box in time to help celebrate Yamaha's thirtieth anniversary!

Foggy was Honda's top rider of the day and Hislop had more TT experience than me at the time so it wasn't a surprise they got the RVFs and I couldn't complain. I'd been beating Joey Dunlop that year and had put in a quicker lap than him in practice, but his seniority and long ser-vice with Honda meant he deservedly took over Fogarty's bike for the Senior after Carl had left the island.

So, I battled on with my Tony Scott prepared, kitted engine, which was substantially down on horsepower having been destroyed two weeks before, in the full knowledge that I hadn't got a chance of winning. I was there as a professional to do the best possible job I could though and was determined to see it through and achieve the highest results I could.

The Formula One TT opened race week as usual and as expected His lop and Fogarty were away and gone on the exotic RVFs. I'd started number ten just before Steve Hislop, who came past me on a charge in the first lap at some rate of knots on record pace, recording a 122.83mph lap from the standing start. He'd done a plus 124mph unofficial lap in practice and my RC30 just wasn't capable of staying with the RVF.

Joey was up front with Fogarty second before Hislop got into his stride. Trevor Nation had messed up his start on the Norton but still put in a 119.54mph first lap which was the fastest ever recorded on a British bike. Robert Dunlop was suffering on the other Norton, having broken his collarbone two weeks before and Fogarty caught and passed him on the road posting a 121.79mph lap on the other RVF. I remember getting a signal that I was in seventh at Union Mills, going into lap two.

Hislop was really flying and passed Fogarty on the road on lap two, which has a huge psychological effect; it destroys you if you're caught and has the reverse effect if you're the one doing the passing. Getting a rider in sight really lifts you, because you know then you've been doing some catching, plus you've now got a physical target to aim at. While having Fogarty as his target, Hislop had raised the outright record to 123.48mph

Meanwhile, I'd moved up to fifth on lap two with a race average of 118.49mph behind the two RVFs, Brian Morrison in third who was on the best bike Yamaha could give them in their thirtieth year and Nation's Norton. I was getting settled in by now, making nice progress through the field and passed Trevor Nation to get into fourth place. I think at one stage we'd both got past Brian Morrison on corrected time, but then the rubber front strap snapped on my petrol tank and I had to hold it on for the whole of the fourth lap, gripping it with my knees and elbows to keep it in place, quite an interesting experience over the bumps at 190mph.

It really made me lose my rhythm and after that I had no chance. We fixed the petrol tank at the pit stop but it was too late by then because Trevor Nation had got past me. I went back out again and finished fifth but in the end I made up another place without trying because Nation was disqualified, due to an oversized fuel tank, so overall I was very happy to get the fourth.

Rob Orme was leading the British 125 Championship at the time and Honda had arranged for me to have the use of his bike plus Rob's expertise to set it up on the island, but it turned up minus all the special factory parts and Rob never showed at all. It had obviously been put back to standard before it was sent, which was desperately disappointing because the thing couldn't have pulled the skin off a rice pudding.

I hadn't been riding a 125 for a while and the last thing we'd needed was the struggle we had to set it up and then fine tune it in practice, but I did my best in the race which Joey Dunlop was favourite to win. A victory would make him joint all time highest TT winner, equalling the late Mike Hailwood's fourteen victories.

The start was delayed by an hour and a half because of rain and a heavy hailstorm, frustrating for me as I just wanted to get on with it because conditions like that don't worry me at all. Northern Ireland has a lot of rainfall and I've had some great races in the wet, one or two of my best ever performances I think.

You've got to be on a different planet to get it absolutely right in the wet though. I can get a bike really moving around on soft wet tyres in the rain, but only if I'm on top from, really in control. The trick for me is to relax because if you're up tight and you lose it, that's it, you're off, but if you're nice and loose you've got much more feel. It's important to soften the suspension so you can feel it all moving underneath you, everything working away. If the suspension is too hard then the tyres are overworking and you can't feel it working; if the suspension is too soft and overworking then you can't feel the tyres and so on, it's all about getting the balance night, especially critical when it's wet.

Even seats are important, because that's part of the suspension; too soft and you start to lose feel, the seat sponge delays the reaction between the bike moving and when you feel it and that's vital time lost, which could be the difference between a fast time and disaster. Plus of course, every rider's different; when Woolsey Coulter rode my Yamaha R6 in 1999, his set up and seat arrangement was completely different, much harder than mine with no padding at all.

It's only when you're on top form and feeling everything that you can win in the wet - outside that, it's only luck. I needed some of that when the 1991 125 TT finally got under way, in cold and wet conditions. I was holding second place behind Joey on the first lap and put in a 102.17mph on the next, but as the sun came out, the temperature rose very quickly and the jet settings let us down with the bike starting to run too rich. Robert Dunlop edged ahead of me and went on to win when Joey's bike developed a fuel pipe problem. With my 125 slowing all the time the temperature increased, Bob Heath beat me into third by 6.6 secs, so I missed the rostrum again.

Having gone second quickest in practice I had number two on my bike and was first away on the road on my 250 in the Junior TT. So I started off with no one in front of me to aim at for the first time ever, just the prize money and the win, but I soon settled into a fast pace, just racing the course. I led by two seconds at the end of the first lap from Brian Reid, Steve Hislop, Ian Lougher and Ian Newton, all of us having a terrific battle in one of the closest TTs for a while.

At Glen Helen on lap two, Brian and I were dead level on corrected time and Steve Hislop followed Lougher out of the race with a seized engine. This elevated Robert Dunlop to third and Steven Hazlett up to fourth with the refuelling stop next. The top guys had got quick release fillers but we were too naïve to think about changing the old fashioned screw top type which was fitted to the bike we'd received. The few seconds delay we had scaling the petrol tank was crucial as Robert was ahead of me after the pit stop, which featured the safety 'stop' box at the beginning of pit lane for the first time.

Brian Reid crashed at Handley's corner and I nearly followed him out of the race with a huge moment at Quarter Bridge, flying down the road speedway style with the bike completely sideways. Dunlop's lead was eight seconds going in to the last lap which I cut back to 4.8 seconds with the fastest (and only flying) lap of the race at 116.75mph, with Hazlett in third, nearly one and a half minutes behind. That lap was only ten seconds outside the lap record which I think I would have smashed if the ACU hadn't banned 'bluegas' fuel, (which allows for a higher state of tune) for the 1991 event. So near yet so far. Show over.

I'd won the North West on the 600 but as soon as we started putting it over the rough stuff at the TT, we couldn't get it to handle. The problem turned out to be the spring on the rear shock but no one had the exact part we wanted to try on the island and we were struggling for time too, with four bikes to prepare. Practice had been wet as well, which limits set-up time and we ended up guessing at settings on the 600 before the race. And of course they were wrong. The bike was nowhere near what we wanted but I brought it home fifth and began to focus my mind on the Senior

Foggy left the island and Joey got the RVF that he'd left behind which disappointed me, but I just got on with the job. Trevor Nation led the 1991 Senior TT briefly at Glen Helen on the first lap before Hislop disappeared again on the other RVF with Joey right behind him, followed by Brian Morrison and me. Joey couldn't believe the power of the RVF "It was pulling the arms off me!" he said, and Hislop and him were on the road together from Ramsey to Douglas on the last lap, giving the fans a rare treat. I held on to fifth on lap two and made up a place when Nation went out on the Verandah with a broken exhaust, causing over-heating problems in the Winkel engine.

Going into the final lap I got a signal that Brian Morrison was only nine seconds ahead on his trick OW01 Yamaha and I set about catching him, sensing a rostrum finish could be on. My final circuit of 121.66mph was my fastest, and made me the third quickest ever at the TT, bringing me home in third place, twenty one seconds ahead of the Yamaha and up on the rostrum for the second time that week. That gave Honda a 1-2-3 in the Senior; I'd definitely pushed myself all the way and was well pleased to put in a lap quicker than Joey on his million pound RVF, finally finishing less than a minute behind him.

I was delighted with my overall performance as I felt this was really only my second TT as 1989 had been my learning year. I'd had a serious go at it in 1990 and won silver replicas in all my races but had now achieved a second in the Junior, third in the Senior, two fourth places in the Formula One and the 125 and a fifth in the Supersport 600 - I could-n't complain.

Following that performance, Honda promised me 'competitive' machinery for 1992 - I'd have to wait and see what that meant, but it was terrific news to get the nod for the following year that early on. Even in that state of tune, my RC30 had such a powerful motor; Honda's engines are wonderful pieces of engineering, it's such a strong company, with a range of good, quality products built to very high standards - just like mine - and some of the best personnel in the industry.

I'd met one of them the year before, a chap called Dave Hancock who Was Honda UK's Sales Manager then. He knew his way around the race world as he'd raced 125's for a while and had been a Yamaha rider and multiple TT winner Charlie William's race mechanic before joining Honda. We got on like a house on fire and still do.

Dave called me up one day mid-summer after the TT and asked if I'd be available for some testing in Holland and of course I agreed. It was a two day trip he explained, so I packed my bags and we travelled together from London out to the famous track of Assen in wonderful summer weather. The circuit was being heavily guarded with security people every-where because what was inside had to remain a heavily guarded secret. Two forty-foot containers had arrived there earlier, direct from the Honda factory's research and development section,

There were wall to wall Japanese technicians and specialists of every description, one on wheels, one or two on frames, a suspension expert, one on engines and so on, all under the control of an R & D boss who was introduced to me as Mr Baba. Every big sports bike of the day was parked at the track; Yamaha's EXUP, Suzuki's GSX-R 1100, Honda's own CBR1000F, all of them, which was of course Honda's opposition of the day. There was a truck full of tyres from every manufacturer you could think of and then the reason for all the secrecy was revealed.

Two Japanese test riders, two from mainland Europe, Dave Hancock and me were to ride and help develop a 900cc prototype sports bike, which was launched on an unsuspecting Western world the following year and called the Honda Fireblade. What a bike, fantastic power to weight ratio and handling so sharp I was very excited by it, I just wanted to tell everyone about how good it was as soon as I got home, but of course I couldn't.

And good heavens it was hard work! We tested everything that was there over and over again, riding timed sessions on every type of tyre, every combination of settings, everything you can think of and you had to be totally consistent. It was really tough going keeping up the pace on the Honda and all the other bikes that the team was demanding over the two days. They made it clear it was useless going slower when the settings were better, so consistency was vital and I impressed them with what I was doing.

They couldn't believe my bike knowledge either, how much I knew about everything from the wheels right down to the seat. It was a real trick bit of stuff already that prototype number one - all black it was - and I really put it through its paces. The Japanese had asked for a rider who knew a bit about what he was doing on the road and Dave Hancock had put his neck on the line when he nominated me, but he didn't regret it.

He trusted me to come along and do the best job I could and told me he'd been worried in case I didn't, in front of the top Japanese R&D men. I saw that the boss, Honda's executive chief engineer Tadao Baba had the complete respect of all the technicians and his new, unfinished bike just blitzed the opposition. Every rider there, was between 1.9 and 2.1 seconds faster on the new Honda than anything else and we were all trying really hard; by the end of the second day I'd have given anything to beat the Honda times on one of the other bikes, but I just couldn't do it. Mr Baba was trying too, so hard in fact that he wrote off one of the Yamahas at the chicane trying to beat his own time on his prototype.

I'd hit it off with him immediately because I could see the job he was trying to do and the bike was a bit of a revolution really. He'd done a bit of racing and engineering before he joined Honda and had been involved in the development of some nice bikes like the CB400 and the big CB750, so he had a great track record. I think he fought the marketing men in Japan a bit, who'd told him the bike wouldn't sell, before he finally got his way in the late eighties and started on the project.

He's a great guy, really friendly and a good rider who still loves doing it. It's amazing that word hadn't leaked about the new model - the security had really worked well - and it did take the world by storm in 1992 because it was really the first bike that went like a bomb in a straight line and around comers too.

I'd had a lot of fun with the prototype, seriously grinding the pegs and exhausts away in the final sessions. I came off the track towards the end and asked Mr. Baba if he wanted me to go faster but he looked a bit shocked and said, "No! This only road bike!"

There were still a few things I wasn't sure of about the final production bike - it was too light at the front end and steered too quick for my taste, I didn't think the brakes were as good as my race bikes' either and I wanted more power.

My good friend, ace technician Dennis Willey and I got hold of one the following year. We put better brakes on it, Tony Scott fully tuned the engine while we slipped in a nice Ohlins rear shock and upside down forks, using RC45 yokes to change the offset (the distance between the fork stanchions and the headstock) from 35 to 30mm. Finally, we changed the front wheel to a seventeen inch which gives you a lower profile tyre and much more feel, because there's a lot less flex. By then it was a real dream to ride. These same changes to the steering geometry and front wheel were eventually introduced on later Fireblades as part of the factory's refinement and development process.

It's now a much more stable bike, but Mr Baba is constantly working on improvements, his dream is that the bike will keep evolving long after he's gone.

It was a real privilege being invited to Assen and being involved with the development of such a superb milestone bike and Dave Hancock was as happy as Larry, pleased enough with my performance to get me involved in quite a few European press launches which is a real honour, representing Honda Britain at such prestigious affairs I raced the Fireblade for the first time on the Isle of Man in 1996, when the Production

TT came back in and already knew about the modifications that were being made. I went to the launch of the 1998 Fireblade at an Italian circuit, Monza, I think.

The bike was unveiled and it didn't look much different to the previous year's model and the press didn't seem very impressed. But I knew it was a very different bike to the previous year's, with a multitude of changes and got up to give an impromptu speech which I think saved the day a bit. The Japanese top brass seemed very impressed with my sudden PR skills and thanked me afterwards, so just for good measure I went out on the track with the press and test riders, had a look at it for a couple of laps because I'd never seen it before in my life and then showed everyone there what a superb package this latest model was by posting some very fast times.

I quite enjoyed doing the launches after that and had fun in Spain when Honda's Hornet and Deauville were introduced, both very nice bikes. It seems to me that Honda are usually just that little bit ahead of the other manufacturers, who occasionally catch up, such as Yamaha did with their 'R' series in the late nineties. The difference is that the Yamahas are really race bikes - I know - I raced the R1 and the R6 in 1999, whereas the Honda sportsters are road bikes with a racing capability, which is an important difference for the everyday rider.

Our first meeting after the 1991 TT was at June's Killinchy 150 held on the Ulster Grand Prix Dundrod circuit, which is great practice for the Grand Prix itself in August. I still hadn't ever won a race there, threatened to a few times but never quite made it, so I was determined to break my duck this time round. Joey Dunlop and I had a good dice in the big 750 race, the Kevin Martin Memorial where I was on the tail of Joey all the way until he put in a 123mph record lap to beat me by five seconds and I thought Dundrod was going to stay my bogey track.

The Regal 600 was round seven of the Championship and Johnny Rea, Dave Leach and I had a big fight in what was easily the race of the day. We kept the crowd on tenterhooks all the way to the flag, where just two fifths of a second covered the three of us and I'd taken the first win of my career at the track.

The 250 was another cracker, but all the racing on the track was between Joey, Ian Lougher and Steven Hazlett as I was off and away to win by ten seconds in the end for a great double, putting paid to all my doubts about bad luck on the Dundrod track. I got a double win on the Aghadowey short circuit the next weekend, moving me up to second in the Regal Championship and I followed that up with three more at the Milverton Road Races held at the Skerries, smashing the course record twice, pushing to the absolute limit in successive 250 heats, fighting with Joey Dunlop all the way.

I won the big race of the day, the Grand Final which was important as it was the race which carried big prize money and felt I'd only got second to Dave Leach on my 600 because the race was stopped twice and finally abandoned.

That was a fantastic Saturday's racing, followed by a 750 win and a second in the Lynster 200 invitation race at Mondello Park on the Sunday. It was a hectic schedule, racing every weekend all over Ireland, even surprising everyone by turning up for the Munster 100 in Cork, just before Joey and I were due to fly off to the Suzuka eight hour endurance race. In top form, I smashed the lap record on my 250, winning both races in that class on the tight little twisty three and a half mile track at Clonakilty, before taking a win and the outright course record on the RC30.

Having missed the Ulster Grand Prix the year before, I was determined to finally do well there, racing my Hondas over the 7.4 mile circuit up in the Co. Antrim hills above Belfast. Joey and I had a magnificent scrap from the word go in the 250 Junior event on evenly matched machinery.

The weather was awful, wet and misty, so bad the start was delayed by half an hour and tyre choice was difficult. Thinking the weather was set for the day, I started the race on full wet tyres and carved out a five second lead pretty quickly before a dry line started to appear and Joey, who'd begun on intermediates began to reel me in as his tyres started to work in the drying conditions. I still had a pretty good lead but my visor had steamed up in the wet and misty conditions, I missed my braking point coming into the Hairpin and went off the track with two laps to go.

I knew if I touched my brakes or tried to turn it it'd have me off, so I let it just run on towards what I thought was just a grass bank, but it dipped down into a bit of a dike and I ended up riding the bike into it, which was lucky, because if I'd fallen off it, I wouldn't have been allowed to restart.

I watched Joey shoot up the road and into the lead as I got a bit of 'unofficial' help out of the ditch with the bike, which I'd managed to keep running and got back on the circuit and fired off up the road again and into the race. I'd been about forty odd seconds ahead of third placed Ian Lougher and I'd restarted quick enough to stay ahead of him and caught and passed Joey about six miles or so later, to retake the lead.

Then Joey's gear linkage broke and I cruised in for the win in the end, but we repeated the fight in every one of the seventy four miles of the next race on our RC30s. I made one of many really outrageous moves up Joey's inside in that race, and left a big black darkie up the side of his leathers during one of them. Joey didn't seem to care about it all and just sneaked the win by a quarter of a second, but his wife went mad at me in the paddock when she found out where the big black mark on Joey's leg had come from.

I had a little Honda 400 NCR30 at the time and run that in the combined 125 and 400 race, winning quite easily before we were out on the 750s again for another big clash with Joey. The conditions had been so bad a lot of riders had pulled in during the second Junior race because of the mist and spray making visibility so poor. I was leading, so it hadn't been affecting me as much; I'm always careful in poor visibility, particularly on the Isle of Man but as I know the island course so well, I try and keep up as fast a pace as possible.

Mist and cloud can come down on the mountain there without warning and a lot of riders knock it off, but with good road knowledge I generally keep going at a fast pace unless it's so bad that it's obvious the race is going to be stopped. I've often used those conditions to my advantage, making up loads of time on the more timid - or sensible!

The second 750 race was a carbon copy of the first, with Joey and me way out in front of brother Robert's Norton; by halfway through the race he was over a minute behind us in third. I could see the crowd going mad as we fought it out, with me pulling every trick in the book, but Joey got me again at the flag, admitting afterwards that it was the hardest he'd ever raced in the wet there.

The Supersport 600 race was one of the closest ever too, with two seconds covering seven of us at the front, Johnny Rea, Dave Leach, Steve Cull, Leslie McMaster, Mark Farmer, Steve Ives and me all fighting it out for over two thirds of the race. Some back markers split us up in the final stages and I was tucked in behind leader Johnny Rea who'd been swapping the lead with me throughout. I was ready to take him on the last lap, when my radiator burst and the engine started to tighten as it overheated, nursing it home to keep my second place.

I got Joey back on my 750 shortly afterwards at the Mid-Antrim 150, held on the Clough circuit, where I won the Regal 600, 250 and the 750 races, smashing lap and race records in each event for good measure, including setting a new absolute course record under two minutes for the first time. I had started a winning streak which was to last for the rest of the year.

I reduced Johnny Rea's lead in the 600 Regal Championship to eleven points in the next meeting at Aghadowey by beating him into second on my CBR The Ace of Aghadowey race was undoubtedly the best of the day though, with a fine scrap up front between Dave Leach on his OW01 Yamaha, my RC30 and Woolsey Coulter on his 250, popping up out of nowhere all the time to get past me on the brakes, before I'd have him back with the power of the 750 on the straights. I led for a spell with Woolsey giving Leach a hard time for a while, but in the end it was Dave and I, tooth and nail to the line in a real good one, which he held on to take by a wheel.

My championship positions were looking good by now with just some ground to make up in the Regal. For the first time in my life towards the end of that season, we started to think about tactics to try and take some championships. I took another crucial Regal win on my CBR600 at the Carrowdore 100, Ulster's last road race of the season, which meant the Championship would go down to the wire in the final round at Nutt's Corner. In the feature race itself, I blasted away from a quality field to win by sixteen seconds, smashing the course record with a 112.97mph lap and then raised it again to 113.35mph the very next time round.

Joey Dunlop and I seemed to be battling it out in every 250 race that season and I think it was the pressure of those encounters that led me into breaking so many records. The 250 event at Carrowdore was another epic fight between the two of us and I took the class record again with a lap of 110.27mph to finish up with a superb hat trick at the meeting

The big race at Nutts Corner, The King of the Corner, was one of my best encounters with Jeremy McWilliams, who was a bit of a late starter like me. He wasn't interested in road racing, just concentrating on the short stuff in the smaller capacity classes, but we mixed it a few times on the short circuits and he was a good opponent.

If you ride against opposition every week you start to work them out and I haven't been living this long because I'm stupid. If everything a rider does, you do something different, it does break them down eventually and you start to get on top. I didn't know Jeremy much at all though and he put up a real interesting fight. It was dreadfully wet. Jeremy was on a 250 and I was on my RC30 which was a real handful in those conditions around that twisty little circuit, which is only about a mile long.

We had a real good battle and I had to pull out all the stops just to sneak it on the line. Superb stuff from Jeremy and it could have gone either way, I'm so delighted that he's finally got the breaks he deserves in Grand Prix and a great shame his talent hasn't been showcased to the world a lot earlier.

That was a long time before his involvement with the QUB (Queens University, Belfast) team, who had done a lot of development work with Yamaha and Irish racing hero Ray McCullough. He'd beaten the best in the world at the Ulster Grand Prix on his 250, when it was still a World Championship round, with help from that terrific team of two stroke specialists at Belfast University.

Ray and QUB helped me with my 250 a lot in the early nineties, even though I was with Honda, providing me with quite a few specialist development parts under the direction of their chief, Doctor Blair, who worked very closely with Yamaha in Japan.

Jeremy had led by over seven seconds at one stage in that classic race, which I was delighted to win in such terrible conditions. Johnny Rea, my opponent to take the Regal Championship overall, had fallen in practice. He hurt his shoulder which was disappointing for everyone because he understandably didn't fancy carrying the injury in the atrocious conditions on the track. In fact he retired quite quickly in the race, unable to control the slides properly I expect and the thrilling final encounter was literally washed out. I was happy to let a hard charging Leslie McMaster take the win in the end, settling for a safe second and the Championship by a single point from Johnny Rea, one of the first tactical results I can remember going for.

Up until then we'd never, ever had a plan for the season; just storm ahead, ride everything, everywhere, flat out for all the wins and prize money we could get! And work day and night too. What a life!

All the English riders came over again for the big money Sunflower meeting at Kirkistown; Rob McElnea on his Loctite Yamaha, Fogarty with his E7D model RC30, Hislop and Alan Carter on their 250s and British 600 Champion Ian Simpson amongst others. I got two fourths in the 750 races and a good third behind Steve Hislop in the first 250 race, pushing Alan Carter into fourth which was superb really as the 250 was only a hobby to me at the time and those guys were top European runners.

I had another great time at the Macau Grand Prix, finishing third behind the two GP500 bikes of Eddie Laycock on Joe Millar's Yamaha and winner Didier de Radigues, who went out in style in the final race of his career on the 500 Lucky Strike Suzuki. Irish riders took three of the top four places with Robert Dunlop finishing fourth behind me.

I finished the season as Supersport 600 Short Circuit Champion, 750 Short Circuit Champion, 750, 600 and 250 Road Race Champion and of course the Regal Championship Winner. All this plus my performance at the North West and the TT had drawn the attention of the race world and I got two separate offers to ride a leased factory 500 Yamaha Grand Prix bike in 1992, which I turned down.

That may have been one of the biggest mistakes of my life; they were only semi-factory bikes though and I would have been a private entry, but they were only offered to selected riders and it would have been a big chance to get on the world stage. The media hype put pressure on Honda Britain and Neil Tuxworth flew over to see me at the end of 1991, to make sure I was staying to ride for Honda for the following year.

In my heart, I wasn't at all sure I was ready for Grand Prix, thinking I needed to build up more short circuit experience in England and Europe before making such a move. I didn't realise I was getting older by the day and that opportunities like that don't come around very often. As I've said, I always like to prepare carefully before taking the plunge into something new, but looking back maybe I should have just gone for it.

It did give me leverage with Honda though, who committed to getting me out of Ireland and into the British short circuit scene, which I felt was my next step up. The deal we cut was that I'd concentrate on the Regal Championship in 1992, but could drop certain rounds enabling me to ride in England at British Championship meetings, to ease myself into the scene there. I was happy with that and signed for Honda in Neil Tuxworth's hotel room at the end of 1991.

My heart was still in road racing you see - sod Grand Prix - that could wait, I had some unfinished business to deal with elsewhere.

6

I thought it was great having a job racing bikes in those days. I remained loyal to Honda because that's how I was built, a faithful hard worker, but what I didn't realise was that they needed me just as much as I needed them. I was full of confidence and thought I was a good rider by then, but I didn't know just how good and desperately needed someone who recognised my full potential and could cut the deals for me.

I had lots of help and sponsorship from various Irish businesses great and small who helped me out for so long. I'm forever grateful for all the sacrifices they made and everything they did on my behalf in those years, Thank you all very much indeed, what we achieved was fantastic, with so little help from outside.

Honda had promised me better equipment for 1992 and I was keen to get hold of it. After a terrific Isle of Man hat trick in 1991, Steve Hislop had asked for a 750 ride in the 1992 British Championships and had held on and on in the hope of getting it, but that particular prize was eventually awarded to Simon Crafar.

Hislop was well peeved off at not getting his way and followed Fogarty out of the team, who had left Honda at the end of 1991. His Honda RC30 hadn't been the most competitive machine in World Superbike the year before, Fogarty had proved that and I think he just felt he was going to be wasting his time on it for another year. We were to have a terrific fight on matching Castrol RC30s at the North West later in the season though.

I made my annual pilgrimage to Honda Britain's Louth headquarters in January to collect a new CBR600 and the really big prize of a new chassis, factory forks and rebuilt factory engines for my RC30. I guess Hislop and Fogarty's departure had an influence on what I'd ended up with, but after a few days in England getting everything together, there was no time to worry about that or any time to lose in preparation for the season. I wanted to do even better in 1992, win the Irish Championships, win races on the roads to get all the money I'd need to survive and the road race championships themselves. I wasn't too worried about short circuits as I was going to England on my 600 and 400 to learn about those and that was it.

But before all that happened I was really keen to get my season going by racing at the Daytona International. Honda didn't want me burning my bikes out over there though and wouldn't give me any official support, probably because they knew the RC30 was finished by then and wouldn't be competitive. But having missed out the year before, I decided I was going anyway and managed to gather up enough money and with a bit of support from the Motor Cycle News team we got out there and I loved the track immediately.

John Reynolds was there with a Kawasaki and Brian Morrison amongst others. They couldn't believe the speed of the place, a really fast track but I was feeling right at home because I was doing those sorts of speeds every week on public roads. I thought this huge big smooth track was a great place. Tony Scott had worked on my engines for a good month before we left for Daytona and had done a wonderful job of hand building them for me, all factory stuff by now of course, (allowable under new rules) even though it was out of date.

So my team consisted of my brother Noel, girlfriend Christine and technician Jim and we weren't very well prepared at all being so far from home. We didn't even have any tyre warmers, just leaving the wheels out in the hot Florida sunshine outside the pits, with someone nominated to turn them over every so often, a bit like cooking toast in front of a fire. There was a good spirit in the camp though as the deal was we were going to party and sightsee for three whole days after the race, which I was going to pay for out of my winnings. In March, Daytona is the place to be.

This was a brand new bike at its first race meeting, so we had quite a bit of trouble getting it right and set up properly in the qualifying heats. Rules prevented us from using our factory flat slide carburettors, but an American team were kind enough to let us try a set of US market flat slides, which were allowed, but they caused more trials and tribulations for us in practice - we struggled to get the bike to run right with them fitted. Plus we didn't know how they were going to affect fuel consumption, which is really important for pit stops in such a long race, so we ended up not using them, reverting to standard road kit and I didn't do too badly in the end.

In the race I took it very easy at the start, feeling my way a bit and not wanting to get mangled up with anyone early on. I knew that long races were my speciality anyway and I'd decided to get settled in and then try and come through the field one by one. It all started to work out nicely, with the team doing well at the pit stops, while making sure our new solar tyre heating system was working properly!

It's about a two hour race, two hundred miles at an average 100mph and it's in the last half hour that the cookie starts to crumble. After a hundred and fifty miles or so at high speed in the sub-tropical heat, bikes start breaking down under the strain and riders lose it because of tiredness and heat exhaustion. My stamina was great though and Tony Scott had done a wonderful job on the engine, with the bike fast enough through the speed traps in practice to get the attention of some Honda factory technicians.

They came over to our pit to see what was going on and couldn't believe our private team just had an engine fitted with regular carbs; 1 was getting good top speed but was well down on acceleration coming out of the turns though. They were very impressed at the high state of tune we'd achieved on our own and our relationship continued with the same HRC personnel at the beginning of the RC45 project in 1994. My secret development work with the Fireblade, combined with this showing at Daytona was really starting to get us noticed in Japan.

Towards the end of the race coming off the banking I was starting to check the giant digital marker board which sits in the middle of the track there and it was giving me in tenth place, then after a few more laps I picked off another bike and the board gave me as ninth.

I went past a couple of crashed bikes quite soon after that and all of a sudden I was seventh, with the lap indicator showing three laps remaining, then the race leader Doug Polen came past me, being chased by Scott Russell in second. Alright I was being lapped and they're pretty big laps at Daytona, four or five miles long but I was pleased it'd taken that long for them to reach me.

They came past pretty quick, but not too fast and I jumped on the back of them, being out accelerated coming out of the turns on the twisty infield section but once we got on the banking I was staying with them and closing up behind them on the brakes at the next corner. They got away from me a bit; world class riders after all, Polen was a World Superbike Champion and Scott Russell American Champion at the time, but I kept hammering away at them.

I was sixth going into the second to last lap when the front end of the RC30 started to shake a bit and little shadows began flying past me. I thought I must have run over something and kept the wire tight about 180mph, ready for the braking point coming into turn one where I sat up, squeezed the front brake lever and - nothing. The trouble is you're braking point is the last possible place you can brake to take the comer and there's no room for adjustment, but there was just no pressure, no feel, nothing.

In a split second I realised the vibration must have pushed the brake pads to the outside of the calliper which can happen after a tank slapper, so I pumped the front brake lever like mad to get the pads onto the disc and - nothing.

The green light had come on in my head by now telling me that this baby wasn't going to stop. The outside of turn one was all Armco barriers and I was still flat out and knew if I went into that I was in serious trouble. You come off the banking at turn one down onto the infield section, but because the Daytona Speedway is a big oval track, you could stay on the banking until it's blocked a couple of hundred yards later, where you re-enter it from the short circuit style infield section.

All I could do was stay on this banking and try to stop the bike somehow - there was still no front brake so I stood on the back and locked the rear up at 180mph, starting to pump the brake then to try and control it and got down a couple of gears before there was an almighty bang and that was it. Show over.

I woke up in the medical centre severely battered from head to toe with my left shoulder blade ripped right off my back. I found out later that my front tyre had broken up following the pounding I'd been giving it at the end of the race chasing Polen and Russell and pulling them back on the brakes. It's quite an abrasive track and at one corner I'd reeled them back by fifty yards and I think it was that that had finished the tyre off.

The shadows I'd seen were the lumps of rubber breaking off the tyre's casing, some of which had sliced into the radiator, but more importantly, ripped the front brake hoses right off the bike. The steam from the radiator, the smoke from the back tyre and my body language as I fought to scrub speed off the RC30 produced some spectacular film footage. We'd changed the rear at every pit stop, but no one changed the front in those days, running the same tyre all the way through the race. They do now. Once or even twice for some teams.

When I got home my doctor was able to slide his hand up between the inside of my shoulder blade and my back so I was pretty bad really, but as soon as the team found out I was going to live after the race they started having a real go at me for ruining their holiday!

They'd had the time to work out that sixth place at the Daytona 200 was worth over twenty thousand pounds including all the product bonuses we would have picked up. And I'd crashed when there was only a lap and a bit to go. How dare I!

We'd bought our Disneyland tickets before the race had even started, planning to go on a spree with the winnings and now the team got their revenge by dragging me out of hospital all strapped up and taking me to Orlando anyway, forcing me on every ride there was at The Magic Kingdom, laughing like mad while I was screaming and groaning with pain all the time, getting some very odd looks from all the other passengers.

So there you go. Just a lap and a bit to go - not even ten miles, at the end of two hours racing over two hundred miles in a really important international event on an uncompetitive bike, about to get covered in glory with a great result on my first ever visit and - within seconds it's all over. Then I'm being tortured by my team, finished off by a bollocking from my team boss Neil Tuxworth for smashing his bike up. Of course, if that tyre had lasted I'd have been the blue eyed boy...

As it was I ended being placed twentieth in Daytona's bizarre scoring system, while Scott Russell had squeezed past Doug Polen for the win.

I came back to Ireland wiser and poorer, with a race problem as big as the medical one, in that I couldn't afford to miss any Regal Championship meetings, because of the rounds I would already be missing by racing in England.

The previous Christmas I'd told my bosses at Food Engineering that I'd be leaving in April to race motorcycles as a full time professional rider. Racing was needing my undivided attention seven days a week by now - being restricted to four was just another handicap and we'd agreed I'd leave the following April, when the season got fully underway. Of course my Daytona accident meant that I wasn't really contributing much to the company in the last couple of weeks. As my happy times there came to an end, we completed the perfect circle - I'd arrived on crutches all those years before and now, I was leaving on crutches too!

Now that racing was to provide my only income it made me even more focussed; it wasn't do or die, but it definitely made me concentrate more, and I was sharper. Up until then it was really still a hobby, something I was doing just for fun, but now things had changed significantly and work was getting in the way. It was getting more serious now, but I was still thoroughly enjoying racing and thankfully that's how it's remained until very recently. I've never raced bikes because I wanted piles of money or success, I've always done it simply because I just love riding bikes fast. If I get paid enough to make a living out of doing it, then even better!

My 'Daytona' shoulder was a big problem and I did miss a Regal round at Bishopscourt and then the Nutts Comer meeting on the Saturday before Easter, featuring the second Regal round, but I was heavily strapped and back just three weeks after my Daytona accident, at Aghadowey. I got a second in the 750 race, the 400 and the Regal Championship round on my 600. I was pleased to get out and race because you're always unsure how you're going to feel back out on the track after a big accident like the one in America, but I felt OK about it and did well, considering

After getting back into it all at Aghadowey I came back with a bang at Easter Monday's Kirkistown meeting with a hat trick in the Regal, Supersport and Superbike Race and a third place on my 400 to really set me up for the Tandragee 100, my home race.

The deal I'd cut with Honda was to give up my 250 racing in order to concentrate on the Regal, while getting into the British Championships on my 600. I was trying to do everything else too, but Honda insisted I slowed down a bit, so I was left without a 250 going into the Tandragee weekend, the start of the road racing season, even though I'd smashed the lap record there on my 250 the year before.

In the week leading up to the race Turkingtons offered me their old 1990 250, I said yes, begged for an entry and got it and the bike was taken off display and hurriedly prepared for its third season of racing! I romped away from the moment the flag dropped and got a good lead over Steven Hazlett and Noel Hudson before a terrible thunderstorm turned the final part of the race into a procession to the line without much racing going on really and I won by over ten seconds.

Parts of the track were still flooded for the Regal 600 race when I got away again from Brian Reid and Dave Leach, who were fighting it out for second when Dave crashed heavily and was seriously injured. The race was stopped while I was ahead by about thirty seconds. Dave was in intensive care for many weeks after that and he'd been touch and go. It was the end of his racing career.

I'd got really close to Dave, fighting so many battles with him over the last few seasons and I felt annoyed and upset that my friend had got so badly hurt during the race. Another old school friend of mine who only raced for fun, Oral Watson had crashed and was killed too. Both these incidents weighed heavily on my mind. I won the 750 race too, to complete a brilliant start to my road racing season, but left the track wishing we could start the meeting all over again.

Dave recovered OK, he tried a couple of comebacks but the accident finished his career really and he was wise to stop when he did. I'd already decided to go and race on circuits and do more stuff in England and when Dave had gone from the Irish scene, so had my main challenge and the excitement. We'd had so many great fights over the last couple of seasons and he was the guy who'd pushed me into so many records every week. It made me want to go to England even more. It was time to move on.

People have asked me if I'd left it too late to go to England to race but I don't really think so, if you keep winning races people don't care what age you are. Maybe I was a bit long in the tooth to get a factory Grand Prix ride even though I'd had the offers the previous winter, but I figured if you were beating enough people up you'd still get it.

When I did start going over to British Championship rounds, I realised getting to England was just too expensive, I couldn't afford to go until I just got really insistent in 1992. What I used to have to do was get four weeks road racing prize money at home together and then go to England to race. There wasn't much prize money involved over there even if you won and the boats, hotels, food and all the other expenses were coming straight out of my own pocket, it just wasn't financially viable. The trouble was I really wanted to do it because I knew it was the only way forward, but at the same time it just wasn't financially sensible without backing. I had half backing but that wasn't enough.

Back at home, getting success at Tandragee on the 250 prompted us to wheel the old girl out again for the Cookstown 100 because I wanted to ride in as many races as possible despite what Honda was telling me - apart from anything else it gave me plenty of practice but it all worked out superbly well. I was enjoying my racing and coasted in for an eleven second win on the 250. Johnny Rea was the only man to give me a hard time for most of the Regal 600 race after Brian Reid's steering damper broke, but I eventually got away to win by eighteen seconds.

The superbike race was a different matter with Joey Dunlop getting a really good start leading for the first couple of laps with me behind which was always a great experience. We were starting to get a really good fight together; he is such a masterful rider with so much talent, it's a good idea sometimes to sit behind someone like that and learn everything you can. I managed to squeeze past him on lap five, raising the outright lap record to almost 107mph in the process, opening up a twenty second lead by the end of the race.

An old airfield had been put back into use and a new circuit opened at Bishopscourt. I'd missed the first meeting there in March because of my Daytona injury but it all went pretty well getting a second in the Regal round there, followed by a first in the 400 and the 750 race. I was starting to get excited about the British Championship races I was going to be doing soon, but there was the small matter of the North West 200 to deal with first, which I felt was going to be the most important race meeting of my life.

The event was getting larger and growing in importance all the time and it was going to be my biggest test yet, with all the top UK riders appearing, the big names I was soon going to be facing in the British Championships.

At last I had full power factory engines for the super quick North West track and practice went like a dream on the 750. I got pole position, relegating Fogarty to second (he'd been drafted in by Castrol Honda for a one off ride on an RC30) and I pushed Joey Dunlop into second too, in the Supersport 600 category.

Phillip McCallen sorting out those top guys. Yes! What a brilliant start and I followed that up with third fastest in the 250 and pole again, this time on the 400. I was really pleased getting a front row grid position in everything I'd entered and I couldn't wait to get going on Saturday's race day.

In practice week leading competitors have promotional work to carry out which includes photo calls with 'Miss North West'. The beauty contest to find the 1992 winner had been won by a Manda McKinley that year, a very pretty girl I remember, who sat on my bike, posing for the official cameraman, whose photos would be released to the press as part of the media campaign. I was struck by how attractive she was, but I already had a girlfriend of course, Christine - and with six races to compete in on Saturday, I had plenty to think about.

I honestly don't remember a great deal about our initial meeting, but Manda, who is now my wife, certainly does, so I think it's best if she tells the story...

"Be careful of this next guy." said the photographer, "It's Philip McCallen and he's a bit of ladies man you know." So I got a warning instead of an introduction to the man I was going to end up marrying - a chance meeting if ever you like. I was at university in Coleraine and had been on a girls night out in a Portrush nightclub when they announced the Miss North West beauty contest and I joined in for a bit of a laugh.

I'd won a heat that year for Miss Northern Ireland and was preparing for the final so my interview technique was pretty good - quite a few girls had gone there just to compete though, so I was surprised yet pleased to win and suddenly wondered what I'd let myself in for. Little did I know that whim in the nightclub was to change my whole life forever. That was about a month before the event and there was quite a bit of promotion to do and a lot of photo calls with the riders, which began on Tuesday's practice day.

I met the photographer and did some shots with the more well known competitors including Robert and Joey Dunlop who even I'd heard of. I just laughed off the cameraman's warning and sat on Phillip's bike ready for the pictures and he appeared a few seconds later. He didn't say hello or introduce himself but stood next to me and asked 'What's that perfume you're wearing?" and I thought to myself, OK, yes the photographer's right, but I told him it was 'Ruffles' and then he asked me what I was doing that night and where I was going, to which I replied I didn't know.

The next time I met him was on the podium on race day at the end of the first race, which he'd won. I had to present all the prizes to the winners and he came up to collect the trophy and as I was putting the laurel garland over his head he said, "Ruffles isn't it?" which I thought showed he had a good memory and perhaps he wasn't so bad after all. He gave me a peck on the check at that stage and said that he'd see me after the next race back on the podium for another kiss; I secretly hoped he was right.

By the time he'd won four more that day, there'd been a sort of progression and he got a kiss on the lips which did not amuse my boyfriend at the time, who was in the crowd in front of the podium. At the organisers' dinner that night, my boyfriend had picked up the fact that Phillip was showing more than a little interest in me and it just happened that I'd gone to the Ladies' at the same time as Phillip had gone to the Gentlemens' and we bumped into each other outside.

There we were innocently chatting away when my boyfriend arrived, told me to get outside and into the car because we weren't staying, he stormed out and that was the end of our night out.

Phillip obtained my phone number from the Clerk of the Course and called me during the TT, in fact he rang a few times after that and finally we arranged to meet in August for dinner in a little secluded place in Gortin. My parents were on holiday, my boyfriend was in Belfast and from that minute on we were in a difficult situation as we both had relationships. We became very close friends and would liked to have been more, but time and our other relationships prevented it.

I met Phillip in Portadown in November on my birthday - my twenty first actually, when he'd just got back from Macau. He'd brought me some silk lingerie as a present, which I put in my car and drove to Coleraine on my own for my birthday party. Everyone was there waiting for me, including my boyfriend and I went straight in. My boyfriend went out quite innocently to get something from the car later that night, cassettes I think and found the box of lingerie and a card from Philip.

He came back into the house holding the offending items, shouting and screaming before storming out of the house in a terrible rage and off into the night in his car. Funnily enough, that was effectively the end of my relationship with him, but it was going to be a wee while before things became more serious with Phillip.

So now you know. Life's a funny old thing - if you'd told me then, back at practice week for the 1992 North West 200 that Manda was going to be my wife, I'd have said never in a million years - I had some races to win, I couldn't be doing with all that romantic stuff?

Honda had promised me British short circuit specialist Alan Carter's second 250 for the TT and the North West meetings, but I ended up using my ageing Turkington's 250, which I'd been winning on in the races leading up to the North West. I was up front from the moment the race began and got into a titanic battle with Robert Dunlop who always had the physical advantage over me on 250s, being smaller and lighter. We swapped the lead constantly in a real ding dong battle but whenever

I got in front I was careful to keep my bike a thousand revs off its maximum when changing up through the gears, knowing this would lull Robert into a false sense of security.

After a bit of this, I knew by the way Robert was riding that he wasn't worried about me getting past him on the brakes, because he believed his bike was faster than mine and that he'd get me back on the next straight. Sure enough, Robert had started to relax, storming past me on the straights whenever he wanted he thought - and I saved it all - and those crucial top thousand revs for the home stretch along the coast road on the final lap, make or break time.

I dived through into the lead at the Metropole, with only a couple of miles to go, but this time I really opened up the little 250 right up to over 13,000 revs and kept her stuck flat out all the way to the finish line; by the time Robert woke up I was too far away for him to pick up my slipstream, the con trick had worked and I took the chequered flag and the win.

Here I was climbing up on that podium - so pleased, just well happy to have got the dream start we needed by winning the first race of the day, that I hardly noticed that girl again (apart from her perfume, as Manda has said), but I got a kiss on her cheek for my trouble and the cameras, and I told her I'd see her in a bit because I was going to win another one. Cocky git.

The first superbike race began immediately, with Joey getting a great start and leading but I got past him before the end of the lap, followed by Fogarty, with Mark Farmer next, who was on the Loctite sponsored Yamaha and Robert Dunlop in fifth on the Norton. Foggy was on the Castrol Honda RC30 so our bikes were well matched for once and we got away from the others, swapping it quite a bit in a good clean fight.

He got past me when I clipped a kerb on the exit from the chicane but things were hotting up nicely when I got him back at the Metropole on lap three, but he slowed up after that with engine problems, just when it was getting really interesting between us. Robert Dunlop started a big charge, passed Mark Farmer in second and caught and passed me too and we had a repeat of our 250 battle, minus the con trick and I pulled away on the last lap to win by over three seconds in the end, getting back on the podium again for another kiss. I was starting to enjoy this and told her I'd go and win another one for her this time, so I did.

But that Supersport 600 event was without doubt the hardest one of my life up until then · maybe the hardest ever, with Mike Edwards, Jim

Moodie, Joey Dunlop and me in a terrific, race long battle, each of us leading and losing it all the way.

With two laps to go someone's bike blew up in front of us and there was a big oil streak in the start and finish area, coming out of the last chicane. I hit it and the whole bike slid from the inside right across the road to the far outside and I thought "I'm gone!" So did the big crowd packed in at the side of the road there, who were scattering with fright as I headed towards them, desperately trying to oversteer it and I don't know how, I think it was God and me who got it back under control and unbelievably, I'd kept the lead too.

Behind me, Mike Edwards said he didn't know how I saved it, but I lost my drive coming out of the turn and the lead by the next corner. On the last lap Joey Dunlop was in front but missed a gear going into Church Corner and I stuck it up the inside of him with Moodie and Edwards going through too. Moodie appeared next to me at the final bend and we seemed to cross the line together. I was given the decision though, having won by the length of my front wheel and I was back up those podium steps again.

The trouble with the North West is it's a very tight schedule and if you're on the podium, which is built on the back of a flat bed truck, off you go on a little trip around the pit area, but your bike's already on the grid with the field waiting for you to get the race underway, so I had plenty on my mind. But I was starting to enjoy being kissed by this pretty girl and the little pocks on the cheek were getting a lot better now, so I gave her a bit of a hug this time and told her I'd go and win her another one.

My little NC30 was waiting on the grid for me and the combined 125/400 race started as soon as the little parade lap around the pit area had finished and I had hit the saddle. The Yamahas of Johnny Rea and Steve Lindsell were slightly quicker than my Honda, which started running far too hot and losing power towards the end of the race, so I had to make up two places going into the last chicane and won it by a whisker.

After that many wins I felt like a God and if that had all been possible, then I was going to do the impossible and win the next race too, which was the second 250 event. I crashed entering the link road leading to the Roundabout, using some new high profile Grand Prix tyres Michelin had given me to try. The front had felt a bit funny in the previous 250 race, but this time it had let go for no apparent reason when I'd tried to turn it in, fighting for the lead with Robert Dunlop and Ian Newton. It wasn't until the TT two weeks later that we found out why.

250s are quick steering and light at the front end and don't put a lot of heat in to a tyre at the best of times. The pointed profile on this new rubber was ideal for scratching around short circuits but didn't suit my style very well. But much more important, the part of the tyre not in contact with the road when the bike was upright was getting cold on the long straights at the North West and the TT, meaning I was getting to the corners flat out with the sides of the tyre cold! We went back to the old profile on the island and have stayed with it ever since, but the accident was actually a blessing in disguise, because it was a slow corner, I wasn't hurt and after I'd picked myself up I suddenly realised how tired I was.

I got behind the fence, sat down and relaxed, taking some deep breaths and recovering for a bit, while I signed a few autographs for the fans there. It did me a lot of good, helping me get psyched up for my next outing, the big money final superbike race, which was the one everyone wanted.

There'd been no time for food, I'd just grabbed a bar of chocolate at some point and kept drinking the salt and glucose drinks my doctor, Fred McSorley had made up for me, because the fluid loss is so enormous at a meeting like that in the summer heat. He's done so well looking after me all these years, I don't think I'd be in one piece today if he hadn't done such a good job for me on so many occasions.

Some RC30s with engine wear used to force a lot of oil out of the breather pipe which exited under the seat tail. Some other riders had protested about it and the organisers had made RC30 runners fit a collector box before the last race, which should have routed any excess oil back into the carburettors to get burnt up in the combustion process. As my engine didn't lose any oil I didn't have any worries, but as a safeguard we'd rerouted the pipe to exit on the engine, because if any oil did escape into the carburettors it would have made the bike run worse.

It was a stupid move and taught us another lesson, because from halfway through the race the bike started moving around and my feet kept slipping off the foot pegs too, so I knew it was oil doing it. At high speed the air pressure was acting like a vacuum and started sucking oil out of the engine through the breather pipe and all over the bike.

Fogarty had gone off like a bullet on his RC30, determined to get his first North West win with Yamaha mounted Mark Farmer hot on his heels and me sitting behind, watching the boys in front fight it out for a bit. Robert Dunlop's Norton broke down trying to stay with us and then Fogarty retired into the pits too, leaving Mark Farmer and me to fight it out up front.

The oil meant I was having to be really careful on the turns but it started to slide so much on the last lap I had to knock it off a bit, but I still overshot at University Corner and he got ahead of me.

That was it - oil or not, there was no way I was going to lead this race for so long and then lose the five thousand pounds prize money on the last lap! The red mist came down and in a do or die effort I got past an oil splattered Mark Farmer at The Metropole and he never got near me again. When I got off the bike I was completely exhausted and it was all I could do to get up the podium steps, but there was that girl again and this time I got a kiss on the lips! I thought, here now, that's a thing, that was a bit cheeky, but I was very happy.

We won about ten thousand pounds that day - the most successful performance of my career up until then, both on the track and financially. No one else has ever won five North Wests at once and a day's wages like that was something I'd only ever dreamed about. Wonderful.

As Manda has already described, I was invited to the organisers' and sponsors' dinner that night and of course she was there. I spoke to her a few times on the phone but she was playing it very cool, my work schedule was so tough and I didn't want to hurt anyone - we were both in relationships at the time, but I called her again in August and she finally relented and let me take her out to that little place near Omagh...

We'd blitzed the opposition, broken the records and torn up the form books at the North West, and everyone was wondering what was going to happen at the TT, not least of them me!

The new Michelin tyres for the 250 Honda they provided me with for TT fortnight gave me a big scare on Monday morning's very first TT practice. The bike turned in really fast for Quarter Bridge and I nearly lost it, feet off both pegs, everything, only a mile or so from the start. Petrol was seeping from the breather at the front of the tank and I thought it must have leaked onto the tyre or something and stopped to have a look, but couldn't see anything dramatic going on.

I kept going and got third quickest in practice, with the thing still pretty wild going into comers at the end of the straights and the next day I burst some fork seals, so I put it down to oil on the tyres this time. It wasn't until the third day's session I sussed it out, went back to the old profile type of tyre and felt immediately at home again, keeping third overall in the 250 plus the 400 and Formula One, topping it off by being fastest on my 600.

With the wins at the North West on my 750 and the island practice sessions, Tony Scott had rebuilt the engine, new pistons, rings, everything at the beginning of practice week, but it was losing a little bit of oil so had to be stripped again and we were running out of time to get ready for Thursday afternoon's session.

The thing had to be run in after the (two) rebuilds and we were so short of personnel. Of course I'd turned down the Yamaha Grand Prix offer in the autumn because of the promises of improved equipment Honda had made. It was my first big disappointment with them. It's amazing to think of it really, but we were Honda's official representatives there, this little bit of private enterprise over from Northern Ireland trying with Joey Dunlop to continue Honda's unbeaten run in the Formula One TT, facing Fogarty on a Yamaha this time and Steve Hislop, who was going to be running one of the super fast Nortons.

Looking back on it now, I think when Fogarty and Hislop, the previous year's double winners had left the team, Honda probably thought deep down they'd lost this year's races already and weren't going to waste any money on it. Honda UK's Dave Hancock had called in all his resources though and his friends in Japan to get anything he could to help me, including some improved four into two exhausts from HRC themselves.

Apart from that and some good wishes, all we had was Christine, me, Jim and of course brother Noel who got the short straw in the end, taking the race bike out to run it in on the public roads. We were just completely out of time and support and Noel was stopped by the Police for speeding. There wasn't a lot of tread on the racing slicks and it turned into a bit of a serious offence. The big fine didn't help our skinny budget too much either.

The race day weather was perfect, hot with blue skies and a big crowd had come to the island wondering if Hislop was going to be the first British rider to win on a Norton since Mike Hailwood's victory in 1961. A 121.38mph practice lap on the Norton said it all.

I was itching to get out there, feeling confident after whipping everyone at the North West and the race began with Fogarty getting off to a great start. He had a thirty seven second lead over me at one stage, with Hislop fourteen seconds further back in third, even though he was having some overheating problems with the Norton. I carved several seconds out of Fogarty's lead on (flying) lap two and then he stalled the Yamaha in the stop box coming into pit lane to refuel at the end of the lap while Hislop stopped his Norton at the 'old' Honda pit and killed the engine before he realised what he'd done. So I made up a few seconds more while those two were having difficulties.

Robert Dunlop's Norton seized and Hislop decided the front mud guard had to come off his to help cool it down a bit and stop the same thing happening. Meanwhile I'd caught Joey up on the road and it took me a little while to get past him which let Fogarty, who was going well, get away again. I really cranked it up then and my signals showed I was reducing his lead and then suddenly they were giving me first place when Fogarty's second gear jammed at the Bungalow. This left me eighteen seconds in the lead, ahead of Hislop who was now flying again on the cooler running Norton.

It all came down to the last lap, but I'd been waiting years for this chance and the British Bike Supporters Club was going to have to wait. Hislop pushed me all the way with a superb 123.3mph final effort, but I recorded the fastest ever RC30 lap on the island at 122.68mph to win by twelve seconds in 1hr 53m 22.4 secs, at a race average of 119.80mph.

Joey was nearly two minutes back in third place. It seemed like it had been so long coming, but then again, everything has to be right, including your luck. It was a great effort from our small, tight, well-structured little team - and I include Tony Scott in that - which had given me the reliability we needed. I'd had a consistent ride and was particularly pleased with the win on the out of date, bogged down RC30.

In the combined 400 Supersport and 125 Ultra lightweight TT, Fogarty was riding Dave Leach's Yamaha and had qualified very well, but was only third behind me, chasing Brian Reid who'd got away with a scorching start. Fogarty came back at me in a tough battle between the two of us, together on the road and we had a good fight from the start of the lap, until the Ramsey hairpin when his more powerful Yamaha stormed off.

I used his slipstream for some of the way until pure power left me trailing behind going up the mountain. We hadn't been able to get any kit radiators for my Honda and it was overheating and losing quite a bit of power in the terrifically hot summer weather.

All three of us at the front had desperately close times though, way inside the old lap record. Fogarty's bad luck continued and he went out at around half distance, but Brian Reid pulled further away from me in the end and I was happy to come in second on what I felt was an inferior machine.

Steve Lindsell was third, but the big news of the day was Joey's 125 win which equalled Mike Hailwood's all-time record number of fourteen TT wins. Super stuff from a brilliant rider.

The 250 Junior TT race was hugely entertaining for the fans with Brian Reid, Ian Lougher, Joey and Robert Dunlop all together on the roads. I would have been much happier using my faithful old 1990 250, but Honda insisted I use the machine they brought to the island for me. Without specialised help, you can't get a bike like that running right in one week with so much else going on and we never got it exactly right.

In the race I was having a long battle for fifth place with Steve Johnson, who's bike was a bit quicker than mine, when I had a big moment chasing him into Kirk Michael with my foot slipping off an oily peg.

I recovered from that little heart stopper, getting past him for the umpteenth time on the Sulby straight, when my 250 seized without warning and Steve narrowly missed running into me. He finished an excellent fourth while my race was over. In our next encounter we both crashed at the Ulster Grand Prix. Steve lost his life in the incident and I was to be accused of causing the crash.

The frustration of not finishing fired me up for the afternoon's Super Sport 600 TT (now called the Junior) which I led from start to finish, one of the best races of my life which I planned to a tee. I'd gambled before the start though, by guessing at some settings after a difficult practice and the forks were very soft, with the front end really bouncing around. I bust Steve Hislop's 1991 record with a 116.17mph lap from a standing start and then raised it again to 116.25mph on lap two, leaving Bob Jackson, Johnny Rea and Steve Ward fighting it out behind me, the nearest over thirty eight seconds adrift after the pit stops.

My next signal showed me even further ahead but then Hislop had got into his stride and came back at me on a charge past Johnny Rea and up into second on the third lap. I upped the pace a bit then, getting it all wrong and sideways at Sulby Bridge in the process, but my cushion was so good going into the final lap, I know I'd done enough to control the race and at times had the bike at half throttle, to cruise in by over forty seconds from Hislop and Steve Ward.

The biggest thanks I got after that were not only from Honda sales bosses Bob McMillan and Dave Hancock, but also from the company's regional sales managers, who knew the huge effect that win was going to have on sales in their dealerships. I'd saved their bacon with the RC30 which was being crucified in the sales stakes all over the world by now and had now followed that up with the 600 win. They all seemed to appreciate what I'd done.

After that record RC30 lap in the Formula One, I was ready to go faster if needs be to win Friday's Senior. That final F1 lap had come together perfectly while I was under the pressure of fighting off Hislop's challenge. On a 750 you're accelerating everywhere on the island flat out, with the throttle on the stop, but there aren't many straights on the course and only two or three places where you're trying to get the thing up to maximum speed in top gear.

We gear the 750 pretty high for one point or two because it's important not to have the engine over revving or it won't last race distance, it'll just blow up. You obviously don't want it under geared or likewise over geared, or it'll never pull top.

There's a big drop down towards Greaver Castle where you can get a 750 flat out, but there's nowhere then until the long Sulby straight and there's usually a big headwind along the mountain, so it's difficult for the bike to pull top gear the way you want and that's about it. There's a fast section between Creg-ny-Baa and Brandish which you've got to get completely right to take flat out; you won't do it anywhere if you don't get perfect drive out of the corner before anyway, only when you've done that is it possible to get the thing flat out.

Get it all right, every section perfect and smooth having already put in the necessary amount of preparation and that's when you get the fast laps. My 122.68mph lap on the RC30 has remained the fastest ever there on that particular machine and that's the way it'll stay unless someone gets really focussed in a future Manx Classic! Maybe I'll have a go at it one day,

And where to next? The change in formula for the big races on the island in the late 90's has made a significant difference as to what machine to choose now to compete on. Increasing the four cylinder ceiling to 1,000cc from 750 has allowed Yamaha's R1 and latest generation big bore Honda Fireblades to go there, heavily tuned to compete with the factory 750s.

These road bikes are getting so good now, so advanced and powerful that this definitely seems the way forward, but I still think a good factory 750 should win but it would have to be a very good one indeed. Parts are so scarce, exotic and expensive though and the risk of failure on such an important world stage for manufacturers' most sophisticated equipment is very dangerous for their reputations. So why take the risk?

I got the dream job at the Plistop nightclub that year. I was in charge of cooling down the girls in the wet 'T' shirt competition though I kept a safe distance, having to behave myself now I was in the limelight.

In contrast to the way that first big race of the week had gone, my 1992 Senior TT was a disaster from Bray Hill onwards, where I must have picked up the stone that holed the radiator. The bike was at a hundred degrees from that moment on and I made the mistake of staying in Robert Dunlop's slipstream which let me knock the power off a bit, thinking that would take some of the load off the engine.

What I should have been doing was staying out in the fresh air and let that do the cooling; I meant to pull in at the end of the first lap but decided about Governor's Bridge that if I did that it was all over and stuck right behind Robert Dunlop for another lap.

Amazingly, my signals were showing that I was still in the hunt and I kept going, but at the refuelling stop it really was all over and I retired at the same time as an off-colour Joey Dunlop, to watch Fogarty and Hislop slug it out in that classic last couple of laps. Hislop's Norton won by 4.4 secs after Fogarty's final 123.61mph record-breaking lap, which beat Hislop's 123.48mph time set on the RVF the year before, when he'd been chasing Fogarty, of course. That lap record stood for seven years until Jim Moodie and Joey Dunlop both broke it on RC45s at the peak of their development.

Back at home, 1992 turned into an absolute disaster. There had been a couple of years' of bad weather at the Ulster Grand Prix and the event had been swapped with the Killinchy 150 at the same Dundrod circuit, in an attempt to get some decent weather and a better crowd. Full of confidence after my TT double, I got pole in glorious weather on the 600 and in the 250 class using my 'old' Turkingtons machine, plus second in the 400 and superbikes.

I'd started well on my 250 in the first race and was lying in second behind Brian Reid halfway around the first lap and all I remember was an almighty bang, my bike started sliding out of control, I was fighting it alongside a hedge and then I was flying through air; that was it and I woke up a couple of days later in hospital.

The news had gone round the circuit like wildfire that there'd been a crash between Steve Johnson and Phillip McCallen and one of them was dead. The worst thing of all was that Robert Dunlop had come back to the start and said that he'd seen the crash and that Phillip McCallen had knocked Steve Johnson off. Then all hell broke loose.

7

By this time Robert Dunlop and I'd had a few run-ins over different things and Robbie seemed to be out to get me over some bits and pieces. His accusation was a serious one to make and I was told it had appeared on the television that night and in the newspapers later on.

I came round in hospital severely battered with a broken shoulder and collarbone to find out about Steve's death and these very scary accusations that didn't go away. It got worse and worse. The bereaved family wanted a full explanation of the circumstances surrounding Steve's death, with Robert Dunlop in constant contact with them, repeating his statement that he'd been right behind Steve and me - which he had - and there was no problem he said, he'd seen it; I'd taken Steve Johnson off the track

I still didn't realise quite how serious all this was until the Police appealed for witnesses to the accident and about fifteen did come forward, unfortunately with conflicting statements. By this time I was starting to get very worried indeed about the consequences of all this. I had a reputation as a hard rider but I wasn't dangerous, just determined. Being accused of something so serious, even if it's behind the scenes is an extremely unpleasant thing and it not only put pressure on me but the whole family. My Mum was desperately upset, my girlfriend was terribly worried by it all - it got to my brothers - everybody was affected.

I tried so hard to think about the accident to see if my memory was playing tricks on me - was I deluding myself with wishful thinking? - but all I could remember was a clear track in front of me which led to Brian Reid ahead.

Even before the inquest began in the Coroner's Court just before Christmas one of the witnesses, a good friend of mine actually, came up to me and told me he had to tell the truth. I said "Well that's good, thanks, that's just what I need." But he told me it wasn't, because I'd definitely knocked the other rider off. Just what I needed as we were being called in for the hearing.

It goes back to the old story of what you see and what you think you see are two totally different things. It started to come out that one of the reasons for the confusion was that I always ride with number nine on my bike and was well known for it, but on this occasion I had the number one plate and Steve Johnson had been riding with number nine on his bike.

He had green leathers and a white bike and I had a green and white bike with matching leathers so who was who at a hundred miles an hour? Some spectators at that part of the course had seen number nine take off number one, but most people had watched Brian Reid going through and then swung their heads backs to see the aftermath of our accident, not what had caused it. There was a lot of confusion, rumour and hearsay about.

Things got worse that morning at the inquest itself when I got onto the witness stand and the Coroner adjourned for a lunch break to give the Johnson family, who'd travelled from England that morning a break, and me time to consult with my solicitor. I hadn't realised just how serious it was all going to get and hadn't organised a legal representative to accompany me. The firm had said if there is any sort of problem ask for an adjournment, but I hadn't got a clue how to do that and rang my solicitor's office during the recess in quite a panic.

For once in a lifetime the entire firm was out at lunch celebrating something and I had no option when the Court reconvened, but to face an accusatory barrister in the witness box for over an hour. He really put me through the mill but I just told the story of what had actually happened and the truth has a funny way of winning through in the end. It was exceptionally lucky that a local doctor had taken some amateur video the day of the race and he'd caught the majority of the incident. It was shown in Court, the footage revealing I was a good bit in front of Steve Johnson going into the comer, proving me blameless beyond question, because Steve had run into me.

Even then the barrister tried to make out that although it was now proven I was leading Johnson going into the comer, hadn't I slowed down deliberately to make him run into me? I was vindicated of course and cleared completely of any wrong doing, bringing to an end an absolute nightmare that had been getting worse for six months as the situation came to a head. I don't know to this day who that doctor and amateur cameraman was, so I've never had the opportunity to thank him until now. Thank you very much.

It was all very nasty, a terrible strain on everyone concerned, particularly dreadful for Steve's family of course.

After a few weeks' convalescence, I finally got back in the saddle at Nutts Corner with a second place in the Regal Championship and was straight back to the Isle of Man for the Southern 100 race meeting which is held on the 4.24 mile Billown circuit over there. I won three events on my 750, including the Southern 100 Championship race, the 400 Supersport and the Regal 600 round too, to complete a five out of five clean sweep. I was back with a bang.

The tragedies of the season were never far from my mind though. Motorcycle road racing is dangerous and that will always bring injury and worse with it. Steve Johnson and Oral Watson's deaths, Dave Leach's terrible injuries and my own close calls were a constant reminder of the dangerous game I was playing.

It may seem strange but the only way that I knew how to deal with it all was riding my bikes, but the next meeting I was due to ride at was the Temple 100 and I have to say that was preying on my mind. I was glad to have missed the meeting by going to Suzuka the year before, because of the terrible crash I'd had at the Temple in 1990. Lying in bed, blinded after that gave me plenty of time to think about different ways to make a living and to go over and over the accident in my mind. I had no memory of the crash itself, but it wasn't hard to work out what had happened and it made me realise that I was pushing too hard for that win.

The Temple's got 150mph jumps everywhere which are only a real problem because the road is full of humps and bumps just before them. The slightest kick in the steering from an uneven surface like that makes it really difficult to get a bike stable, then lined up properly and ready to jump at 150mph or more.

I was pleased not to have to go back the year after the crash, but I knew now I couldn't walk away from it in defeat and fear and I had to confront it one more time. I was a long way from fit and knew the 750 was going to be far too big a handful there in my condition, so I took my 600 and the 250, promising myself I'd win some races and overcome my apprehension.

James Courtney got away fast in the 250 before Brian Reid and I overhauled him. I tracked Brian into the approach to the Rectory corner and dived up the inside to sneak a win. He was upset about the move and lodged a protest which was thrown out by the stewards, another example of the pressure I was under and the effect it was having on my reputation.

I led the Regal 600 race from start to finish, which improved my Championship position immensely and rounded off the day with a second place on my 600, behind Derek Young's 750 in the superbike race. It's safe to say the Temple was not my favourite track, because it was impossible to ride there as I really wanted, but I'd come through unscathed and finally put my fears to rest.

Many people have asked me which is my favourite circuit of all and it has to be the Isle of Man, six laps in the big races there, two hundred and twenty five miles at over 120mph, that is the ultimate buzz, there really is nothing like it, plus I've had the privilege of picking up a big cheque at the end of it all to reward me for it. What an amazing job! If you've never been to the island yet, stop putting it off! Being part of the great festival there is an unforgettable experience and so is riding the wonderful island course.

The Regal Championship was blown wide open at the Mid-Antrim 150. A popular rider called Alan Irwin took the first road race win of his career after I'd done a bit of racing off the track while leading, the bike actually ending up on top of me. I got going again to finish sixth and keep a thirteen point lead in the Championship. This was crucial, as I was to miss the next round at Bishopscourt, because I was finally going to compete in England on my 400 and 600 at Cadwell Park's Supercup that weekend.

It was a significant trip. I felt like I was leaving everything behind, all the upsets, tragedy and pressure, with a whole new world opening up in front of me. I'd missed the previous British rounds I was entered for because of a bout of 'flu I picked up after the North West and then the Ulster Grand Prix accident. I'd seen Cadwell Park many years before, but hadn't been back, even though it was so close to Honda Britain's headquarters. I was in good company at the meeting with Jeremy McWilliams, Woolsey Coulter, Mark Farmer and Robert Dunlop all riding in various classes. I've always loved having somewhere new to ride and got into the groove immediately, finishing sixth in the 600 Supersport encounter, but crashing my 400 which put me out of the race.

There was no time to lose getting back to Ireland and preparing for the Ace of Aghadowey meeting as I was now trailing Alan Irwin in the

Regal, with Johnny Rea right behind me following Alan's win and John-ny's fourth in the Bishopscourt round I'd missed. In the end the meeting was washed out and I was tempted to ride at Scarborough's Gold Cup the next weekend, but travelled down to Killalane instead. I took the 250 Irish Road Race Championship with a win on my 250 and was never headed in the 600 and 750 events for a wonderful hat trick, bringing my tally of wins for the season to twenty-seven.

I brought my 600 home fifth in my second British Supercup meeting at Brands Hatch the following weekend, finishing thirteenth in the 400 race, returning to Ireland ready for the final two Regal encounters of the year at Bishopscourt.

All I had to do was get a good top three finish to make sure of the title, but I totally destroyed my Honda Britain CBR600 in a big accident while leading on the final corner. I was so angry with myself, I just could-n't believe I'd done it, but then I wrecked my spare 600 in the second Regal event that day, luckily escaping injury. I'd written off two bikes, completely destroyed them, including one I'd paid for out of my North West 200 winnings and lost the Regal title all in one go, ending up third behind Johnny Rea and Alan Irwin. You win some, you lose some, you smash some up.

By now my sponsors, Turkington Systems Windows had generously offered to invest in a new 500 Grand Prix Yamaha plus support to take on the likes of Wayne Rainey and Kevin Schwantz in GP racing the fol-lowing year. It was a superb offer from them and looking back now I regret not taking it - who knows where it would have led me? Hindsight is a wonderful thing, but at the time I still felt I didn't have enough short circuit experience and needed to do more in England, plus race in a few events on the Continent, before moving in to Grand Prix the following year. Then Honda Britain made me an alternative offer.

Fogarty had gone off with his privateer Ducati and Simon Crafar had been riding a Honda Britain RC30 in the British Supercups with limited success in 1992, even though it was so long in the tooth by now. A sin-gle, beautiful RVF750 was being made available to the team for 1993 though and I should have put up a bigger fight for it, but Steve Hislop announced he'd finished with road racing and cut a deal to ride it in the British Championship, what was known then as The Supercup, with one eye on a move into World Superbikes in 1994.

"I've done my time here," he said about the Isle of Man and his RVF was promised to me to ride at the North West 200, TT and Ulster Grand

Prix plus Crafar's old RC30, 'improved' they said, for a competitive British Supercup campaign. We knew by then that HRC were hard at work on the RC30 replacement too, which was due to make its first appearance at the 1993 Suzuka eight hour endurance race. I was tempted.

Moving to Grand Prix meant I'd be leaving Britain with only two TT wins to my credit. My love of road racing and the prospect of competing with the RVF on the island and the other big road events, made me decide that I wasn't having that and I signed for Honda Britain again. That was a decision I often think about.

The media launch in Ireland was held at The Culloden Hotel near Belfast and featured the trick RVF750, Honda dignitaries, Ronald and me. Here was a winning bike, the message said and this young man's going to ride it to victory in the big road races. I think they thought they'd finally cracked it with me - here was someone who would ride anything, anywhere. But what they didn't realise was that I did know what I was doing all those years before and the successes had come because the team was prepared right, the machines were prepared right, everything, down to the last detail.

The deal entailed me living in England, being based at Honda's race headquarters and meant the end of so many things. Jim McMahon's young family meant he couldn't make the move from Northern Ireland with me, and my brother Noel got left behind too, with Honda only prepared to consider my older brother Ronald being part of my team.

It was all change - bikes, job, team, country of residence, race tracks, everything and for the first time ever, I travelled to Honda Britain's Louth headquarters at the beginning of the year and didn't come back, moving into a little house we called 'The Bungalow' close to the workshop complex.

Ronald joined the team as a full time technician and we left our younger brother Noel behind, perhaps feeling a little left out of our team's development. We shared the house with Steve Hislop and technician Ian Richards (who'd finished second to Mike Hailwood in the 1979 Senior TT) who was a good lad and turned into a great friend. But with my old team and helpers all gone, without all that expertise and support and the familiarity of having a strong team around me missing, everything quickly fell to pieces. As I've always said it's the strength of the team that is of paramount importance and the rider is only one piece of that jigsaw. Road races can be won with an average bike, courage, skill and determination, but try that without meticulous preparation on a short circuit and you're on a road to nowhere.

It turned out that the season before, Simon Crafar had refused to ride the RC30 I'd now inherited, as it was totally out of date. I still believed in myself and thought I'd ride it and do well, but of course I couldn't do it. The bizarre thing was the season, even preseason testing had started really well. I was only half a second down on Hislop during shakedown tests at the Welsh short circuit Pembrey in early March, even though he was on the RVF.

He was a bit disappointed really, the engine turned out not to be the awesome unit we'd hoped, just a factory RC30 motor with some trick internals and the legendary twenty five thousand pound set of carbure-tors. The bodies were milled out of solid magnesium, beautifully made, with needle roller bearings for the slides - some bit of kit! The chassis was good though, hand built, the real thing, so the bike had a much bet-ter power to weight ratio, riding more like a 250 than the big RC30.

The first race of the year was at Brands Hatch, a support race for the World Superbike Round and very wet, which I won by thirteen seconds, leaving Hislop and the RVF, literally in my wake. I was pleased but of course it caused a little bit of friction in the team. It didn't look partic-ularly good for Steve, or the team manager; the fact that an RC30 had whipped the RVF didn't look good for anything.

It was a false start all round, the weather and my wet road riding skills masking the fact the RC30 was dead and gone by then. The pace had suddenly upped on the track with a tranche of new models, the Yamahas were going well then, but the team green Kawasakis were probably the pick of the bunch. In 1992, Crafar's Honda was maybe capable of run-ning in the top six; by the time I inherited it in the following season, it was struggling to stay in the top ten, I was in trouble and it wasn't long before we found that out.

It was wet again when the season proper started at Knockhill. I hadn't raced there since 1989, but I started well, fighting it out with the boys at the front until Hislop, who being Scots was a bit of a specialist there, eventually caught and passed me on the inside, towards the end of the race. I came back at him, moving so close going through the chicane I was going to run in to the rear of his bike and I had no choice but to pull my bike over and slide off and that was the beginning of a deterio-ration in the relationship with my manager.

Nick Jeffries was there, just having a bit of fun warming up for the road races but had crashed earlier on, a crank in Hislop's engine had broken as well, so it was turning in to an expensive meeting. I'd slid off in practice too, trying so hard to make up for the deficiency of the machine and trying to get to grips with the Ohlins suspension, which was new to me. I couldn't get the bike the way I wanted it at all; I was used to riding an RC30 with conventional forks and Showa suspension, I couldn't cope with the Ohlins kit. It just didn't work on the RC30 - or the RC45 for that matter.

My manager made it clear that from then on I was just to ride round and ease up enough to reduce the chances of more accidents. Of course, I wasn't at all happy with that, just wanting to work harder and harder to get things right.

How I missed my old outfit. Ronald was a good mechanic but we were lacking the support of our conscientious team from back home. And now we had this team manager who was very economy minded, feeling that spending money on the old machinery wasn't worth while, plus you couldn't crash, because spares were in such short supply. I'd turned down Grand Prix offers in consecutive years to stick with Honda, I'd given up a lot, left my homeland, dismantled my hugely successful team and effectively sacrificed my relationship with my girlfriend of five years and felt terribly frustrated by the lack of progress.

The whole team felt the same including Steve Hislop who was nowhere near fighting for the lead in the British Championship, which was where he'd been hoping to be. It took ages for one of his technicians to understand the importance of the settings on the bike and not to make radical changes the night before the race, which caused Steve some big problems.

I kept believing I could make this bike handle and make the results happen and was so frustrated because no one would listen to me, saying the problem was me and my riding style.

The races weren't any harder than I was used to at home, the circuits were different but my racing in Ireland was a much heavier schedule, really relentless work. I knew in England that my talent was not going to be enough and that we had to have everything perfect with the machinery to even stand a chance of winning, because all the other teams would be spending days and weeks getting every single thing exact.

My team's thinking was that Simon Crafar had ridden my bike ok the year before, so it was nothing to do with the equipment, it was all my fault. But of course it was the bike. Apart from anything else, Craft's style was totally different to mine, he liked his bike quick turning and solid and I like mine to be movable and flexible.

My bike of the year before, the one I'd had great success with had been earmarked for Nick Jeffries' road racing campaign. I'd wanted to keep it though, because it had been new at the beginning of the previous season and we had done all the work on it, perfecting it to suit me.

I wasn't prepared to give in though - no way, but I just couldn't 'feel' the bike I'd now been given to work with. I hadn't felt comfortable with it from the moment I'd sat on it, with judder from the front end when I was pushing hard into turns. It was only later that I realised the upside down Ohlins forks were just too stiff. The RC30 had a very rigid chassis and the more flexible standard forks and Showa rear shock suited it and me much better. I didn't see it then, but looking back that was the problem; I was used to lots of feedback from a bike moving around underneath me, but was getting nothing at all through this set up, with disastrous consequences.

In the first lap of the superbike race at Mallory Park, another early round in the British Supercup, I was coming through the esses where you drop right and left coming up towards the hairpin, I gassed it coming out of the left and it high sided me right in front of the following pack. The left hand side of the tyre was cold and I couldn't feel the bike move until it was too late you see. The race had to be stopped because of total carnage - my crash had wiped out the rest of the field that was behind me and I took a real beating, waking up in Leicester's Royal Infirmary.

By this time of course I realised what a mistake I'd made and really started living from that moment on the prospect of this trick RC45 coming out ready for next year. I made myself believe we'd be winning on it every week and everything would turn out fine in the long run. What a surprise we were to get when that bike did finally come out.

At least I could look forward to my first outing on the RVF at the North West 200 where I'd been so successful the year before, but the disastrous season was to continue back in Ireland too. I hadn't had much time on the thing, only a couple of short sessions on it before, but it was immediately apparent on the first night of practice that there was something wrong, because it had no speed at all. I told the mechanics that there was a problem and it probably needed jetting up, but as usual they said no, it was fine and this time I went completely berserk, saying that no one was leaving the garage that night until the bike had been stripped in front of me. I was so mad.

Once the heads were off, lo and behold it was immediately apparent that the engine had cold seized in its previous wet race at Oulton Park and dragged the pistons and rings, marking the barrel with aluminium. There was hardly any compression at all. I was right.

Luckily, Tony Scott had been preparing another engine for the TT and he got it finished just in time for it to be sent over. We ran it in using a road bike and some helpers and fitted it in time for a few unofficial laps in the final 250 practice session, including one at 119mph. I'd qualified fourth on my 600 and on my 250, the class which traditionally opens Saturday's programme of races

I was in a good position in the first event, swapping the lead with Robert Dunlop, James Courtney and Woolsey Coulter. It was turning into a real classic North West battle, with me just ahead of six other riders all abreast of each other, when Davy Johnson ran into the back of my bike braking at The Metropole, sending both of us off the circuit. The melee had let Robert Dunlop get away a bit and I rejoined well down the field to set about clawing back the gap and couldn't believe it when Johnson hit the back of my bike again at Church Corner on the next lap.

He'd got it all sideways coming into the corner and had a choice between hitting me or the high kerb. Tough choice, but I ended up as the soft option and this time he fired me off the bike and onto the road, where I lay unconscious for a few seconds.

I'd hit my head quite heavily (thanks again Arai) and damaged the muscles in my left shoulder. I got it looked at and had some painkillers but was still a bit shaky, so took the doctor's good advice and didn't start in the first superbike race, but felt well enough to compete in the rest of the events that day.

The record books show I was seventh in the 600, fifth in the 400 and second in the other 250 race and finished the big superbike race of the day, which was stopped on lap four, in third place, fractionally behind Robert Dunlop and Carl Fogarty, both on 888 Ducatis. I'd love to say that I had them beat and was just biding my time before I picked them both off, but I couldn't ride at anywhere near my best due to the earlier incident.

My left shoulder had taken a lot of punishment over the years. Smashed, broken, beaten and bashed. It had been badly damaged at Daytona and now I'd hurt it again at the North West with so little time to recover before the TT. I put my mind to work on getting it healed and with intensive physio in England and help from my medical guru Fred McSorley, we got it into some sort of shape ready for practice at the TT.

We had the beautiful little RVF set up OK, but had switched back to standard RC30 carbs and then back again to the factory equipment to try and get it running perfectly. In my mind I felt his was my show now and in complete control. My other bikes were going well too in practice and I headed the field on my 250, was third fastest on my 600 but crucially, ended fastest on the 750 with a 117.17mph in early practice with conditions far from ideal. I followed it up with a 118.54mph lap in the final session, quite a bit in front of Simon Beck and Robert Dunlop.

I could have gone a bit quicker on one lap but my visor was out of tear-offs and had suddenly picked up a lot of flies and I couldn't see very well at all, just when it mattered. Towards the end, I'd caught up with Joey Dunlop on the road, but didn't want to pass him to give anything away about me or my bike, so I sat on his tail.

I remember he suddenly braked much earlier than I expected going into one corner and I grabbed hard at my anchors and felt this awful pain in my left shoulder, really bad and knew that something had hit it. When I came back into the paddock I got my leathers off and asked my brother if there was any bruising, but there wasn't. In fact something had just snapped inside, ligaments or muscle damage from the earlier injury I guess, that was obviously nowhere near healed.

Honda had won the last eleven Formula One races and I started as favourite to record their twelfth win, putting in a great opening lap with Mark Farmer on a Ducati flying too and Nick Jeffries quicker than he'd ever been on my old RC30.

The shoulder was giving me real trouble heaving the bike around in the faster corners, which is where you can make up so much time, but I kept up a relentless charge on the second lap, hauling myself up to second place. The Tony Scott engine was in a lighter state of tune than Hislop's trickier motor for reliability, but strong enough for the job. A rear wheel bearing failed on Farmer's Ducati, leaving me just a few seconds behind new leader Nick Jeffries and ready to take over at the front after the pit stops.

Everything was going smoothly, riding well within myself and protecting my shoulder as much as I could and pulled back Jeffries within ten seconds on lap three. At the second pit stop my helmet technician mixed up a visor change and broke the locating fittings inside my helmet. The problem was I'd had two different Arai models with me, each of which needed different visors.

Panic ensued after a complete helmet change was shouted for and the ensuing debacle cost me so much time. My helmet was being pulled off my head and it felt like my ears were going with it, plus the strap hadn't been undone properly and it all cost me so many vital seconds. I rejoined the race and did my absolute best, eating into Jeffries' lead with a 119.73mph last lap, but it wasn't enough to make up all the time we'd lost with the helmet fiasco and I finished second, just thirteen seconds adrift behind my own old bike!

I pulled out of Monday's Supersport 400 TT in a bid to rest my shoulder before Wednesday's Junior TT, in which I made one of the most embarrassing mistakes of my whole career. I was in fifth place when I caught a rider called Dave Milling who was in about eighth and I just couldn't shake him off. I got totally absorbed in this fight, really peeved off at how long it was taking to get away from him. I fought him off all the way down the mountain and finally got rid of him coming round Signpost corner and The Nook and I was so desperate to keep him off my back wheel by then, I kept going instead of coming in for fuel. As soon as I crossed the finish line I realised what I'd done.

Apparently my whole team's jaws had hit the floor as I came screaming through and I thought about turning back, reversing it up pit lane but in my heart I knew it was all over. There were too many people at the bottom of Bray Hill to turn left and get back so I just kept going, with the forlorn hope that a miracle might happen and I could make it all the way around the next lap.

No chance of course, but by the time I got to Ballacraine I'd really convinced myself that I might even make it and I kept on riding - it was too humiliating to pull in anyway. She finally spluttered to a halt coming into Quarry Bends and I couldn't believe it, I'd coasted to a halt right in front of one of the television cameras, who capped it all by interviewing me there and then. "What's the problem Phillip?" asked the reporter. Hmm! Difficult.

My luck only improved slightly in the 600 race, finishing a lowly seventh place with my mind already focussing on Friday's Senior TT. I was so desperate by this time, still so wound up by losing the F1 because of the helmet cock up, nothing was going to stop me winning this race. The weather was bad enough on Friday morning for the race to be postponed, then called off until Saturday and the extra twenty four hours rest did me good. I knew I didn't have the strength to last the whole six laps, realising that maybe I could manage two flat out at the most and that this was my best chance - put in some fast early times and see who was prepared to live with me. In the end, no one was.

I went off like a rocket, the fastest I'd ever ridden from a standing start recording a 120.65mph lap with very wet patches all over the place and mist in others, quite thick from Guthries to The Bungalow. I was the man on the mission that day and came charging flat out into the last corner before Ballacraine, which is a sixth gear right-hander and there was a big damp patch bang in the middle. The bike went sliding completely sideways all the way across the road and I hung right off the side of it, using every bit of strength and willpower I had left to get it straightened up again, one of my best ever 'saves' against all the odds.

"Wow!" I thought, if I can do that, I can do anything and then the same thing happened when I got a huge highside on more water in fifth gear this time at the thirty third, but I held onto her again and knew it had to be my day. What a beautiful bike the RVF was to ride, light and nimble; it'd only taken a short while to get it just how I wanted - on something heavier I think I would have been in a lot more trouble during those two incidents.

Everything started to flow nicely after that and I caught and passed Simon Beck on the road, then blasted Nick Jeffries into the weeds, to lead by sixteen seconds from Mark Farmer. His Ducati ran out of fuel on the second lap leaving me ahead of Joey Dunlop by twenty four seconds, with Jeffries much further back and I raced the course on my own for a good while, keeping the pressure up with a hot pace.

Joey slowed with an oil reservoir problem, I caught and passed Steve Ward who was in fourth at that stage and I was leading by sixty seconds at the second pit stop. Three of my first four laps had been at 120mph + in pretty poor conditions and that had won the race for me. No one could get close by then which was handy, because I was riding in great pain and struggled to control the bike towards the end, praying I could bring the RVF home for my third TT victory. I won by over a minute from Jeffries, Steve Ward was another minute or so behind and justice had been done. The champagne had never tasted sweeter.

I was exhausted, shattered, crippled with pain but happy to have finally got the win both the bike and I deserved and so was Honda, who saw how far gone I was and gave me some time off work. I hung around Douglas for a couple of days, to try and wind down a bit.

I went home to Portadown mentally and physically drained and wandered into a travel agency on a bit of a whim, asking what late bookings they'd got available. The single supplement was really steep for the places I fancied going, so I had a quick think and asked if I could borrow their phone.

I'd only seen Manda a dozen times or so by then. Luckily she answered the phone immediately and I said "Hi, do you fancy going away somewhere?" and she ummed and ahhed a bit and said, "Yes, OK then!" which surprised me quite a bit.

"Right then!" I said and gave her some options. She chose Crete, I promised to call her later and the travel agent gave me a really funny look. I rang her up later on the same day and said we were leaving Saturday and she said "What!?", really surprised but I talked her into it and my friend Davy Hamilton drove us down to Dublin airport. We didn't want anyone to get hurt and of course had to tell some white lies to prevent that happening.

Rested, stronger and fitter, my first race back in England was at the Supercup at Snetterton. I'd taken out my CBR in the Supersport 600 practice more out of frustration at being back on the RC30 than anything else and I smashed the lap record. The time was quick enough to have netted pole position by a country mile, but of course I wasn't allowed to ride in the race as I was supposed to be a superbike rider.

It did prove I was fast and on the pace though, showing another dismal performance in the Supercup on the old and ill-handling RC30 was machinery based and very little to do with me.

My final official 1993 outing on the RVF was to be at the Ulster Grand Prix and I left England feeling like I still had something to prove, rather than being on the crest of a wave as I'd hoped. A seventh on the RC30 at Donington Park the weekend before had been a bit of a morale booster and one of my better results that year, but I was glad to be back in Ireland and on a road racing circuit with the hand-built bike. Hislop had done very well in the same race at Donington because the team had started to get the RVF well sorted by then.

Practice was blazing hot, so much so the field was warned about melting tar at the hairpin and I finished up fourth on the superbike grid behind Joey, Ian Simpson and Robert Dunlop. I was second fastest on my 600 and in pole position for the 250 race on Paul Brown's Honda Britain bike. I suddenly realised during practice that I was just about pain free for the first time that year and felt in pretty good shape.

By race day the Dundrod weather had taken on a more traditional feel and the Regal 600 was run in damp conditions. I got a great start on my trusty CBR600 and led from the line with Championship leader Ian King harrying me all the time in the first three laps. I had a bit of clutch trouble from early on and a mystery engine stutter which must have been carburation; King retired on the fourth lap and Simpson put in a charge towards the end, but I was never headed and kicked off the day with a very pleasing win in front of a huge crowd.

I managed another flying start to lead the Junior too and got away from the field a bit, breaking the class record with a 113.86mph, but Robert Dunlop raised it again and got right up to my rear wheel at one stage. I held him at bay though and pulled away again when it started to rain quite heavily, before taking the chequered flag when the race was stopped early, due to the worsening conditions.

Two out of two, with the superbikes to come, knowing I might have the edge with the RVF as well. The race turned into another fight with Robert Dunlop and his Ducati this time. I put in a scorcher on the first lap to lead Dunlop over the line with Simon Beck in third and Joey fourth. The Ducati was fast and nimble and Robert got past me on the second lap, so I gave the RVF its head and chased the big Italian 888 on lap three, taking a second off Joey's outright course record in the process at 119.35mph.

The pressure told and I took the lead, Robert started to fade with Joey moving into second behind me, followed by Simon Beck and Nick Jeffries. Suddenly, the motor began overheating, so I started to protect it a bit just doing enough to keep in front, under pressure all the way until the top three finished only a second apart. At last! My first Ulster Grand Prix superbike win, which had been a long, long time coming and the celebrations went on into the night.

The highs and lows of motorcycle racing were never more clearly marked when we returned to the dismal reality of the British Supercup. I was now being described in the Northern Ireland press as the 'Portadown Exile' - the rider who'd gone to England to race on British Championship short circuits and hadn't made an impression. I was so down hearted, knowing I was a match for any of the riders in the Supercup races and it was obvious my supporters and fans were disappointed too. They'd all been hoping I'd blaze a trail of glory in the British Championship and keep up my winning ways, but it just wasn't happening.

The majority of the Press realised all I needed was the right equipment, but it annoyed me when a few reports tagged me as having 'failed to make my mark'. Tenth and twelfth place was all I could manage on my RC30 at the Cadwell Park Supercup meeting and another poor showing at Brands Hatch the following week did nothing to help my spirits

As soon as I was back on the roads at the Killalane end of season event though, things clicked immediately into place and I led the field on the RC30 from start to finish, not caring about the thing bouncing around the road from hedge to hedge. Nothing was going to stop me winning that race and I did it again with my 600, although Johnny Rea pushed me all the way this time, and I broke clear very early on in the Junior event to win quite easily and complete the hat trick. I was looking forward to the The Grand Final to see if I could complete a clean sweep and end the season with a bang and I was leading pretty comfortably when the race was red flagged. We'd come in because of an oil spill, which was bad enough to end proceedings, the race being declared null and void so I was denied my fourth victory of the day, but left still delighted with my hat trick.

1993 saw the start of me doing a lot of road safety work with bikes, just trying a little bit to improve motorcycles' reputation with the public. I do quite a bit of work with the motorcycle police and it was around about then that the Honda ST1100 came out and I spent some time at the English Police Instructor college in Essex

My job was to help train the motorcycle police in high speed riding techniques and we spent a lot of time rewriting the rider's guide manuals too, which were terribly out of date, giving gear changing advice, for example, that would quickly destroy a gearbox.

In full police 'dress', the ST1100 was a big bike, but surprisingly quick and we had a lot of fun out on the road together. It was a great education for me too and I quickly realised what a superb job the traffic police do, trying to keep people safe on the roads and controlling two wheeled tearaways like the young Phillip McCallen.

That started a lot of subsequent road safety work with Northern Ireland's police service, something I'm always very keen to help promote. I'm very proud to have been of service to them and hope in the course of our work together we might have contributed to helping prevent some accidents and injury.

Macau's traditional end of season Grand Prix was a very short-lived affair for me as my RVF's lightweight drive sprocket sheared on lap one of the first leg, forcing me to start from the back of the grid in the second leg. I had a terrific ride trying to make up the deficit though, slicing through the field like a man possessed, putting in the fastest lap ever recorded by a four stroke bike, and I ended up fourth. Another couple of laps and I would have caught the leading trio at a really fast pace, but I just ran out of time. Unusually, we had one more event that autumn, the first ever Indonesian international race in Jakarta.

Our road racing circus had been brought to shakedown test the new track at Sentoul itself, but a stomach bug decimated the field and turned the event into a bit of a lottery. Everyone was affected and a lot of riders couldn't compete because of it, being really ill with terrible diarrhoea. One competitor had an extremely embarrassing accident while he was dancing in the hotel's nightclub one night. Poor chap. I'm sad to report that incident just about constituted the most fun I'd had all year. Says it all doesn't it?

I ended up eighth in the race though and really enjoyed it, determined then that I'd try for some World Superbike rounds the following season, with the fabled new RC45. I knew it'd be no good without some top threes in the British Supercup first, so I signed for Honda again with all that in my mind, plus I was contracted to race for them on the Isle of Man and at the North West and Ulster Grand Prix meetings too.

Brilliant, let's put 1993 behind us, I thought. I've learnt all the new English circuits I hadn't seen before, now there's a whole new year in front of us, with a brand new superbike from the world's biggest manufacturer and it's all finally going to come right. Were we in for a shock.

8

My RC45 finally turned up late February 1994 which put paid to any thoughts of riding it at Daytona. After my good showing there two years before, I'd had an approach from an American dealer offering a well sorted Ducati and a great package to ride there. Honda wouldn't have been too impressed if I'd taken them up on that offer though and it would have been in contravention of my contract, so, reluctantly, I had to turn them down and just waited for the RC45 to arrive.

Looking back, I gave up so much staying faithful to Honda. Fogarty had made the smart move by getting out at the right time, before the machinery had become uncompetitive - Hislop had tried to get out and couldn't and we'd completely blown 1993.

And the joke was when the RC45 arrived we quickly realised we'd blown 1994 too. My race bike had been taken out of a crate and was quite simply a road bike from top to bottom. My teammate Steve fared a little better and was allocated the only sets of kit suspension, forks and parts that had arrived, because he was definitely due to compete in some World Superbike rounds.

I had to make do with a standard road bike, fitted with just the few parts that were available, because my duties lay in the UK road racing scene and the British Supercup. The fact of the matter was, there just weren't the parts around, with other Honda superbike teams like Medd Racing trying to have trick parts manufactured in an attempt to be competitive, but nothing was working.

Doug Polen and Aaron Slight had been signed to race for Castrol Honda in World Superbike, continuing Honda's commitment to base its big four stroke racing in the UK, so my dreams of a chance in the World Series had evaporated with that announcement. My team manager tried to convince me we were in exactly the same parts situation as Polen and Slight were in their tests at Phillip Island. I started developing a good relationship with those boys though and they denied it, it just wasn't the stuff they were using. What we had was great for road work, but not good enough for British Supercup pace.

I'd been waiting a year for this, in fact the whole motorcycling world had been waiting for this bike to come out and no one could race it, nothing happened with it in World Superbike, in the British Supercup, nowhere. I had no alternative than to try though, with all thoughts of riding in some continental World Superbike rounds gone, I just buckled down and tried to get on with the job.

In the final few Supercup rounds of the previous season I had basically given up trying to be at the front, because I'd proved to myself it just wasn't possible. I just rode within the limits of myself and the bike, finishing where I could, in an effort to keep my bike and me in one piece as I'd been instructed. It wasn't my style at all, I'd never approached racing like that before in my life and it definitely took the fiercely competitive edge off me.

And now this, my big hopes for the new bike lying in pieces. We just couldn't get the thing to go right or handle, really big problems. I was in hot water very early on in the season when I borrowed a spare set of Hislop's Ohlins forks, worth several thousand pounds, in an attempt to get mine to go around corners and totalled the bike at Cadwell Park in the process. There was a big row because the front discs had sliced the forks into pieces in the crash, but it eventually all came to a head at Mallory Park.

The Medd Racing team, which had bought RC45s from Honda for the season were also having great difficulties with them. In the Supercup meeting at the Leicester circuit, every member of their team smashed up the new bikes, Robert Dunlop, Ray Stringer and James Haydon totalled their RC45s one after another and Steve Hislop dumped his for good measure.

It was obvious this couldn't continue, Honda UK bosses got involved and subsequently did everything they could to improve the parts situation and I was able to gradually improve my bike. It was a long, long process though, I was badly detuned from the doldrums of the previous season and nothing that was happening with the RC45 was helping.

Steve Hislop was doing a lot better than me, I'm not moaning about it, but he did have superior parts, and our machines weren't really matched until the last month of the season, by which time I was totally exhausted and in no real fit state to take advantage of them. What a desperate disappointment.

Steve is his own man and has a reputation for being candid about the machinery he rides and he was less than complimentary about the RC45 in the press. He'd done a road test report on one that summer too, pitched against a Ducati 916 and he'd reported that the Ducati was the better bike. I don't know if that was directly connected to Honda and he parting company at the end of the season, but it couldn't have done him any favours. Double World Champion Doug Polen fell out with Honda over the bike too, even he struggled to ride it with any success.

Don't get me wrong, it was a good bike, a great piece of equipment, beautifully engineered, but it just wasn't on the British Superbike pace and nowhere near competitive in the international series. I just stayed quiet though, kept riding with my head down and tried my hardest.

We really had two teams within a team that year, Steve's effort was totally separate to mine, which was now missing my elder brother Ronald. He is a superb technician and engineer and had been offered a job with the World Superbike team at the end of 1993, putting him in a difficult position. He couldn't turn it down though, twice the money, HRC training over the winter in Japan and the prospect of building Doug Polen's WSB engines was hard to resist.

It wasn't at all helpful for me though, meaning I had another added difficulty that I really didn't need. Again I was having to start the season not only with a new, untried bike that needed huge development work, but a brand new team once more, the last thing I needed under the circumstances. The personnel problems went on for a while and contributed to an unsettled first few weeks. It's so important to be in control of what you were getting and what you're being given - all my previous successes had come from having complete control and our team setup was just not working.

I rode the new bike to the limit at Snetterton early in the season and qualified quite well funnily enough, fighting it out in the first two laps of the race with the two Nortons. These were the bikes that had dominated the championship the year before and I was doing everything I could to stay with them, finally losing it at the chicane in the battle, the RC45 fairing me off with a vicious highside, giving me a huge beating just to remind me who was boss. It certainly wasn't doing what I wanted it to.

Steve Hislop had tried a couple of World Superbike rounds but couldn't get in the running with the bike; I was so sorry for him because he desperately wanted to follow our old team mate Fogarty into a full time World Superbike ride and it just wasn't happening.

The feedback was useful though and we got more help after the WSB round at Hockenheim regarding the high speed stability problems we'd been having. This was critical leading up to the super fast North West 200 meeting. It was hard, hard work trying to get the RC45 set up; each team was trying every possible combination, kit forks, Showas, Ohlins. I was trying everything too and every combination of mechanics - three in the first couple of months and nothing was working.

Sometimes the bikes would run well and then mysteriously go off song and it wasn't until the end of the year that we tracked it down to the fuel injection system. The electronic management was over sensitive to temperature fluctuations and wildly affected the overall performance of the engine. This was a superb bike in road trim, but a nightmare once you started tuning it for pure performance.

80,000 spectators lined the nine mile North West 200 circuit that May for the traditional TT curtain raiser, which had become by far and away Ireland's biggest sporting event by then. I qualified pretty well even though we were a long way from getting the RC45 properly sorted, with only one practice session available due to poor weather. I ended up second on the superbike grid.

Padgetts kindly stepped in with the loan of a 250 when the original bike I was due to ride disappeared, and Saturday's first 250 race was an absolute cracker, held in beautiful summer weather that had continued from the second practice session.

Woolsey Coulter got a flier of a start and led early on from Ian Newton, James Courtney, Joey and me, beginning a race long fight for the lead. On more than one occasion we were all leading! - five abreast coming into the braking area and with a pace so hot something had to give and it was James Courtney crashing at the chicane.

Woolsey was riding the same Aprilia Ian Newton had taken the lap record with in 1992 and it was still very fast, being used to good effect against Newton's own newer model. I always did have a power disadvantage against Woolsey when I first started racing him to Technical College on our FS1-E

Yamahas all those years before and it seemed like old times scrapping with him on the roads - no oncoming traffic this time though!

The Aprilias really did have the edge on my Honda even though I was doing everything to stay with them in third; Joey went out on the last lap, a back marker caused some confusion at the front, but not enough for me to get close enough and Woolsey and Newton crossed the line together, just in front of me in a photo finish, with my old college mate getting the decision.

I led briefly on lap one of the first superbike race by about half a second, but it quickly became apparent that the RC45 was down on power from practice and it wouldn't even pull top gear on the long straights, with me having to use the rev limiter and keep it flat out in fifth. Ian Duffus and Robert Dunlop got past me on the Medd team's RC45 and I overshot at University trying to stay on terms, letting the new boy David Jeffries through this time. I put in a 121.84mph final lap to get right back on terms and level with the first two, but I was taking some big risks trying to make up for this mysterious power loss and got it all wrong at Coleraine, while trying to make a pass for the lead and I had to settle for third.

The Supersport 600 was another excellent tussle and kept the massive crowd enthralled throughout, with another battle royal raging between me and Mike Edwards, Mark Farmer and Ian Simpson. Their Yamahas seemed to have the edge on power and top speed because once again my Honda just wasn't the same, fast bike I'd dialled in during practice.

I had to try so hard that I went grass tracking at the chicane, with 'Simmo' smacking into the kerb in the heat of the battle. Nothing I did could stop the Yamahas taking the top three slots though, my bike just seemed to have lost its edge, with quite a big power loss and no punch coming out of the comers. The Aprilias of Coulter and Newton were too hot for my Honda in the second 250 race and I finished in third place behind them again.

Ian Duffus had done nothing in practice and was a real surprise package again in the big final superbike race of the day. It was Joey Dunlop, Michael Rutter (on the lap record holding Ducati that Fogarty had used with such success the year before) and me away from the line. David Jeffries got past me, but even though my bike was still well down on power, I fought back to lead by around half a second on lap two ahead of Joey, David Jeffries and Rutter.

I was doing everything I could to make up for the power loss, but dropped back to third behind Ian Duffus who'd moved up on a very fast bike, which had seemed too quick to be true to me in the first race, even on my struggling RC45.

I'd complained to my team manager after the first superbike race, but he wouldn't do anything about it; this was my prize money, my reputation and prestige I was fighting for, so after the second superbike race I put down the protest money myself (you have to pay for the privilege of protesting which stops things getting out of hand). I had finished third again, but was elevated to second after my protest was upheld, the Scot admitting he had been running a 1,000cc motor in the races. It was too late to protest about the first race where I should also have been promoted to second, but at least justice had been done.

I'd been on the podium four times but I was desperately disappointed not to have won, telling the team that the bikes were definitely off. They didn't believe me of course, because they'd been so quick in practice and nothing had been changed. I was determined to get to the bottom of it though and first thing Monday morning insisted the bikes were put on the dyno at our Louth headquarters and proved I was right with my 750 8bhp down and the 600 down 5bhp.

We changed everything we could think of that day, tested everything we could but had run out of ideas by the evening; the only possible thing we had left was fuel. So, we went up to the local filling station, bought two gallons of fuel, put one in each bike and they went instantly back onto full power.

We'd run out of the fuel we'd brought with us to the North West after practice and had bought some super unleaded from a station near the circuit. Not many people in Northern Ireland use super unleaded and I went back to the same filling station the next week to ask when they'd last had a delivery. It had been months and months before the North West 200 and what was in their tanks had simply gone off during its lengthy storage. That had been the most expensive fuel I'd ever bought in my life. We were really careful to carry enough of our own fuel for all practice and race requirements at each meeting after that.

All this time we were thinking about improvements to the bike for the Isle of Man, now only a few days off. I was really on for beating Hislop who'd stayed away from the North West but had decided to return to the island that year. "Now we'll see," I thought as we got ready,

We were so nearly fair and square this time, although he'd got far more factory kit parts, including all the suspension springs he needed, whereas we didn't have anything for my RC45. To try and close the gap, I ended up having some manufactured in Northern Ireland and practice went superbly; I was getting quicker and quicker all the time. I opened proceedings fastest with a standing start 120.44mph lap and ended it still ahead of an improving Hislop with my quickest at 121.15mph, which equates to just under eighteen and three quarter minutes for the complete lap.

I knew then that the 125mph lap was achievable. I just had to have the bike set up better and get the perfect lap which I had yet to achieve - absolutely everything perfect, every corner, every apex, every one of the three hundred and seventy gear changes and twenty nine braking points bang on, and I felt I could definitely do it.

I ended quickest in the 250 too, with a fast 114.64mph and was very pleased with that; this was one event I was particularly keen to win to make amends for my refuelling debacle of the year before - everything seemed to be coming right at last.

On Saturday's Formula One race day I was ready to try anything to win and went off like a bat out of hell from the start in perfect conditions and was just five seconds off leader Steve Ward at Ramsey, when the heavens opened, making for treacherous riding on the slick tyres. The mountain section contributed fog to the poor conditions and most riders stopped at the pits at the end of lap one to change tyres. I went on to full wets and back out at a tremendous pace, leaving Joey, Hislop and Steve Ward behind me in the pitlane, refusing to go out again.

Initially, the organisers just ignored them, but eventually took the decision to red flag the race seconds before the rain eased off and hazy sunshine broke through onto the Glencrutchery Road. I was very disappointed at the decision, there was nothing that bad about the roads or the conditions by then and I was absolutely flying.

The race was rerun on Sunday and I went off like a bomb again, but I struggled from the word go. Now the roads were dry and speeds were increasing, I couldn't make the bike turn, couldn't get the power on coming out of the corners - nothing. Something was wrong, I just wasn't feeling the bike at all, which was so odd because we'd had it perfect in practice. I held second place though, just eleven seconds adrift of Hislop at Ramsey and started to think that perhaps it was me, unable to find my rhythm.

Hislop put in a good first lap around 121mph and led me by twenty seconds over the line and I continued to edge backwards with the bike still not doing what I wanted at all. Two lengthy pit stops gave Steve a bigger lead and I was struggling to find the smooth rhythm you need around the mountain course - I just wasn't confident enough to flow with the bike even though my final lap was the fastest of the race at 122.08mph. It didn't pull Hislop back by much, but was enough to keep ahead of Joey the maestro, who finished third.

I apologised to my pit crew and said it was my fault, Hizzy was smoking it and I just couldn't do anything about it, couldn't get myself together on the day and that was it. It wasn't until the bike was stripped the next day that the technicians found the spring in the rear shock - one of the ones we'd had manufactured ourselves - was loose inside its mountings, slapping about the shock housing itself.

The nuts were locked OK, nothing had come loose, the spring had just collapsed, presumably when the unit had heated up during the race or at the very end of practice. Whatever, it had reduced the ride height at the rear of the bike by over an inch, which had affected the handling enormously.

It was a big relief to find out what was wrong, why I hadn't been able to get the bike settled and it made me more determined to get everything right for Friday's Senior. On Wednesday evening's practice I went off like a maniac with all new suspension to set up from scratch again and I have never ridden that fast to this day on the Isle of Man, or anywhere else for that matter. We had some new brake pads to try too; Hislop had been trying some and I'd been using different types of EBC product and was running with a harder compound type on this occasion, with a brand new calliper set up too.

I'd always had a superb relationship with Andy Freeman and Michael Brandon of EBC the brake specialists, another of the manufacturers I've been involved with in development work, doing a lot of testing for them from the early nineties onwards. Sometimes we'd be working from week to week and the latest kit wouldn't be ready until the Saturday before race day.

Occasionally we'd meet halfway to cut down on journey times, usually at motorway services where this little box containing the latest generation would be pushed across the table to me. I'd try them out on Sunday's warm up to see if I could use them in the race and sometimes we won, sometimes we lost.

On this occasion in practice for the Senior TT though, the new pads were cooling off too much between braking points and taking a split second longer to come in when I needed them - and I was going like a complete lunatic. I was faster everywhere than I've ever been, or will ever be again, so much so that spectators who'd seen me go past weren't at all surprised when they heard I'd crashed.

Sometimes I can get a very smooth lap which turns out to be very fast without me realising it but that's unusual. But I always know when I'm on a super quick lap like that one was, getting it right everywhere, holding it on the perfect line, every single corner absolutely right, getting the gas on as early as possible and keeping it up for twenty minutes. You always know when you're on it like that; in the race all that the signals tell you is place and plus or minus because the lap times themselves are academic.

The accident happened coming across the tram lines up to the Museum over the mountain when I came into the corner at the absolute maximum, touched the brake and nothing happened for a moment. The bike was hardly touched, I got up and walked away OK, but the crash did have serious consequences.

When the pads did finally heat up and bite, the back wheel came right up in the air with the bike leaned over into the corner, so I had to let her run on or I'd have been off and I spotted some grass beyond the corner and thought "That's good I'll head for that." and slow her down as much as I can, but ended up in a ditch that I couldn't see from the road, nearly hitting photographer Tony Breese on the way, who leapt out of the way like a Jack in the box.

You see, I'd been on the pace all the way round the lap until that point and by then, I'd worked out everything I'd needed to do with the bike to get it perfect - a bit more damping here, a bit more preload there, everything was in my head ready to adjust the moment I got back to the paddock to have the bike perfect for the race. The accident was the worst thing that could have happened, because it knocked all that information, everything I'd worked out and logged ready to make the changes, clean out of my head.

Now we were out of time, I was going to have to start the race without the bike set up properly and just ride for the best result I could. Hislop had a big advantage of course with set up time, as he only had one bike to concentrate on, whereas I had to spread my practice time between three machines. Plus, he would be starting on a bike he was very confident with and on which he'd already won.

Hizzy got away with a superb 122.50mph lap, just ten seconds outside the lap record but I was second quickest, four seconds ahead of Joey, but tailing Hislop by nineteen seconds. With the rear suspension problems in the F1 and basically one lap of practice on the 750, we'd just run out of time and luck and my bike was nowhere near right again. I probably could have ridden through it - I was in fact, being second place in the biggest race on the toughest course in the world, but the combination of a poor set up and the fact that Hizzy's bike had the edge was just too much to overcome.

I lost some more time in the pits when we had to remove a dead bird from my radiator and the signals told me all I needed to know - I was gradually slipping back all the time, but fought my way all the way to the chequered flag to hold on to second, finishing seventy one seconds ahead of Joey.

It was another frustrating result, particularly as I'd handed Joey his seventeenth TT win in the Junior race earlier that week, which I'd controlled from the word go, leading Joey by six seconds at the end of the first lap with Ian Lougher and Brian Reid close behind. I'd started piling on the pressure and increased my lead to fifteen seconds by Ramsey on the fourth and final lap and barring disaster, knew I had it in the bag. Joey admitted he'd settled for second by then with a loose footrest slowing him up and I was cruising over the mountain when the bike coughed and spluttered to a halt, out of fuel with just five miles to go. I couldn't believe it; leading the race and now this, two years on the trot.

The bikes point downhill slightly in the pits, especially the little 250s and it's the duty of the crew member concerned to time the gravity fed fuel refill to ensure enough has gone in to complete the next two laps. My crewman didn't time it and mistook some air bubbling out for a full tank of fuel, but it wasn't full up and it was a bad mistake. He snapped the filler cap shut, which was my signal to get out of there, but I was missing that crucial last couple of pints of fuel and it cost me the race.

You see, I took all the beatings there were to be had, all the bad luck, the humiliations and most of the time I took the blame for things that weren't my fault; there was always a reason behind everything that happened. All I needed was some good luck for a team who were so keen to succeed and prepared to do anything to help their rider to win. I learnt it all the hard way, that's why I've been such a good manager in the short time I did it.

That's why Jim Moodie, Michael Rutter and Ian Simpson all loved riding my bikes and the reason we had so much success in such a short time. I was prepared to spend the money, even quite a bit of my own, which I saw only as an investment. It was quickly repaid with success.

The only success we had in 1994 was on the roads. In any form the new 750 was a handful on short circuits, but it was a great road bike even straight from the crate. There was no doubt about that by then, but we proved it beyond question at the Ulster Grand Prix. Records tumbled that year, but not just in the superbike class.

Practice was good and I ended second quickest on my 250 behind Joey, but fastest in the Regal 600 and superbike qualifying sessions too. The first superbike encounter was an absolute classic with Welshman Jason Griffiths getting a terrific start, leading me and Joey when the race was suddenly stopped because a car tried to get on the course at Hairpin Bend! The race was restarted over the full distance and I took the lead this time with Griffiths and Joey in tow. My old adversary came storming past at Deer's Leap missing an oil flag and losing it a bit, ending up a slip road somewhere.

He broke the lap record then with a 123.75mph, caught up with Griffiths and the pace got hotter still with us all recorded at 175mph through the speed trap - what a fast course it is at Dundrod. He raised it again and passed Griffiths to get on my tail and then passed me on lap five, so I stuck there with him, planning to slipstream him right at the end of the race and we were side by side at the Quarry Bends, where we banged into each other quite hard. Joey held me off and got past a couple of slower riders better than me right at the end, to win by a couple of tenths of a second. The crowd had been going wild with it all and were delighted Joey had got it in the end.

I raised the outright lap record to 125.99mph in the second superbike race, in a duel with Jason Griffiths who was very quick on his Kawasaki. I'd got away from him a little bit in the last lap, but just held onto a huge highsider and slide at The Windmills, preparing for the climb up the back of the circuit. It made me lose my drive which let him get back on my tail again. It was just a no-holds-barred dogfight then all the way to the line, but I held him off to win by a bike length. He'd obliterated the course record in the course of the battle, with a superb 126.01mph.

I put in a really fast opening lap in the first 250 race and opened up 2 three second gap over a hard charging James Courtney, then put in a record breaking fifth lap which was enough for me to come home for the win. Joey put me under a lot more pressure in the second 250 encounter, forcing me into breaking the class record for the second time that day, with a 119.64mph lap.

It was one of those meetings where everything clicks and each victory was increasing my confidence for the next race. The Regal 600 encounter was another cracking confrontation, where I fought it out with 600 TT winner Ian Duffus and Steve Ward, even though my bike wasn't running perfectly until about half distance. I was riding out of my skin to stay in touch with them in third place and when the engine suddenly cleared and I was back to full power I blasted the class record in that event too, recording a 119.00mph lap. The crowd had certainly got their money's worth that day and so had I, the only man ever to have won four Ulster Grand Prix events at the same meeting.

Strangely enough, the records and victories were a bit of a double-edged sword for me. It was great to get the four wins, earn some prize money and pump some sort of life back into our racing, but it also increased the talk that I was just a road racer who couldn't make it on the tracks. It just wasn't true, I was as fast as anyone else out there, I just hadn't been given the chance to prove it.

I would have given my eye teeth for one of those race wins to have been in the British Supercup if nothing else than to shut the critics up. People were making ill-informed judgments on me, based on nothing more than half-baked opinion with no real knowledge of the true facts whatsoever.

In my heart I knew that I'd been dancing on thin ice at the Ulster Grand Prix and that the following week it was going to be breaking again back in England. The bike remained totally uncompetitive on short circuits and so, therefore did I.

Towards the end of the racing year, Steve Hislop and I had heard through the grapevine that a new manager was going to be taking over the British Superbike racing side of the Honda team for the next season, so I began 'considering my position' as the saying goes and started to look at every option available.

It was all off the record stuff and nothing had been said officially, but you didn't have to be Einstein to work out that someone had to take the rap for the dismal showing of the much vaunted new bike. Steve Hislop and I didn't have to go further than the bathroom mirror to work out who it was going to be.

At the end of the 1994 season a summit meeting was held with sponsors Castrol at Honda's London headquarters where Neil Tuxworth announced I was no longer needed for the Company's road racing effort as he'd signed Steve Ward and Nick Jeffries for the TT. It cheered me up enormously when I heard that the Castrol personnel present responded by saying that they didn't believe either of those riders could beat Phillip McCallen. I was eventually offered machinery from Honda just for the Isle of Man, but I decided to turn the offer down and ride elsewhere; it was clear by then I was realistically out of a job.

With Tuxworth concentrating on the world series, Colin Seeley was formally appointed to take over management of Honda Britain's British effort, announcing he was going to do for Honda what he'd done for Norton by bringing 'his' riders Ian Simpson and Phil Borley with him. They'd finished first and second in the 1994 Championship but didn't make the same sort of impression with the RC45 in 1995. As expected, McCallen and Hislop didn't feature in the Seeley plan at all, paying the price for our failure.

While a rejuvenated Steve Hislop took a Ducati to the British Super-bike Championship in 1995, the winning dream team of Seeley, Borley and Simpson were to struggle; in fact the only real success they were to have was on the roads again; and isn't life strange, I was the man who was going to give it to them.

The Thunderbike 600 Supersport series had been launched to support the Grand Prix circus and that seemed an exciting route to take. My long-standing sponsors Turkingtons agreed to continue their support, I pulled some strings and was lucky enough to get an entry in the series. I set up meetings at London's traditional winter Alexander Palace road and race bike show venue, with two rival manufacturers willing to support me with competitive machinery for the new Thunderbike series.

I'd had a great ride on Joe Millar's 500 V4 Grand Prix machine at Macau, finishing second. I liked the bike immediately, people had said 500s were really difficult and it would be unridable but it suited me very well, feeling like a big 250 really, just a bit harder to flick around. I'd got a bit hacked off with being the fastest 750 rider at Macau every year, always being beaten by 500 GP bikes and I enjoyed turning the tables this time around and considered a deal to compete on the bike at the 1995 Isle of Man TT.

In early 1995 I drove over to England to drop my Honda company car back at their London headquarters on my way to the 'Ally Pally' show in the north of the capital. I was just dropping the keys off inside when I was asked up to the boardroom and walked in to find sales chief Dave Hancock and boss Bob McMillan waiting for me. They agreed to back me with spares and bikes to ride in the new World Thunderbike cham-pionship, part of the Grand Prix support series, if I'd race their super bikes at the North West and the Isle of Man under Colin Seeley's new management. Better the devil you know I thought - and I agreed.

9

There wasn't enough money. That's life I guess, same for all of us except the very lucky few. I was contracted to do all the rounds in the new Thunderbike series and race on the roads for Honda too, which would give me the opportunity to boost my earnings and help the budget.

The schedule was going to be very tight indeed because there were calendar overlaps and it got very demanding, very quickly. The budget for a second mechanic never materialised, which would have made life much easier and the European travelling schedule became gruelling. It all meant I was qualifying pretty well, but starting races desperately tired, doing well initially but often fading in the second half through sheer exhaustion.

The first round at Jerez was the shape of things to come. I'd finished pretty well in an early season British 600 Supersport round at Mallory Park a few days before, ending up a safe and measured sixth after an attritional race with three restarts, while putting the finishing touches to the bike.

The original, feasible plan for the year was to road race for Honda Britain under the superbike management and have two of my own mechanics for the new Thunderbike campaign. They would share the driving to each round on the Continent and I'd then fly out for the meeting, arriving refreshed and ready.

No chance. The skinny budget, which was relying on road race prize money in the first place was just too small to get the personnel we required, so I ended up grinding around the roads of Europe in the big new motorhome come transporter we'd acquired courtesy of Turkingtons, arriving at each new circuit tired out before I'd even started. I realised how tough it was going to be on that first journey down to Jerez as soon as we hit France, knowing there was a thousand mile drive ahead of us.

Barry Sheene's father Frank had come along for the ride and we were very glad of his help, but he was shouting at me to slow down all the way through the mountain roads of southern Spain, saying I was going far too fast for safety. I'd been doing that on public roads for as long as I could remember and ignored his advice.

I'd just started taking over driving and felt a bit of vibration at the back of the truck and it was really lucky I decided to stop, because both back wheels were hanging off the truck, with just a couple of loose studs holding them on. I don't know how much further we would have got; a mile or so at most, I would have thought and we would have crashed on one of those frightening mountain passes without question. That sixth sense has saved me more times than I care to remember.

We'd been making good headway, but the delay really didn't help us. Arriving at the circuit dog-tired in the early hours of practice day was a taste of things to come that year. I learnt the Jerez track pretty quickly and qualifying went well, but my race settings transferred too much weight to the front wheel and the rear end was so light I couldn't get any grip coming out of corners, finishing well down the field.

The series was immediately very competitive, top European Champions and other good riders with some big well funded private teams in the paddock wielding major budgets which allowed for constant development programmes. Our little team was doing what it could, concentrating on engine and exhaust configurations with Micron and Tony Scott, brake development with EBC and we had begun working closely with Avon on tyre technology.

The first tyre deal I ever negotiated was with Andrew Wheeler of Avon tyres in 1988; you have to use treaded tyres in the Manx Grand Prix, so cut slicks are the order of the day. Andrew thought I was going to win and Avon kindly supplied what I needed for my 350, thinking I was worthy of their investment as a good prospect. The relationship continued in 1989 during my races with Kawasaki, us Avon were their official sponsor and I did like their equipment, good grip and feel and an excellent production tyre, a full blown race product.

When I cut the deal with Michelin-sponsored Honda later in 1989, the only way I could get slicks from the French company was if I took their production tyres too, so that was that and I remained happy with them for most of my career.

Michelin and the others Dunlop, Pirelli and Metzeler really concentrated on the production market then, having cottoned on to the fact that they were losing huge numbers of road tyre sales and started playing catch up with Avon, putting all their slick technology into their road rubber, and the gap eventually closed.

I like plenty of feel from my bikes and I'm often asked why I never used Dunlops more (which I'd tested on some years ago) but I'd always stayed with Michelin, thinking if they were good enough for riders like Mick Doohan they were good enough for me.

Tyre technology has raced ahead along with the machinery. When I began racing, production tyres were road tyres and that was it. Now there's a choice of compounds and grades, wets, intermediates and soft road tyres carrying the barest minimum of tread needed to make them road legal, a perfect example of how racing develops products that make everyday riding (and driving) safer.

I was delighted with the product Avon began supplying us in 1995 and worked hard on development. Tyres were not a problem but our overall budget was impossibly small and it turned into a classic vicious circle; there wasn't enough money for an extra mechanic and the air tickets we so desperately needed for me to arrive really fresh and ready to put in a decent performance. The itinerary was punishing to say the least. Back at home the North West 200 clashed with the Nurburgring Thunderbike round but we worked out that it was going to be possible to do both if I gave up Thursday's North West practice session for German Thunderbike qualifying instead.

Germany's race was on Sunday, the day after the North West's race day, so on this occasion, the airlines were going to get my money and I was looking forward to it all.

So I only got Tuesday night's practice session to qualify for the North West and my 250 wouldn't go at all well and then blew up during that single session, meaning I wasn't going to get a grid position at all. I'd been given Nigel Bosworth's 250 by Honda for the meeting and the Ulster GP and the TT. The machine had been a real flier in the early season, a very mean, fast bit of kit, but we didn't realise what had happened to the bike before we took delivery of it until the Isle of Man TT a little later that month.

With my mechanic and Thunderbike outfit travelling by road to Germany, I'd arrived at Portrush to establish myself with yet another new team, having been allocated what was supposedly Phil Borley's Castrol Honda RC45. His fellow superbike rider Ian Simpson was also going to be competing on his own bike which had different exhaust systems and parts and was definitely faster than the one I was given.

Set up was a struggle - everything I wanted to do, I was being told "No, we don't need to do that." But I knew what needed to be done to the RC45 to get it to work properly for me. It had taken us a whole year to finally achieve something near to what we'd wanted the previous year, but this team was doing things completely differently, trying to base their settings on the Nortons of the previous year, but the RC45 was a totally different bike.

It was surprising just how different things were on these bikes to when I'd been riding them only a few months before - totally different braking systems for example, but it hadn't done them any good. They were last season's championship winning team and sure they could make the RC45 competitive. The bikes were no better than when we had them.

This was my first time on a big 750 since the year before don't forget and it was set up very differently and just didn't suit me, so getting fourth fastest and a front row grid position in just three laps a time that thankfully no one improved on in the second session which I missed - was pretty good. I hope I don't sound like I'm making excuses for all these performances. What I am trying to do is tell the truth and explain all the obstacles I and many others have always seemed to have to over-come throughout our careers, and perhaps give a little insight into what was going on behind the headlines and race reports. The journalists and pundits can only ever give one person's interpretation of a complex story.

I was second quickest on the two laps I got in on my 'spare' 600, the number one bike being in Germany and had to lodge an application to start from the back of the grid in the 250, which was granted.

I'd never ridden this bike before it had seized on me after half a lap in practice. Thankfully Dennis Willey, the Honda Britain technician who'd looked after me so well when I first started racing for Honda in 1989 had come over to support me and the team and had personally rebuilt the bike. Dennis had become a good friend; he'd been helping me out a bit in 1993 and 1994 after he'd come back from working with an Italian team.

We'd stayed in touch and he'd give me his professional opinion on various things and by 1995 he was starting to become a full time part timer if you like. He had great respect for Foggy who he'd worked with for so long and he liked my style too, but he'd become a little disillusioned with the dodgy employment prospects of a career in racing, but still loved working on bikes. I loved riding them and always did my best to win which he appreciated. We were both doing it for the love of it and that paid dividends in so many ways.

Dennis had worked with HRC in Japan in 1991 on Foggy and Hislop's Suzuka eight hour RVF (which finished third in that top class event) and knows his way around a Honda V4 better than anyone else outside the place that makes them. He's been an invaluable technical help, friend and guide to me during my career, helping out at the North West, the TT and other big races and I'll always appreciate what he's done for me.

The 250 was supposed to be a little pocket rocket and it wasn't. We'd been misled. Dennis rebuilt it as best he could while I was at Nurburgring, looked after my 600 with my friends from Ireland and represented me with Colin Seeley regarding my 750, trying to get the thing closer to how I wanted it. I flew back from Germany, having to leave half way through Friday's final Thunderbikes qualifying session and things were pretty good, I was lying seventh when I left. The journeys back and forth to the airport in Germany were a nightmare as I was riding pillion on a local TT fan's Fireblade, making the connection each time by the skin of my teeth.

Because of my record at the North West, the Clerk of the Course kindly allowed me to start from the back of the 'A' grid on the 250 in Saturday's first race of the day. I just had the warm-up lap to get used to the bike on which we hadn't had any time to sort out suspension settings, there'd been no plug readings to set carburation, gear ratios - everything was an educated guess based on the records we always kept from previous years. Trouble is every bike is different, particularly the pure bred race two strokes and so are the conditions, with set up being largely about 'feel'. So, I was at a big disadvantage.

I knew if I didn't get on terms at the front early on I'd be struggling to get a finish. There was only one thing I could think of to do and I walked up the grid just before the race and asked the riders in front of me if they'd be kind enough to leave a little gap for me to get through at the very edge of the track because this bike was so fast, I wasn't sure if I could stop it coming through! The riders in the three rows in front of me agreed and it all went according to plan, starting like a bomb and going into the first corner in the top three and suddenly I was in second behind Ian Newton on his super quick Aprilia.

Having been sold a pup I was still under the delusion this Honda of mine was a really trick bit of kit - it wasn't - but I think that frame of mind gave me the confidence to pull off some amazing stunts in that race. I managed to get past the Aprilia at Coleraine on the final lap, doing enough to stay ahead by Portrush, before the final blast down the coast road where the power of the Aprilia got back at me. We were side by side coming into the chicane at Juniper Hill, but I kept the advantage and held back another big charge in the final section to win a dramatic race in front of a delirious crowd, setting a new lap record for the class at 116.57mph.

The first superbike encounter was a superb thriller for the tens of thousands of knowledgeable race goers at the North West. Ian Simpson's bike definitely had the edge over Michael Rutter's Ducati and me on the second Castrol Honda as we fought it out in brilliant sunshine. There was nothing between us for lap after lap and once again I was having to ride through the problems with the bike, which were all down to lack of practice and set up, plus of course I hadn't been near it or the team before. It just wasn't dancing how I wanted it.

I started to get a very worrying brake fade in the last two laps, but felt I'd worked the other two riders out and that the win was mine for the taking. But 'Simmo' had the better of a gaggle of back markers at Portrush on the very last lap. It enabled him to get away just enough to leave Michael Rutter and I to sort out the places

The brakes in the six pot callipers on my Honda had gone clean off by that stage, there was just nothing left there at all, leaving me no alternative than to back off or fall off and Rutter took full advantage. Under the circumstances, I was very pleased with the third place and took my revenge in the Regal 600 using my own bike, set up how I wanted it and no one even got near me.

I'd only got a couple of practice laps in on it and it had been a cold evening session. The race day temperatures were soaring sky high though and I had a bit of a scare in warm up and actually made some last second suspension adjustments on the starting grid in a bid to get the Honda perfect. My start was good and I led on the first run to Portstewart, with Mike Edwards in hot pursuit. I piled on the pressure though and with the familiar bike beautifully prepared and the Tony Scott motor running sweetly I put in a relentless effort, shaking Edwards off my tail and leaving the rest of the field far behind with two consecutive record breaking laps at 118.04mph and 118.28mph.

After the first lightweight race I'd told the technician who was helping out with the 250 to retard the ignition slightly and drop the jets down a fraction as it was running a little bit rich. This was to help the top end of it and what did he do? - advanced it instead. What a disaster, the bike just wasn't the same, I should have known better and left well alone and couldn't do any better than fourth.

But the 750 had improved between races and was going well enough for me to put on another crowd pleasing performance in the big North West 200 race itself, although the brakes let me down again in the last two laps. It turned into a race long battle between Ian Duffus, New Zealander Robert Holden and me.

We swapped the lead so many times I lost count, but Holden was leading on the last lap and I'd timed everything to perfection and had got ahead a bit coming into the chicane. I braked hard for the corner and there was nothing, not a whisker of stoppers and I overshot going up onto the grass, gave it a big handful of throttle to try and get back at him because I was fuming by now, I really wanted to win so much.

The RC45 high sided instantly, spitting me right up into the air sideways, but I held on to it somehow with the huge crowd gasping at what must have looked like a certain accident and I stormed back after Holden, but it was too late by then to get back on terms and I was furious to have lost that win.

The team had got my feedback from the first race, knew that I'd only lost that because of brake fade and had used a different compound this time. When the brakes were stripped we found they were completely shot to pieces, no brake material left at all, just metal. That had cost me the win and several thousand pounds, which I could have used to good effect in my Thunderbike campaign.

I was still happy though, a 250 win, a 600 win and the lap record, plus a second and a third place on a superbike, which along with the 250, I'd never seen before. I'd only had a single practice session on all of them. I bounced around in a light aircraft for hours that night, flying back to Germany for the Thunderbike round, arriving at the track at four in the morning totally exhausted.

I didn't do too badly, but I was frustrated at being so strung out all the time. The bike was fast enough and so was I, it was just the punishing schedule of the travelling, particularly the driving that was getting to me and it was badly affecting my race performance. Things were going to get really awkward at the TT because race week clashed with the Italian Grand Prix at Mugello featuring another of my Thunderbike rounds.

I had to do the road races for Honda and the money; apart from loving them, I was actually finding them easier too, but if I was to race in Italy, where Thursday and Friday's practice clashed with the Senior TT, I was going to have to cut a deal with my Honda bosses, so that I could leave the island early. I persuaded Honda chief Dave Hancock to agree that if I won the opening Formula One race, he'd let me leave for Italy after the Junior TT on the following Wednesday.

I was so pleased I said I'd throw in wins in the 600 and the 250 race too for good measure which was a tall order, but I knew the way my 600 was running and how I was riding it, that no one would be able to touch me, plus if we got this fabled rocketship 250 running right too, then I'd be hard to beat on that as well.

Once on the island I wanted lots of different things putting into the 750 and I needed big changes to the settings too, but the new team set up just wouldn't do it, thinking they knew best. The profile of the front tyre was useless for me as well and they wanted to do all sorts of crazy things that were way beyond what I wanted. Then the RC45 they'd given me broke down at Glen Vine on Monday's first practice lap and I went completely mad at them, because their attitude was endangering everything we were there for.

It quickly became apparent no one in the team was happy with their bike. Steve Ward and Nick Jeffries were also proven TT riders who were struggling to get the machines to do what they wanted and team manager Colin Seeley was asked for more help. On the British short circuits the team were struggling to get the Hondas to run as well as their Nortons of the previous year.

We couldn't carry on like this but thankfully Honda UK's Managing Director Bob McMillan became involved and his input was a positive influence on the whole team. Dennis Willey was there and stepped in at this stage to get the bike into some sort of shape, although it was still a long way from perfect. While Dennis set up my bike how I wanted it, I got the front tyre I needed to stabilise the thing and my lap times started to improve so dramatically that the whole team then adopted the same tyre.

My best contact at Honda UK, Dave Hancock had arrived by then. Dave knows his stuff and usually got his hands dirty whenever he turned up at my garage, particularly with the 250 which always seemed to be running behind schedule ever since I'd given up riding it full time. We were always playing catch up with it on the last night before the race, usually travelling up to Jurby, (which is an old disused runway complex perfect for high speed testing) trying to get it set up right and Dave would always be with us there late into the night, sleeves rolled up and pitching in, a real enthusiast.

This year Dave came by to help out as usual and it was in our garage, working on the 250 together when we found the engine markings showing it was a 1993 motor, not the 1995 powerhouse we'd been led to believe. The trick engine had been taken out before I was given it to ride. There is no excuse for doing something like that. It was Honda Britain's bike, they wanted it to win for themselves and Castrol and the best road rider they had (me, [allegedly]) should have been given all the help he could get by every member of the team.

I'd been deceived and palmed off with an old spare engine from the back of someone's workshop. No wonder I'd had to pull out all the stops at the North West 200. That was why the works Aprilia I was up against at the time seemed so incredibly fast.

We ended up rebuilding it four times in three days and it still wouldn't pull more than 12,000 revs, so I couldn't even get it into top gear, the bike only being good enough for tenth place in qualifying for what had now become the Lightweight TT, as the 600 Supersport machines had superseded the 250s as the Junior TT class that year. My CBR600 was a different story though, well sorted and fast and I headed the practice board to start as clear favourite.

After a dismal start on the 750 in Monday's first session, Tuesday was made difficult by rain showers dotted all over the course, but I did get in one flying lap of 120.84mph on the RC45. That time ended up my best of the week, (some thirty seconds up on any other rider), as I really concentrated on my 600 on Thursday and only put in one more lap on the superbike. What we had was what we'd got and it was time to get on with the job.

Saturday's weather was dry for the crucial blue riband Formula One event which I knew I had to win at all costs. I started with a cracking 120.85mph opener from the standing start, passing Nick Jeffries on the road on the way, but it was still only enough for a 3.7 second lead over Joey, who was as smooth and fast as ever, coming back at me in the second lap to turn the tables and lead by a fraction going into the pit stops.

We were both having our own separate problems, mine was vision caused by sweat and insects and I made the first of two helmet and glove changes that cost me precious time. Meanwhile, Joey had lost one of the fresh air tubes that loop over the tank and into the airbox on the RC45, there was no spare in pitlane so he had to go out again with it still missing, which would have reduced his airbox pressure and affected performance.

I did settle after the pit stop and started to control my pace a bit according to the signals, caught and passed Steve Ward on the road and built up a nice cushion of over thirty seconds going into the pit stop; with the luxury of such a lead I thought I'd change into a nice fresh helmet again and thought how easy it was with all the luck finally going my way. And then it ran out.

Dennis Willey was my wheel man and changed the rear for me during the stop and torqued it all up properly - you can hear the airgun clicking away in the video - (I know, because I've checked) and I blasted away up pitlane still comfortably up on Joey and looking forward to controlling the race from the front. I hadn't even got to the bottom of Bray Hill though, when I felt the bike start to weave and I immediately knew something was wrong, but I didn't back off because I just had to win this race.

I was riding through the problem but the weave was getting worse bit by bit on the fifth lap and was slowing me down. Joey must have sensed he'd suddenly got a chance from his signals because he started to reel me in and my boards were telling me he'd closed to within eight seconds towards the end of the lap.

I'd had a good cushion but it wasn't enough to allow for anything going wrong. I knew I couldn't pull in because if I did I would definitely have lost the race; I knew I couldn't lose the race because that meant I would have to stay to try and win the Senior on Friday; I knew I couldn't do that, because I had to be at the Italian Grand Prix for my Thunderbike race.

The big 750 was squirming and sliding around so much by this time that when I came storming down the Glencrutchery Road towards the line, I was totally gutted, knowing I was going to have to pull into the pits and God knows what we were going to find. It was obvious there was something dreadfully wrong with the bike because it was all over the place - really wild; no one could believe it when they saw what had happened after I stopped. Eventually. Because I had to win this race. So I kept going.

Dymag had sent a new batch of their superb wheels over to the island, some of which had never been checked or fitted to the bike before. There was a little bevel on the inside of the wheel that lets it fit right up onto the hub; trouble was the bevel hadn't been taken back enough so it wasn't a perfect fit and didn't seat properly. Dennis Willey's wheel change was smooth and unhurried and had seemed perfect.

One big nut holds the rear wheel onto the single sided swinging arm on an RC45 and because the wheel wasn't a perfect fit on the hub, there was slight movement, enough to loosen the whole assembly which spun around the spline, the nut chewing right into the hub of the wheel itself. The whole thing was only being held on by the remains of the nut, tight up against the fragile little sprung 'R' clip that slots through a drilled hole in the nut and axle, which is only designed to stop the nut coming loose, not to hold a whole wheel on.

I didn't know what was wrong; I was in such a state of nervous tension it's difficult to describe. The only similar situation I can think of is if you can imagine you're the pilot of an aircraft. Now imagine it's got a terrible problem, you're hurtling towards the ground fighting the controls all the way, knowing any second now you're going to crash. The feeling was pretty similar. All I knew was that I was absolutely petrified at what the bike was doing every time I was trying to brake and slow down; it felt like the frame had cracked or something. Whatever it was though, I realised it didn't seem to be getting any worse and it wasn't until a good way around the last lap I worked out that it must be a loose rear wheel.

The big problem was on the overrun going into comers with the throttle knocked off when it went absolutely crazy, huge tank slappers which I was struggling to control, wondering if one of them was going to pitch me off. Joey had the bit between his teeth by now and was only seconds behind me and I started to try everything I could. Going into a bend near Cronk Urleigh just before Kirk Michael, I tried keeping the throttle turned on slightly, keeping just a little bit of power on and used the rear brake at the same time, enough to keep the whole drive train loaded up going into the comer and the bike was still misbehaving wildly, but just a bit calmer.

I don't remember the second half of that lap to this day. I think my mind has blanked out the terror of it all; coming into those challenging comers on the island at 150 or 160mph, fighting this animal of a bike all the way. I was somewhere else for those last ten minutes or so, way, way over the edge. The record book shows the lap was timed at 119.71 mph, which was complete madness under the circumstances. At the chequered flag I'd beaten Joey by over eighteen seconds and came up pitlane having won the race which is where my memory does come back in.

I remember being so overcome I couldn't get off the bike at all and when I finally did, I couldn't stand up. There was none of the huge adrenalin rush, the amazing buzz of winning a big race at the highest level, the feeling was unreal; just sort of floating like I was back on land and I shouldn't have been.

I settled down a bit amongst all the hell that breaks loose after a TT in the winners' enclosure, where the bikes get put up on the podium and on their axle stands. I looked at the offending wheel for the first time then - what a state it was in, a real testimony to the strength of Dymags. It was very loose indeed, flapping about and just being held on by what was left of the nut up against the little wire 'R' clip as I'd been praying. Everyone near that podium, and everybody who saw it later was staggered by how much it was wobbling around, completely off the axle.

No one could believe I'd ridden the bike in that condition. Colin Seeley was dumbfounded when he kicked the wheel after I'd asked him to and he respected me after that. He now knew what I was capable of doing, knew I'd transformed his bike to get it right, that I'd done what they couldn't do to get the bike perfect for me and so much better for the other riders. Dave Hancock was bowled over too, so impressed with what I'd done he said there was no question of not letting me go over to Italy for the Thunderbikes, in fact if I wanted to leave there and then it was fine by him. I stayed though because I still had a job to do.

The 250 was struggling for speed and to make matters worse I seemed to be fighting traffic for most of the race, getting held up by slower riders all around the course and Joey was flying away at the front. I had a good long tussle with James Courtney on the road on lap four, the only flying lap of the race, but the duff 1993 engine was simply outclassed and I finally brought the disappointing bike home fourth, fifty six seconds behind Joey, Courtney and Gavin Lee.

On my last lap in practice on my 600 the bike had stopped on the mountain and I'd had to nurse it home, spluttering back to the pits because the carbs were full of dirt from some poor fuel. My Thunderbike mechanic who'd been working on it left to go to Italy, to prepare for my arrival there on the following Wednesday. He'd washed out the fuel system before he'd left but I hadn't had time to test the bike at race speeds, and from the moment I started the Junior TT it started stuttering going down Bray Hill at 10,000 revs and wouldn't pull anything higher.

I was the red hot favourite with the talk amongst the other top teams about who was going to get second place and now this. Here I was full

17. Manda and me on our wedding day - 1996. (Ed Winters)

18. Manda and me after I was voted Northern Ireland Sports Personality of 1996 at the Belfast Telegraph Sports Awards. (Belfast Telegraph)

19. With Tadao Baba, Honda Fireblade Designer, in the TT Paddock, 1998. (Phil Woods)

20. Airborne on my RC45, 1997 Formula One TT. (Tony Breese)

21. My final pep talk to Michael Rutter (Jim McMahon's on my left) on the grid of the 1998 North West 200 Production race. He won the crucial battle against Yamaha's R1 with my Honda Fireblade. (Gavan Caldwell)

22. Fighting with James Courtney's Ducati on my F1R1 at the Tandragee 100. (Gavan Caldwell)

23. My last win, fittingly on my home track, in the second superbike race at the 1999 Tandragee 100. (John Legge)

24. The ultimate Honda, the RC45 hand built by HRC Japan for me to ride at the 1998 TT, during Honda's 50th Anniversary celebrations. Injury prevented me from ever turning a wheel on this beauty. (James Wright, Double Red)

25. Carl Fogarty and me in the pits, 1997 Brands Hatch WSB.
(Phil Woods)

26. The end of the roads? Manda and me after my third place in the 1999 Production TT. Not bad with only one arm working - it hurt so much, it felt like time to call it a day. (Gavan Caldwell)

27. Very pleased with myself after my 1988 Newcomers'
Manx Grand Prix win. (Eddie Beater)

28. Dennis Willey, friend and technical maestro, here performing some amateur physio on my injured left shoulder. 1999 NW200 grid. (Gavan Caldwell)

29. Coming in to Kirkmichael on my way to winning the 1996 Production TT. I won on the same bike the following year.

(James Wright - Double Red)

30. Discussing tactics with Honda's Dave Hancock at Oulton Park, 1997. (Phil Woods)

31. 1996 - This is how it feels to win all five races at Ulster Grand Prix.
(Gavan Caldwell)

32. 'Don't drop it!' - Master engine tuner Tony Scott (wearing sunglasses, centre) keeps a watchful eye over one of his engines, Oulton Paark, 1997. (Phil Woods)

of confidence, having qualified much quicker than anyone without having to make a huge effort, ready to give these boys a whipping and I couldn't believe it.

It improved a little bit on the second lap, running up to around 11,000 revs and I knew it had to be either electrical or probably the same fuel problem I'd had in practice. I was doing everything I could to make up time, but was struggling without the top two and a half thousand revs which is where the bike made so much of its power. I was in fourth place when leader Iain Duffus, who'd started twenty seconds behind me, caught me on the road and got past at Ramsey, but it gave me a target and some slipstream and I stuck on his tail all the way up, over and down the mountain and we came into the pits together and left in the same formation too.

The new fuel improved matters quite a bit, the original stuff must have been contaminated with dirt which had blocked one of the corrector jets, stopping it from running right. The new batch of clean fuel was obviously flushing it out - it was still a long way from right but I was riding out of my skin, not even knocking it off for the corners. I kept the thing as flat out as it would go and got past Duffus, a class act who'd won the race the year before and I even started to draw away.

Then, at Ballacraine the CBR cleared completely and with the rev counter finally swinging all the way round to the 13,500 rev maximum I suddenly had all my speed back, that vital punch I'd been missing coming out of comers and I was on it, I was going to pull this time back. I really started piling it on then and knew I'd carved eleven seconds out of Duffus' lead between Ballacraine, where it'd cleared and Ramsey alone because I got a P2 (second place, nine seconds behind) signal in the town's Parliament Square. I knew then all I had to do was pull back those nine seconds over the mountain and the race was mine.

Commentator Fred Clarke had timed me unofficially from Ramsey to Ramsey at 120mph on a bike that hadn't run right until Ballacraine! I was screaming by now, right up on the banks, using the verges everywhere and couldn't have pushed the thing any harder, totally at one with the 600 which I'd been taking to the limit during the Thunderbikes all year.

I was sliding it into every comer, including the 150mph turns, using every bit of my gearbox, the back brake to the full, totally making out the front - there was nothing left, nothing more that the bike or me could give, real manic short circuit style stuff.

I came hammering into the Waterworks in fourth gear absolutely on it, changed down into third, it slipped straight into neutral about seventy miles an hour and down I went, straight on into a wall. I'd lived to tell the tale of my Formula One encounter and hadn't crashed when I was most expecting it and now I'd crashed when I'd least expected to. I was without a doubt on my way to the first ever 120mph lap of the island on a 600 machine - such a shame to have missed out on that achievement. What a way to earn a living and what a massive beating that was. Another free helicopter ride to town, but the trouble was I had run out of time.

I had a four o'clock flight out of the island to London to connect to Italy that afternoon and I hadn't allowed for this. Crashing wasn't part of the schedule. I did everyone's usual trick of telling the doctor it didn't hurt, of course they knew otherwise but somehow I convinced them to let me out of there and I made the flight, changed at Heathrow and changed again at Milan in a great deal of pain.

I remember having my bags with me and passing out at the top of a big elevator in Milan airport and tumbling all the way down for my second beating of the day. I was lying at the bottom, with no strength left at all, trying to pull myself up a wall in an effort to stand up and a little grey haired old lady, sixty if she was a day but with the strength of a horse, grabbed me under my arms and helped me to my feet. I had another flight to catch and somehow got to the track at Mugello where they couldn't believe the state I was in.

The taxi driver helped me out of his car and I couldn't walk, I couldn't talk, I couldn't sit down, I couldn't stand up and I couldn't lie down because I was in so much pain. The only bit of me that wasn't damaged in the crash was my head, thanks to my Arai again, but just for good measure I'd developed a huge abscess in my gum on the way over to complete the head to toe effect. The Grand Prix medical centre took over and found a broken bone in my foot, bruising everywhere else - I was a long way from race winning condition. I did race in the end, but it was fated to be a washout before I even started.

The schedule of racing at the North West 200 and the TT is tough enough without having to travel thousands of miles back and forth to races in Europe in between and it had taken its toll on me; the crash was really the final straw. I recovered a bit to do better at the French round in Le Mans, although I slid off there too, but came back to England for Donington Park's British Grand Prix where I finished eighth, but could have had a fourth. The learning curve was continuing, getting used to the hotter continental conditions and we started experimenting with over-sized radiators and oil coolers.

We were learning a lot in this tough environment and improved again at the Czechoslovakian round in Brno, a long, fast, technical track which I really loved, qualifying on the second row and fighting it out for third place in the race, with a group of five riders. The hectic schedule continued with a visit to a British Supercup meeting at Cadwell Park where I just missed out on a win, finishing second because of confusion in the team over the number of laps there were remaining.

The signal mix up arose over the old supersport format of thirty minutes plus two laps format; I was in second right behind Dave Heal, thinking I was ready to pick him off at my leisure for the win. My signal board had said two laps remaining but as we came into what I thought was the last lap there was the chequered flag. It was desperately frustrating to lose because of such a simple error, particularly as Manda was with my team in pit lane and I so desperately wanted to win for her too. I was still pleased to have beaten the cream of the British Championship competitors though.

I was able to squeeze in the next British Championship round too at Brands Hatch and qualified in pole position with an unofficial lap record, but I was taken out by Ian Macpherson, another Thunderbike runner who I'd been competing with all year. He tried coming underneath me at Clear ways while we were fighting for the lead in the race and took me out with him - I was bitterly disappointed as my first win at the Kent circuit and in the British Championship was looking probable.

From seven starts at the Scarborough Gold Cup road races the following week I finished second three times and won the other four, including a superbike win on Medd Racing's RC45. All good stuff.

I'd got into a spot of bother with Honda for doing so well at Cadwell Park. Not only had we failed to take the win from Yamaha man Dave Heal with our lap counting cock up, but I'd also finished in front of Honda's main championship hope Mike Edwards. Everyone had just ignored me when I'd turned up, thinking I had no chance, so I hadn't been fully briefed on the championship position.

I was sorry about the crucial championship points I'd cost Honda, but secretly delighted to have whipped all the top boys in Britain including Mike Edwards. Mike and I had another fantastic battle later on in the season at the 29th Macau Grand Prix, which everyone described as the most exciting one there had ever been. I'd taken pole position on the tricky 3.8 mile Guia circuit riding Joe Millar's Grand Prix 500 machine again, which I'd previously chosen in favour of the ROC Yamaha, which Mike Edwards was riding.

The race was to be run as a single fifteen lapper instead of the traditional two heat contest and I much preferred it. Mike and I got away from the field with third place man Andreas Hofmann of Switzerland eventually being nearly half a minute adrift. It turned into a real thriller between Mike and me, and I broke Steve Hislop's 1993 course record on the eighth lap, pushing Mike Edwards into immediately raising it again as we fought it out tooth and nail.

The pace got even hotter when we started tearing into the back markers towards the end of the race and I raised the outright lap record again to 89.28mph, letting Mike slip past as I'd got it all worked out by then. I decided to track him until the second to last corner of the race, which is exactly where I got him. I left my braking until about five yards too late though, running only fractionally wide, but it was enough to let him come back at me and I lost the race by a tenth of a second. You can't win 'em all as they say, but by this time I was starting to wonder if my Macau outings were jinxed.

Manda and I had continued seeing each other and our relationship was steadily building; she was waiting for me at my Mum's house when I got back from Macau and it was her birthday, so I took her straight into town and left her in the car outside the jewellers.

She thought I was picking up her birthday present, but I'd planned the whole thing weeks before, getting the right ring size for her engagement finger and choosing the ring I hoped she'd like. It was all ready and waiting in its box, so I went outside and brought her in to the jewellers and with all the staff watching in amazement asked her if she'd like to try it on.

She nearly died with embarrassment - I guess I could have chosen somewhere a little bit more romantic - but there you go, what's the point of beating about the bush!? After all those years of our clandestine affair and so many thousands of miles apart, Miss North West 1992 and I were officially an 'item' from the moment the ring slid on her finger.

Turkingtons pulled out of bike racing at the end of the season, deciding to back two young family members in four wheeled motor sport instead, so it was time to take stock of the direction I wanted my racing to take. I'd proved that I could be competitive around short circuits in world class company and knew I could do much better in Thunderbikes in 1996, but I would have to turn my back on the pressures of my road racing if I was to have a serious chance at the Championship.

After our eleventh hour agreement earlier in 1995, I continued to deal with the sales, rather than the racing side of Honda and began talks again with bosses Dave Hancock and Bob McMillan. We had lots of ideas flying around in 'silly season' but then it was announced that a Production TT was being reintroduced to the Isle of Man for 1996, as the new breed of race bred road machines were now considered capable of racing the mountain course safely. A production based event hadn't been run at the TT since the death of Phil Mellor and Steve Henshaw in 1989.

An International Production TT Championship was introduced in Britain too and suddenly the prospect of racing a Honda Fireblade at the TT and in a major championship became a reality. My contact at Phoenix Distribution (Arai Helmet's UK importers) Wendy Bradley was in discussion with one of their customers, Motorcycle City, an English dealer chain who were looking for a Fireblade rider for the Production TT. Wendy suggested me and I met up with the Company at the NEC Motorcycle Show and opened talks with them regarding the Production TT and new Production Championship, expanding the discussions to include a 600 British Supersport campaign, which I was really keen to take on, if I wasn't going to be racing in the Thunderbikes series.

Castrol had pulled out of British Superbike racing after Colin Seeley's team failed to improve the short circuit performance of the RC45. Honda UK, left without a sponsor, were very much in favour of the proposed deal with Motorcycle City, being prepared to lend support if I'd race an RC45 in Honda Britain colours for them in the major road races of 1996.

At thirty two I was too old by now for a debut Grand Prix ride, having blown that by choosing the British Supercup (superbike) option with Honda three years before. Ironically, failing to make an impression in that series for whatever reason had now blown my chances of a World Superbike or British Superbike berth as well as a Grand Prix slot. Hindsight is a wonderful thing.

I really felt Thunderbikes was my best way forward but I'd learnt that road racing as well was impossible and at the end of the day, knew from experience that the sort of budget we needed to have a proper crack at it was well into six figures. That sort of money is hard to come by and it wasn't forthcoming in the winter of 1995/1996 so the deal with Motorcycle City was struck.

Many of their suppliers were already sponsors of mine and very supportive and we added a few more. They thought quite rightly that if

City's bikes were winning on the track using their products, then they'd see a direct benefit through sales in City's showrooms and clothing stores.

Since the original development work on the Fireblade at Assen, I'd been doing the Fireblade press and dealer launches and we'd built a couple of trick ones ourselves, so we knew how to go one stage further and prepare one for the track. Dealing with the sales side of Honda, instead of their racing arm was suddenly paying dividends both ways, building on the proven link between my road racing successes and CBR600 sales, The media coverage from winning on the 600 at the North West in 1991 had put sales up through the roof and they were boosted again when we won on the 600 again at the TT in 1992, now we had a chance to duplicate that with the CBR900RR.

With Colin Seeley gone and Neil Tuxworth still concentrating full time on World Superbikes, we were going to have to build the 750 ourselves, using a 1995 bike and a mixture of some good new spares and some old stuff, with overall control from Dave Hancock.

We now had a nice tight set-up, reasonable funding and even better support from Honda and the wonderful luxury of time.

10

Now I was starting to concentrate on Production racing in 1996 and was only going to be doing a few superbike races, I was very lucky to have contracts with two tyre manufacturers. I remained with Michelin for my superbike requirements, and signed with Avon for my production based Fireblade and CBR600 tyres. Southern Europe is the place to go for preseason testing as low track temperatures in the British winter and early Spring prevent tyres from getting up to racing temperature. Avon came along to support the test programme and everything went very well with the bikes and the tyres, ending quickest in the South of France on the 600, with the CBR900RR fast and stable too.

We arrived at the first British Championship meeting of the year at Donington Park with a focus and set up more professional than we'd ever been, helped by additional support from Portadown based Francis Neill Motors.

It was so important to get a flying start in the Championship, which had been renamed Thunderbikes to mirror the Grand Prix support events I'd raced in the year before, (although they retained the old Supercup format of thirty minutes racing plus two laps). I started the race in seventh place on the second row of the grid, but with no signalling mistakes this time, I rode the perfect tactical race, 'saving' my tyres while keeping up with the leading pack at the front early on, in a classic 600 battle with Paul Brown, Pete Jennings, Ian Duffus and Dave Heal.

Heal and I broke away from around mid-distance for an epic show-down all the way to the chequered flag, which I took for a win by just three tenths of a second. The fight wasn't even over then as I had to defend myself against a protest from Heal, which I won.

So here I was in front of the gathered press and paddock pundits who'd pigeon-holed me as only a road racer, winning at the most presti-gious motorcycle race track in Britain, beating a top quality field in what was becoming the most competitive class in British racing. My new spon-sor Motorcycle City's Chairman Allan Hemmings, celebrating the twenty fifth anniversary of his founding the Company was there to witness his first full time rider provide him with his new team's first win. Honda were happy as I'd beaten a Yamaha into second place in a terrific duel and things were looking very good indeed.

My superbike and World Thunderbike lessons were really paying off. I'd realised how much of an advantage we were gaining from painstaking preparations and practice, so the next stop was the Cookstown 100 to shake down and dial in the new RC45 to get the feel of everything, ready for the major road racing.

A huge crowd had turned out at the Sherrygroom circuit but a punc-tured rear tyre forced me to pull out of the first superbike race. I hadn't been to the Cookstown for four years, but was really enjoying myself and romped away on the RC45 in the main event, the Cookstown 100 itself and had another very pleasing win in the Regal 600 round, destroying the whole field, with Championship leader Derek Young, Alan Irwin and Jonny Rea picking up the places behind me. It was great to be racing at home again but I was keen to get back to Easter's round two of the Thunderbike campaign in England, my first visit to the tough Thruxton circuit in Hampshire.

Qualifying was difficult, with set up and tyre problems as we got used to the fast speeds and the track's abrasive surface. My fifth row position was a big disadvantage in the race, giving a chance for the leading group to get away but I made good progress, learning the circuit all the time but lost grip towards the end, with my tyres completely chewed to bits. I ended up in ninth position, picking up enough points to carry a three point lead going into the next round at Oulton Park.

I qualified well at the Cheshire circuit, which I really like, a fast hard riding track and got a good start in the race storming off downhill around the long left hander called Cascades in a bunch of riders jostling for position at the front. Mike Edwards accidentally clipped my handlebars trying to come past and I was off and out of the race. I was bitterly disappointed because I'd really been looking forward to this encounter on one of my favourite circuits and was so desperate to win the British Championship.

I won the next round at Snetterton to make up for it, fighting Ian Duffus and Paul Brown right at the front when the race was stopped around half distance. The Thunderbike rules meant there was no two parter, just another fifteen minute race plus two laps at the end, so I rode even harder in the second race, overhauling early leader Ian Duffus on lap two and then led all the way to take the win by a quarter of a second, which was important for my Championship hopes. I'd only picked up seven points since the Donington round, but this victory drew me up to within three points of Championship leader Mike Edwards. I loved all those tracks by now and felt I could win on all of them as long as everything on the bike, including me, was right.

My brand new 250 had arrived at Snetterton courtesy of Padgetts, just in time to be run in ready for the annual North West 200 carnival with a 100,000 crowd flocking to the northern coast to watch some of the hardest road racing there is. The technical complexity of 250s had started to increase quite dramatically and we had some fuel starvation and setup problems in practice, ending up a few rows back from the leaders.

I was fastest on the 600, a bike we'd built especially for the mid-season road racing campaign and was quickest on the 750 too, recording a 116.38mph lap which I couldn't improve on in Thursday's session, as the bike developed a misfire, Iain Duffus just edging me out of pole position. Hot on our heels were the fast and powerful Ducatis of Michael Rutter, Jim Moodie, Ian Simpson and Terry Rymer, all of whom were going to be a big threat in the two superbike races.

It was the first 250 ride I'd had for a year with the handicap of starting way back on the grid, but it felt like the old days as I fought my way through the field to try and get on terms with Woolsey Coulter. His Aprilia was super quick though, plus he was riding it every week which makes a big difference. He rode it superbly well to take the win while I was happy to settle for second. Unusually, the second 250 encounter of the day was the final race of the meeting and once again I was lying in second behind Coulter, but much closer, feeling this time that I had a really good chance of taking him on, when my clutch burnt out, forcing my retirement.

I got away well in the first superbike event amongst the leading bunch, headed by Michael Rutter whose big engined Ducati, a great bike, was as quick as we'd been expecting. He built up quite a good lead while I was in a superb tussle a bit further back with Ian Simpson, Ian Duffus and Jim Moodie. Once I'd finally got away from these three, I started to haul Rutter back in and was right behind him at the Metropole when his engine cut out, forcing him out of the race.

On the last lap I was comfortably in the lead by over a hundred yards from Ian Simpson coming into the final Juniper Hill chicane, with only a couple of hundred yards to go to the flag and I knew I had the race won. For the first and last time in my life I lost concentration and slowed fractionally, starting to think about the next race, planning how I was going to win it and Simpson, who couldn't believe what he was seeing, came round my outside on the last corner and I lost the race. I was so mad with myself, my team was furious with me - they couldn't believe I'd thrown it away like that and Ian Simpson couldn't believe his luck. It was my own fault and I've never let it happen again.

I'd thrown it all away by just drifting off and losing my concentration which just wasn't good enough and nor were the two second places I'd collected so far. I was still furious with myself at the start of the 600 race and promised myself I'd get my first win of the day come hell or high water. All the anger and frustration combined to blast me away from the start and with the bike running beautifully, no one got near me, with Simpson and Duffus scrapping for second and third places a long way behind me from very early on.

This really put me in the right frame of mind for the main race of the day, the North West 200 itself. Ian Duffus was left on the grid with clutch problems while I didn't get a very clean start, lying fourth behind Ian Simpson who was trailing Jim Moodie, with Rutter on the third Ducati getting away first. The sheer power of the big Italian twin enabled him to build up a three or four second lead while I was kept busy fighting past Simpson before setting about Jim Moodie, finally getting into second place at Portrush.

It was tough keeping Moodie and Simpson behind me while concentrating on catching Rutter way up ahead, but whereas before I'd only been catching glimpses of his bright yellow bike and leathers every so often, now I was starting to see him clearly and knew I was catching him all the time. Our fight for second, third and fourth places allowed Terry Rymer and Robert Holden to catch up and join in the fun, when suddenly I flashed past Rutter's Ducati as it slowed and stopped again on the run between Portrush and Portstewart with a lap to go. There was no way I was going to give this one up this time.

I really piled on the pressure and rode relentlessly for the last few miles, holding off the rapid Duckhams Ducatis of Scotsmen Simpson and Moodie, to romp home by four seconds for my tenth win at the North West 200. I collected our biggest prize money for one race ever at the North West, Honda were delighted at another win for their CBR600 and RC45, plus I'd been on the top of my form for the whole meeting and everything was looking promising for TT fortnight, now only a few days away. Just as I'd written myself into the history books at the famous Portrush venue in 1992, now I was destined to do the same on the Isle of Man in 1996.

The RC45 that had run so well at the North West, apart from the little practice hiccup, started to give us bigger problems on the Isle of Man. Tony Scott had done a beautiful job preparing the motor as usual, with the rest of the machine built up to the best specification we could manage. We'd used all sorts of bits and pieces, good stuff mostly and all brand now, but a mixture of 1995 and 1996 parts which helped cause lots of silly little problems that wouldn't have been too troublesome on their own, but combined were to cause me some serious trouble.

The air sensors in the airbox assembly were malfunctioning enough to send the engine management and fuel injection system haywire; this plus some niggling electrical problems made the bike very temperamental, cutting out in the pitlane stop box in the big races and making it difficult to restart after the pit stop. The worst symptoms were when it would only run on three cylinders, cutting in and out at the most dangerous parts of the TT course, just to keep my attention,

Honda's domination of the Formula One TT began when Phil Read won the inaugural F1 race for them in 1977. Only Graeme Crosby's 1981 win for Suzuki and Hailwood's legendary 1978 Ducati victory had prevented a complete whitewash. Our job was to continue Honda's success and fight off the very real threat of the big Ducati in Michael Rutter's hands and Jim Moodie had arrived on the island with John Reynold's Reve Kawasaki World Superbike, a machine capable of out-running my kitted semi factory RC45.

I had the additional responsibility of carrying Honda's flag in the reintroduced Production TT, (for which there were seventy four entries) on the Motorcycle City sponsored Fireblade. The rules allowed some alterations to the suspension, but we'd tested on it in the early season in

France without problems, but had no real idea as to how it was going to behave on the mountain course.

We'd taken some advice and had two differing sets of forks made in Europe, but as usual we were short of practice time with so many bikes to dial in, a situation made worse by appalling conditions in practice week. Tony Scott had checked the engine over, making sure all the tolerances were spot on (drag in an engine can cost a lot of power) so we took the Fireblade for granted really, while concentrating on the other bikes, particularly some new parts that had only just arrived for the RC45.

Because Monday morning's practice starts at 5am it's always a good idea to take your most reliable bike out first to make sure you get some laps in. You never start with the 750 because it's better to get round a couple of times on a smaller bike to get dialled in, so I did two laps on my 600, good enough for fourth place, then switched to the 250. Our preparations for practice had run late into the night before and then into the early hours of the morning and one young technician had been left the final job of putting in the 600cc of oil the 250's gearbox required, but he had actually only put in 60cc.

As soon as I got on the bike early that morning I thought it sounded a little bit odd but put it down to the strange acoustics you get in the stillness of the early morning summer air on the island.

Half way down the straight at Cronk-y-Voddy it seized solid. I got the clutch in but it was the gearbox that had seized and the back wheel stayed locked up at about 130mph. Luckily it was wet and I managed to control the huge slide and get it stopped.

Had it happened another three hundred yards later at the sixth gear right hander at the end of the straight, I would have been in real trouble. I headed the evening session on the 750 with a 119.20mph lap then only went out for one circuit on the Fireblade to see how it would handle, which wasn't too good, a bit scary in fact, ending sixth quickest overall. I was happy to then bring the 600 in second fastest, just behind Ian Duffus.

On Wednesday the CBR600 picked up a rear wheel puncture on the mountain and there was very little practice time remaining when I'd finally got back to the pits. My crew fitted a new rear wheel in a hurry and I went off like a rocket and stuck in a 119.80mph lap with a new, cold rear tyre from a standing start which was something else, compared to Duffus' 1995 lap record of 117.87mph.

This super lap was the second quickest of the entire practice week and better than my quickest qualifying lap on the 750! Surely with a performance like that this year the race was going to be mine? The rest of the field certainly thought so because that fast time had sent such a shock through the paddock, the talk was of who was in the running for second and third places.

The very real threat of the big Ducatis became patently clear when Robert Holden posted the quickest time of 120.38mph in the F1 class compared to my 119.26mph best effort. His challenge was never to materialise though, as the likeable New Zealander was tragically killed in an accident during Friday's final practice session, casting a shadow over the paddock and the whole fortnight.

The terrible weather conditions failed to dampen the enthusiasm of the forty thousand fans who'd brought fourteen and a half thousand bikes onto the island, but the rain had ruined a lot of practice week and continued into the Formula One race itself, with the start delayed for an hour because of a heavy downpour at Kirk Michael. I made a good start on the intermediate tyres and everything was going well, leading the race from Ian Duffus and Nick Jeffries until the gremlins got to work on the RC45. It stalled in the stop box at the end of lap two coming in for fuel and fresh slicks and I lost precious time paddling the machine to my crew's position.

There isn't a lot of room in the TT pit lane and I'd got boxed in by Ian Duffus stopped at the neighbouring V&M team's position, whose attention was all focussed on the desperate trouble they were having with the rear wheel nut on their Honda, which quickly put paid to Duffus' challenge. Manoeuvring my bike away from our position cost me more invaluable seconds though and then it was difficult to restart the bike, but worse was to come.

Pit lane was becoming a nightmare which had started with poor Joey Dunlop, who'd come in at the end of the first lap, as he felt the track was drying enough to change onto slicks. But his team wasn't expecting him that early and hadn't got the wheels ready, which effectively cost him the race there and then as he had to go out again, having achieved nothing during the stop.

Some distance into lap four my RC45 developed a bad misfire. It felt like fuel starvation with the engine cutting in and out from three to four cylinders, the bike not pulling enough to get anywhere near top speed only reaching about 120mph at times, instead of the 180mph or so I should have been getting.

By this time Lee Pullan, in an extraordinary performance riding in a privateer team was chasing me down in second place, about forty seconds back and closing. I nursed the RC45 back to the pits, weaving a bit to get what I thought were the remnants of fuel into the injection system, praying it would make it to the refuelling stop, and it cut out as I approached the stop box again, so I paddled her the last few yards to my crew and breathed a sigh of relief as the fuel cascaded into the tank.

The bike was terribly hard to start once more, even with two technicians shoving me down pitlane and I was heartbroken to find the misfire was still there as soon as I got back up to speed. Just as I was cursing my bad luck though, Lee Pullan's had run out with a replacement wheel problem in pitlane, which gave me a bigger cushion back to Nick Jeffries, who was over fifty seconds behind me.

My misfire was worsening all the time though, with the dashboard lit up like a Christmas tree showing the ignition system had switched into 'get you home' mode, but then I got some luck back as I caught up to the back of Michael Rutter's bike on the road. He wasn't sure of some of the corners as it was only his third TT and we got into a real scrap; I'd rush past him on the turns where I was still relatively quick and then he'd come storming past me on the straights so I could jump into his slipstream, which was the only way I could keep up any sort of reasonable pace on the last lap.

Nick Jeffries appeared with us during the last lap too, where my lack of power meant I couldn't keep the front end lightened up over the rough stuff and the jumps and with the front so heavy I was taking a terrible pounding keeping it under control, with both hands terribly blistered at the end of the race.

My signals still showed me leading, plus I was picking up the other two riders' as well and I know if I could just keep them both in sight I could win and I came home 50.6 seconds ahead of Nick Jeffries, with Michael Rutter nearly thirty seconds further back. We traced the fault to the airbox sensors, which help determine the fuel / air mixture in conjunction with the fuel injection and engine management system.

Even though I'd had those serious bike problems, I'd managed to lead the race from the word go and picked up a prize money bonus for that achievement.

The poor weather continued to dog the festival, delaying the Lightweight TT for a day, which turned out to be a real blessing as I'd been in terrible pain with a wisdom tooth the night before race day, not getting any sleep at all. The postponed start enabled me to see a dentist who ended up practically standing on my chest, swinging and pulling on the tooth with a big pair of pliers. I couldn't risk any side effects from heavier medication and only had a local anaesthetic - all in the line of duty!

After my practice fright on the 250 I'd eventually qualified fastest with a 113.75mph lap, just ahead of Joey. Still feeling like I'd been hit in the face with a hammer the race finally got going and there was nothing between Joey and me during the first two laps, coming into the pits just a couple of seconds apart, with me just having the edge. He'd started the race first on the road which can be a handicap, or an advantage depending on your point of view, but one thing's for sure, it does mean you get your signals later than usual as your timing crew has to wait for the riders behind you to come through, before they can give you a time difference.

I got boxed in again at the pit stop, even worse this time, by Ian Lougher who'd parked his bike right across the front of mine. I was furious because it lost me lots of time and I smoked away, accidentally catching the leg of another pit crew member with my footrest on the way out. As I blasted off down pit lane I was worried that I'd hurt this guy, but it turned out it was a wooden leg, so he hadn't been hurt at all!

We hadn't got the 250's gearbox rebuilt until Wednesday which had limited our practice time and this race was really tight, meaning I was pushing the bike to the limit. I'd softened the suspension a bit for the race so the bike had a bigger suspension stroke on it too and I was heeled over so far at some corners the bottom of the expansion boxes on the Grand Prix exhaust system were trailing along the ground.

The left hand chamber suddenly holed on the third lap which took a huge amount of power out of the bike, making me try harder on the corners which made the hole bigger and the performance worse. I came home fourth, another 250 race lost. I just didn't seem to have any luck on the 250 at the TT. We'd been working on it late the night before at Jurby airfield, running in some pistons and doing some final low speed tests.

Manda and Honda's Dave Hancock were sitting in my car chatting when I came off the 250 at the far end of the airfield, trapping my foot and leg underneath the bike. I hadn't been wearing any leathers either and hurt myself a bit, but they were so engrossed in conversation they didn't notice I'd stopped coming past so I got myself and the bike upright after a while and limped back.

The Junior TT was reduced to a three lapper and I tore into it from the word go breaking the lap record at 118.94mph from the standing start, but Ian Duffus was staying in touch and elected to refuel at the end of the first lap which confused the signals a bit. I'd destroyed the opposition psychologically with my practice lap, but I wanted a safety margin in case something went wrong and kept up a terrific pace just in case, putting in a 118.67mph second lap with the CBR600 really on song. A clean pit stop kept me well ahead, enabling me to control my position on the final lap and roll home at a less frantic pace for my second win of the week.

In the limited amount of practice time we'd had with four bikes to prepare, the least time had been given to the Fireblade which hadn't been handling at all well. This was the first time I'd raced with a rear tyre of such a size plus a sixteen inch front wheel and I was far from comfortable with the feel of the bike. I was under quite a bit of pressure from Japan to succeed, with the Fireblade's creator Tadao Baba sending me a message, telling me he needed the Production TT win for his bike.

With the part I'd played in the development of the Fireblade, I felt it was my duty to win the race for Honda but the handling problems were a real worry. At the very last minute I decided to put the bike back to standard and a set of forks were rushed over from England. We fitted them on the bike, I set them up just by feel and it was the best Fireblade I'd ever ridden, a testimony to the strength of Tadao Baba's original design.

It was surprising I didn't feel all the pressure I was under from my new sponsors, Avon and Honda that year. I had to win the F1 for the big prize money, my original deal with Motorcycle City was to go for the win in the Production TT, I wanted to win the 250 for myself and Padgetts, plus I couldn't lose on my 600 as that was the bike I was riding in England every week.

I enjoyed the Production TT immensely, feeling very fast and safe on the bike I'd helped bring to the marketplace. All the faith we had in that landmark, groundbreaking road bike was repaid ten times over with a wonderful win.

I started fast and smooth, getting into a good rhythm very quickly but got a signal that I was a second or so down on Ian Duffus at Ramsey, so I wound up my pace a little bit, recording a 118.93mph second lap. I caught and passed Lee Pullan on a big Yamaha, while Duffus got in a bit of a battle on the road with Jim Moodie's Suzuki GSXR750. The team contributed a good, clean pit stop and got me away into the final lap still two seconds up and I piled on the pressure, getting a signal at Ramsey that I was five seconds clear.

I knew I needed to conserve my strength for the six lap Senior TT still to come that day and I came over the mountain controlling the race to take the win in the end by six seconds - a hat trick of victories - could I now pull off a record fourth win in the afternoon?

Duffus, Moodie, Jeffries, Rutter and Joey Dunlop were all going to be major threats, plus privateer Lee Pullan had been a surprise package in the F1 six days before, so I knew it was going to be tough. I took it relatively easy for the first half of the opening lap, having spent the morning riding the Fireblade to victory, being careful to settle down on the powerful, different handling RC45.

We'd worked hard on the bike, fitting all new electrical parts and air sensors and it was running well, but I got an early 'P24' signal (second place, four seconds behind). I knew I couldn't afford to let leader Jim Moodie get away on his WSB Kawasaki, which definitely had the edge over my machine, so I had to get my finger out once I'd adjusted to the bike.

Duffus went out with a problem very early on and I got a 'P1' signal at Ramsey halfway around the course, getting into a good rhythm on the climb up to the mountain section. I turned up the heat for the rest of the lap, catching Bob Jackson and Lee Pullan at Creg-ny-Baa, getting past them nicely and flying across the start / finish 7.2 seconds clear of Moodie, with Nick Jeffries another 12.5 seconds further back.

My lap speed was 121.69mph from the standing start, proving how hard I'd ridden over the mountain and now I was in the groove, I decided to keep up the same pace to see who could live with me. The flying start to the second lap helped me increase my average to 122.14mph and my lead to 20 seconds and I knew, baring a mechanical problem that I'd got the race sewn up.

Moodie, Joey and I were all in the pits together at the end of lap four for the refuelling stop and I was looking forward to a bit of a scrap with them, but Jim stayed put with a mechanical problem and Joey, who'd been getting quicker all the time blasted away ahead of me. I caught him on the road after a while and with Jim Moodie out, I was now leading the race from Joey in second place, by nearly a minute. We did a whole lap together which was a tactical mistake as I started to lose my own natural rhythm, because I was too busy watching Joey instead of concentrating on what I was doing.

You should really try to pass the other rider in situations like that and go on, because it's difficult to pick your lines and go fast when you're behind someone. It's the only time I've ever done it in my life and I remember losing my concentration, thinking I had a good lead and I actually began drifting off a bit. It wasn't like my episode at the North West, when I'd been mentally alert but in the wrong way, concentrating on the next race.

I think it may have been fatigue after a long fortnight of practice and racing, having completed fifty near forty mile laps, about two thousand race miles all at a minimum 110mph, plus of course another hard race that very morning.

Joey was in a tight battle for second place with Jeffries, only a couple of seconds in it and he started to up the pace a bit and then my bike wouldn't rev out all the way out again, so I let him go, being forced to knock off the pace quite a bit and concentrate on getting the bike home again. The flag seemed an awful long time coming, but I won at an average 119.76mph by over a minute in the end, with Joey getting a brilliant second just under a couple of seconds ahead of Jeffries.

No rider had ever achieved four TT wins in one week and I was overwhelmed to have surpassed the likes of Joey Dunlop, Steve Hislop and Mike Hailwood, each of whom shared the record of three TT wins in one meeting. To commemorate the achievement, I was immensely honoured to be informed that I was to appear on the Isle of Man's coinage, A new fifty pence piece was minted featuring an image of me racing in front of Joey Dunlop, which made the honour even greater for me.

I'd won all those races but it was such hard, hard work. I could have lost each of the four quite easily if the tiniest bit more luck had gone against us. I decided there and then that firstly we'd have our own 250 for the following season, because I was being handicapped every year having to get a different bike working properly. The holed exhaust would have been foreseeable if we'd had the preparation time, but it was still a bit unlucky.

Secondly, I swore I'd definitely never race another 750 at the TT that had been pieced together like that. I told Honda I wouldn't ride on the island in the following year without a proper new bike, complete with a factory engine. The fact that the Ducati superbikes had put up such a threatening performance against the RC45 at the North West 200 also helped convince them to organise what I wanted and they began making all the right noises about 1997.

A fraught Thunderbike round at Brands Hatch saw me crashing my 600 at Druids hairpin bend, eventually coming home tenth on my spare bike, having started from the back of the restart grid. This dropped me a place to third in the title race, a few points behind Heal and Duffus, but my Championship hopes paled into insignificance with a momentous occasion coming up, my marriage to Manda McKinley.

Manda had booked Clanabogan Church for our wedding, which is close to Manda's home in Omagh, her family parish, on one of the only weekends in the summer of 1996 that I wasn't racing.

I let a cat out of a bag during my speech at our reception by telling everyone the story about the time Manda stole over to the TT to be with me in 1995. It was one 4am practice morning and I was so tired I just couldn't get up. Manda started bouncing around on the end of the bed and the dawn light suddenly came pouring through the windows and her eyes lit up with the morning sunshine. Ever since then, my nickname for her has been 'Twinkle' - those eyes are still bringing light into my life today.

I did the absolute classic and forgot the rings; Manda's brother who was with me and my best man Davy Hamilton on the way to the Church said "Manda's going to kill you!" but I didn't panic, figuring I could borrow a couple of rings from someone, and that she couldn't make a scene at the altar in front of the whole congregation anyway! I thought I'd just slip a ring on and she wouldn't notice, but Manda's friend Sandra saved the day - all of us boys had got changed at her house and had breakfast. She'd spotted the rings I'd left behind and got them to the church in the nick of time.

There's a tradition at home, I've no idea how it started, that bridegrooms to be are captured by their male friends for some harmless fun (unless it's you being humiliated!) and unfortunately, I'd been involved in a lot of them before and now it was pay back time. The pack of lads who'd come looking for me surprised me one afternoon as I was at home working on my bikes in my Mum's garage, getting everything ready early for the Ulster Grand Prix, as practice started the Tuesday after the wedding.

About a dozen of my friends came to get me and I dived out of the back of the garage and over a fence at the bottom of the garden, leaving half my new pair of Diesel jeans on the barbed wire and sprinted away for my life. I ruined a great new pair of shoes too, running for miles through hedges, across rivers and over fields inside a triangle of roads all about a mile long.

These guys were going to get me and I was running for my life, but the pack had split up into cars and were circulating the three roads, while another lot had formed a posse to flush me out. After about an hour of running I knew what a fox must feel like with a pack of hounds after it. I was completely finished, with five of them right on my tail when my Aunt's car appeared for the rescue, ready and waiting with the back door open on the other side of a gate.

I cleared the gate and dived across the back seats head first in one leap and we roared off up the road with the hands of my pursuers pulling at my ankles. The July wedding was a brilliant affair and Manda and I rode off on a pure white Honda Gold Wing with the photographers snapping away, all fairy tale stuff.

What a wonderful life! Four TT wins, a beautiful new bride; how could life be better? I was on the crest of a wave, having won three races at Scarborough's Cock of the North meeting shortly before getting married, plus I'd beaten many of the world's best Thunderbike riders at the British Grand Prix round.

The honeymoon had to be delayed though, as practice for the Ulster Grand Prix began on the Tuesday following the wedding and my superb run of luck was set to continue.

It all started with a massive dogfight in the 250 race at the Ulster Grand Prix, between me and Ian Lougher who was desperate to beat me on my home ground, feeling he had a score to settle after our little run in at the TT. He nipped inside me at Tournagrough and I could see he was riding very hard, eventually crashing at the hairpin. Phelim Owens took over second place and made up some ground behind me, but I raised the lap record to 118.88mph to put me beyond his reach.

I won the next race, the first of two superbike encounters pretty easily from Simon Beck and lap record holder Jason Griffiths, which put me in just the right frame of mind for the Regal 600 encounter. I started with the same bike I'd set aside for my road racing campaign at the beginning of the year, the one I'd smashed the lap and race records on at both the North West and the TT. I took the lead quite early on in the first lap and set a new record of 120.04mph on lap two, raising it again to 120.45mph on lap three, the first time the 120mph barrier had been broken at Dundrod on a 600 machine.

After that I was racing the track and myself and raised the overall race average record to 119.30mph to complete the road race hat trick I'd set my heart on. With three wins under my belt already, now there was no stopping me in the second 250 race of the day which I led from start to finish, disappointed not to really be troubled as Lougher failed to start and Phelim Owens went out on lap one.

In the final superbike encounter of the day, the main race, I was looking for my fifth win, a feat no one had ever achieved before but it turned into the fiercest race of my day with Bob Jackson, Jason Griffiths and me in a tight battle for the lead. I got a slow start and had to fight my way past Dave Goodley and Simon Beck from an early fifth place, my worst position of the whole day's racing.

Jason Griffiths made all the early running at the front, but by lap three I had got ahead and piled on the coals, posting the fastest lap of the race at 125mph on my seventh circuit. Jackson got past me in the closing stages and Griffiths was snapping at my heels, but I fought my way back past the big green Kawasaki for a record fifth win. I'd won each of my five races, having covered over forty racing laps on three different bikes, the equivalent of eight laps of the TT course.

The crowd at Dundrod had never cheered me so much, roaring their approval at my extraordinary feat and furiously waving their programmes as I rode past - what a terrific way to wrap up my road racing season. So, finally, feeling tired but elated after rewriting the history books with another record breaking number of wins, I was able to spirit my new wife away for our honeymoon at last, far away from the frantic world of the race track.

11

My Thunderbike campaign continued well during the next round at Cadwell Park, where I took the CBR600 to a tactical fifth place, having held third for the majority of the race. Most of the opposition was in dire straits with tyre wear and there had been a lot of crashes - I was determined not to join the DNF list.

I had learnt that my old do-or-die style was not the way to win Championships and I let a couple of fast finishing riders come past me, ending up fifth in the race, but heading the title chase by five points, with three rounds remaining. I was in third place in the next round at Mallory Park with four laps to go and plenty in hand, very comfortably placed and ready to challenge for the lead, when the front wheel suddenly tucked underneath me at Gerards Bend for no apparent reason.

It was quite a big accident and I broke my shoulder in two places, furious with myself for throwing away the race and enough points to send me further ahead at the top of the table. My amazing run of good luck and fortune was starting to change, with the shoulder injury sidelining me for the next round at Silverstone. But with everything still to play for I raced two weeks later at Brands Hatch, still injured, where the front tyre punctured on the first warm up lap, forcing me to start from pit lane after the rest of the field had disappeared into the distance. I charged through the field up to eleventh place before sliding off after being forced wide to avoid another rider and the Thunderbike Championship had slipped from my grasp.

I picked up a stomach bug just before the final round of the season at Donington Park and was feeling really off colour in the race, finishing eighth, leaving me fifth overall in the Championship. After leading the title chase, taking those short circuit race wins against the toughest opposition and fighting it out at the front all season, I had finally proven beyond question that I was a complete racer, as happy and competitive on short circuits as I was on the roads, for which I had become so famous.

I had one more road race to complete in 1996, the Macau Grand Prix, and I was looking forward to the chance of getting my revenge over Mike Edwards, who'd pipped me in our previous encounter there. Millions of TV viewers watch the Macau action live in the Far East and they weren't disappointed with the Grand Prix again in 1996.

For the second year running I was riding a Joe Millar V4 500 Grand Prix Yamaha, the machine on which I'd smashed the Macau lap record with the year before, the same bike Eugene McManus had been riding in Grand Prix. The carbs flooded on the grid before the start of the race, stranding me on the line as the field shot off on the warm up lap, but we finally got the bike fired up and I hurriedly took up my position.

Mike Edwards had grabbed pole on the 500 ROC Yamaha machine and everyone was looking forward to another classic encounter between the two of us. Edwards got the holeshot and I tucked myself into third position to get settled in before making my move, taking the lead as soon as I got on the pace and was never headed in the race again, with Edwards shaving my lap record, then crashing in his attempt to catch me.

After so many years of trying I'd finally overcome my run of bad luck at Macau and climbed the winners podium to collect the trophy, reflecting on a year rich with success and personal happiness; it just doesn't get better than that.

My road racing successes were unique and very important to me, but I was still keen for a British Superbike Championship ride in 1997, to lay the ghost of my two lacklustre seasons on the ageing RC30. I'd proved that I could win on the same circuits in the fiercely competitive Super Sport class, on what was basically a home built bike. I knew I'd never be competitive on a superbike constructed by our little outfit and that the factory route was the only way to get a chance at the blue riband UK championship.

Numerous offers abounded after the season was over as usual, but nothing more concrete than the one from my sponsors Motorcycle City, who were keen to continue their support in 1997, having been delighted with the media exposure our racing success had won for them. Honda offered me the option of an NSR500 GP machine for the TT, which I turned down in favour of a full factory engined RC45, knowing the 160bhp grunt of the HRC prepared superbike would have the edge over the more nimble 130bhp two stroke when the chips were down.

My loyalty to Honda remained strong and agreement was reached for me to repeat our 1996 short circuit and road race campaign, plus I was to continue racing the Honda Fireblade in the new British Sports Production Championship. 250 race bikes were getting more complicated every year and our knowledge getting less; Honda realised that if I had the right preparation time on a bike of my own from the beginning of the season, then I could perform and win and they agreed to supply a new 250 for 1997 too.

Back at home I was shortlisted for the Belfast Telegraph Sports Star of the Year Awards and was staggered to beat four wheeled Formula One star Eddie Irvine, Joey Dunlop and golfer Darren Clarke into top spot at a glittering awards ceremony at Belfast's Europa Hotel. I was really surprised and quite overcome by it all and hadn't prepared anything to say. I made a little speech though, explaining that I thought only famous people won such a prestigious award, which brought the house down.

I was very proud to become the Texaco Motor Sport Star of the Year too, at an awards ceremony held in Dublin, where the horse rider Tony McCoy and swimmer Michelle Smith won the other categories. I felt I was in very exalted company and suddenly realised that even if I wasn't famous, I was about to be and the phone didn't stop ringing for a long time.

We headed practice times in preseason tests at Cartagena in the South of France and arrived at Donington Park focussed and ready to start the season with a bang. In Friday's practice session, I went out and took unofficial pole immediately. All my World Thunderbike and previous season's experience, plus the preparation we'd had was coming together nicely and I came into the pits to make a few adjustments, went out again in the second half of practice and dumped it big time with a vicious high side, pushing the cold tyres beyond their limit. I went back to the hotel that night nursing what had really begun to turn into a nagging injury - a badly damaged, heavily swollen left shoulder.

I rode the perfect tactical race carrying the injury though, starting steadily then moving through the field smoothly and calmly, passing the opposition one by one and then breaking clear and forging ahead, building up a good cushion for a comfortable win. Dialling in new suspension in qualifying at a wet Oulton Park had left me twenty first on the grid in the next round, but I rode a blinding race, taking the lead with four laps to go.

After Jim Moodie crashed behind me trying to stay on my lap record pace, I had built up a ten second lead - what a dream start to the season, a win at Donington followed by a rout of the opposition in the second round with just a cruise to the line ahead. There'd been a little front end patter from the bike throughout the race; I'd open the throttle and it would go, but coming into the tight right hander at Knickerbrook on the last lap but one, the symptoms started again, I gassed it and I was suddenly fifteen foot up in the air, watching the bike catapult into the crowd. It was really lucky no one was hurt, including me.

Angry with myself I made my way back to the pits brushing off the gravel, dirt and straw, meeting Honda's Dave Hancock who asked if I was OK. Once I'd told him I was, he said "Right! Now you're in trouble!" and gave me a good telling off for losing the race from such a strong position.

The two factory engines, mine and the one allocated to Michael Rutter's V&M RC45 only arrived a few days before the North West 200, so there was very little time to practice, just a few laps in a private session at Donington Park before the first big road meeting of the year. Not only was the opposition getting stronger every year, but they also had the advantage of winter testing and three or four races to perfect their machinery, whereas my superbike wasn't arriving until the last minute.

It was difficult getting a traffic free, clear lap in practice at the North West too and the bike had a slight weave in a straight line. We didn't have time to perfect the handling though and it handicapped me a little, but the factory 750 engine was powering the big RC45 through the fifth gear section where the speed trap was sited at 176mph. The trap had remained sited at the drop down to the Metropole which is no longer the fastest section because of the new chicane at Magherabuoy. On the fastest sixth gear part of the course going down towards Coleraine, the RC45 was touching 200mph.

I was happy enough to finish third on the grid, behind Jim Moodie's Suzuki and Michael Rutter's RC45, both of whom were riding their bikes every week in the British Championship

The course was a little damp for the first superbike race which was thrilling battle between Rutter, Moodie and me. I was a little way from riding flat out on the brand new bike which I'd hardly ridden, plus it wasn't handling perfectly and the three of us swapped places throughout, but I took the lead at York Corner in Portstewart on the final lap and kept the Scot and the Englishman behind me to take the win.

My 250 seized solid on the warm up lap putting me out of the light weight race, but I led the 600 encounter from the start to the final corner, where I took a fractionally wide line, enough for Michael Rutter to dive underneath me and sneak the win.

Michael and I were so absorbed in another race long duel between the two of us in the Production event, we let Ian Simpson pull away ahead of us on his Red Bull Ducati and allowed Jim Moodie to get on our tail. By the time I'd shaken myself clear of them, it was too late to get on terms with the leader and I had to settle for second.

For the main race of the day I had a problem with the fuel injection system and couldn't get the RC45 fired up in time for the warm up lap, finally getting it running in time to start at the back of the field from pit lane on cold tyres. I rocketed out past Ian Simpson who had been left on the grid and stormed through the field, losing a bit of time overcooking it at one corner, which meant by the time I got on terms with the leading bunch of riders it was too late to challenge for the win; running wide had cost me a podium finish, but I still felt my fifth place was remarkable under the circumstances.

New qualifying rules at the TT meant that practice times dictated start positions for the Senior event, so I was determined to just get the RC45 dialled in and finish down the placings, ensuring I wasn't going to be a target for the rest of the field in the second major race of the Isle of Man fortnight. Proving once again that my fastest laps around the course can seem the most unremarkable at the time, I posted a 121.52mph time on a lap where I was forced to slow down to a twenty mile an hour trickle for half a mile past an accident at Greeba Castle and again, past another incident later on the same lap.

The factory engine was fast and furious and we'd got a lot of information from Honda's World Superbike outfit on set up, with team member Aaron Slight visiting the island for the first time. The factory Showa rear shock was working superbly well, (set up with 10mm extra travel for the humps and bumps compared to Koscinski and Slight's WSB settings). The Ohlins front suspension was sharp and positive with all the development work the Swedish firm had put in, to make the RC45 work at its best.

I was pleased to have chosen the 750 over the NSR Grand Prix bike, (which could only be run in the Senior anyway) although Jim Moodie was proving threateningly quick on it with a 120.16 mph best practice lap, just behind Michael Rutter on a V&M prepared RC45. Joey Dunlop was being less successful in practice on his 500 NSR, preferring an injured Nick Jeffries' RC45, feeling instantly at home with the Englishman's setup.

I started the Formula One calmly for once, wanting to get settled in with the heavy fuel load and my first signal showed me in third behind Rutter and Joey. The gap was a bit too big for comfort and it spurred me on to cross the line with a four second lead at the end of lap one, knowing I had started to take control of the race. During the first stop, I hadn't realised Joey's pit crew had run into rear wheel problems and I went off like a bullet after mine, because we'd lost a lot of time during the stop trying to refit the fuel filler cap.

I stayed calm and controlled and really started to enjoy myself, with the team making up for the first pit lane debacle with a really slick fourth lap fuel and tyre change. I controlled the race for the final two laps, knowing there was a long week ahead of me, winning by over a minute and a half with a time of 1hr 53m 16.8secs and a race average of 119.90mph in front of Michael Rutter, who I'd caught on the mountain on lap six. Bob Jackson came in third on a Kawasaki.

I had the benefit of a new sponsor for my 250, Bell and Howell, but I hadn't brought them any success at the North West. I'd been so close to winning a TT on a 250 so often, but I'd never quite pulled it off, so this year I was determined to win for my sponsor and myself, feeling there was still a hole in my TT records. I decided to go for a tyre change strategy at half distance which is unusual, but I figured a softer compound rear in the warm conditions would give me maximum grip on the last lap, enabling me to smoke away anything else that was still living with me.

It was very tight between me and Joey from the word go, neck and neck at Glen Helen with Jim Moodie only a second behind the two of us, before he went out with a problem and it became a two horse race. Joey flashed across the line at the end of the opening lap with a one second advantage which I'd pulled back by the time I came into the pits. Joey's Crew got him refuelled very quickly, while we lost more time than expected, encountering a problem changing the rear wheel and my first signal on lap three put me eighteen seconds behind Dunlop at Glen Helen.

I lit up the little 250 then, riding so fast that I'd taken seven seconds out of Joey's lead by the time I'd reached Rhencullen. If I'd just settled myself and spread the catching up over the last two laps, I'm sure it would have been a different story, particularly as Joey's rear had gone off on his final lap giving him a lot of problems, but I was greedy and wanted it all there and then. People who'd watched me going through Rhencullen on that lap couldn't believe how fast I took it. I'd never been through there as quick as that in my life on a 250 and something had to happen which of course it did, at Quarry Bends just a few miles later.

Usually, I'd be knocking the 250 down into fifth gear going into that section just using half the road; I'd always wondered if you could take it in top and decided now was the time to try it, flat out at over 150mph, thinking I'd worry about slowing it down to get round the next left when I reached it. But the theory didn't work out.

For a long time, I thought that was the problem, just overcooking it going into the first comer, but it wasn't until some time later I found out from an eyewitness that the front end had kicked fractionally going over a white line in the middle of the road, as the tyre went onto the opposite adverse camber; the bike was heeled over as far as it would go and the front end broke away.

Another factor only floated out of my subconscious for the first time recently too; I remembered seeing hats flying off the heads of the crowd out of the comer of my eye as I was going into that section and the strange noise the crowd made when I lost control, then their total silence, even before I hit the road.

It was windy that day, gusting quite hard at times. I think hitting the white line and getting that little kick happened at the same time as a big gust of wind got under the side of the bike, an unlucky combination that took me off. My Arai helmet, Furygan leathers and Alpine Star gloves and boots did a superb job, but I was seriously beaten up going down that road, following the racing line thankfully, burning a big hole in the back of my leg and getting cut to bits all over. I was very, very lucky to survive.

When I finally came to a halt, I got up, which was a serious mistake because I could hardly stand with the pain, but the crowd was applauding me by then so I gritted my teeth and waved the only arm that would work at them and collapsed into the marshals' post in a heap. The leg was a serious injury, but I'd crushed my left hand badly between the bike and the kerb stones and it ballooned immediately.

It was nobody's fault but mine and all down to pride. I'd never ridden a 250 at that pace before in my life because this was the one race in the world I needed, I'd been so close so many times and wanted it for me, Honda and my sponsor. I was driven back to my hotel that Monday afternoon and was in terrible shape, with my left arm and shoulder not working at all. I remember the agony of Manda scrubbing the debris and gravel out of all the wounds as I sat in the bath, thinking how the rest of the week had suddenly taken on a very different complexion.

The doctors and Adrian, my physiotherapist did a superb job on me for the two days leading up to the Junior TT and I had to make a decision about whether to ride or not. If there was one race you'd pick me to win that week it would be the Junior and everyone had worked so hard around me I decided to give it a go and see how I got on in the early stages of the race.

The medical team had got a bit of power back into my left shoulder and arm and killed the pain with whatever they'd given me, but the hand was badly damaged, swollen and useless. There was just no way I could pull the clutch lever in, so it was pulled in for me on the start line, my hand wrapped around it and I let it go, changing gear without it for the rest of the race.

I caught and passed Jim Moodie quite quickly and was fourth at my first signal and kept going, but Ian Simpson knew I was injured and had seized his opportunity, putting in a superb record first lap from the standing start, to really put the pressure on me. At the end of lap one I was 9.8 seconds adrift and struggling, basically riding one handed.

I fought my way up to second place, knowing Simpson was closing behind me on the road, having only started three places back and he finally caught me on the last lap, steaming past quite easily on a power section coming over the mountain, with a bike a little bit faster than mine which surprised me. Pure pride got me back past him with a short circuit manoeuvre at Signpost Comer and I crossed the line in front, but I knew it was all over and took second place behind 'Simmo's' well deserved win.

He took the early lead on a Ducati this time in Friday's Production TT, which was reduced to two laps because of poor weather, a real sprint of a road race. I promised Honda's Dave Hancock on the start line that I'd win the race for them, but still handicapped, I rode the first part of the race really steadily, knowing I had to save some strength for the afternoon's Senior finale.

I got a 'P2 -5' (second place, five seconds behind) signal at Glen Helen though and after that I forgot about caution and went hell for leather. I was riding so hard the Fireblade was fighting me all the way until just after Ginger Hall, where there's a left hander before a jump; the Honda kicked and took off sideways in fourth gear, well over a hundred miles and hour and tried to highside me when it hit the deck.

I twisted the handlebars and fought it so hard the bike immediately fired the other way. It took so much strength to save it I physically bent the steel steering yokes which twisted the tops of the forks out of true, altering the steering by about thirty degrees. After that I was having to guess what angle to hold the bars at, coming in to land after the dozens of jumps there are on one lap of the TT course, but I was still absolutely flying and by Ramsey, halfway around the lap I'd pulled ten seconds back on Simpson's Ducati, leading the race by five seconds. I pulled further ahead by the end of the lap, crossing the line over eleven seconds in the lead.

Ian told me later that it was the huge pressure I'd put on him by making up ten seconds over less than half that lap in drying conditions that had beaten him psychologically, He couldn't match that sort of pace and I took revenge for my defeat in the Junior two days before.

I got off the Fireblade and onto the RC45 for a Senior race I just had to win. Unbeknown to me on the first lap, the scrutineers had tested the fuel left in the Fireblade's tank and all hell had broken loose, with Ducati lodging a formal protest about what we'd been using. We'd learnt our lesson on fuel the hard way at the North West a couple of years before and now always carried our own to every meeting, enough for all the bikes, practice and race day.

We'd done everything by the book in practice week, given the relevant officials information on what fuel we would be using, including samples. As the Fireblade had a standard, low compression engine, the high octane fuel we ran it on didn't give us an advantage anyway, exactly the reverse in fact as the engine couldn't burn the hydrocarbon rich fuel properly.

Ducati sensed a chance to have the result overturned and their bike elevated to first place though, with all the benefits in showroom sales that would bring them. For once, all the drama was in the paddock and not out with me at the front of the field, having started first on the road in the Senior, sporting the number one plate.

The rule book stated that only super unleaded fuel purchased from a public filling station was allowable for the Production race. We'd bought our super unleaded from the filling station at the Silverstone circuit, which is open to members of the public, a fact verified over the telephone during the inquiry.

Super unleaded wasn't available to the general public on the Isle of Man - there wasn't enough of a demand, so the rest of the field had been buying theirs from the TT paddock garage, which wasn't open to the public! We'd been open and honest, registered the fuel we were going to be using and proved we'd been abiding to the last letter of the rules. My team proved the case in my absence and the result stood.

Fuel was to play an important part in the Senior TT, still raging while the protest inquiry into the Production TT result was going on. Kawasaki's Bob Jackson had secretly fitted a thirty two litre fuel tank for the Senior which was within the rules, with a plan to only make one stop, while we ran into terrible refuelling problems. Joey Dunlop and Jim Moodie were now mounted on the 500cc Honda two stroke NSR Grand Prix bikes and Moodie led at Glen Helen on the first lap, with Michael Rutter in second, having started very fast at number two right behind me on the road, knowing I was handicapped both physically and mentally after Monday's huge accident. As a professional racer I'd always thought accidents like that didn't affect me, but I knew how lucky I'd been to get away without serious injury and I was treating Quarry Bends at least with more respect.

Rutter had taken the lead at Ramsey where I started to pile it on a bit over the mountain just ahead of him as I knew how important it was to ensure he didn't get a glimpse of me, to spur him on to catch me. I needn't have worried so much, because a build up of crankcase pressure spewed oil onto his rear tyre at Signpost Corner and he crashed unhurt, but out of the race. I flashed over the line at the end of that first lap 5.4 seconds up on Moodie's 500 and started to turn the screw then, letting the factory RC45 really have its head.

The flying Scot kept with me though and I'd only drawn away by a couple of seconds more when we came into the pits at the end of lap two. I'd no idea Bob Jackson was going to go straight through without a stop because of his huge fuel tank, and I was stunned when my first signal after the pit stop told me I was eight seconds behind him, in second place.

It didn't take me long to work out that he must have gone straight through and I wasn't too worried about the NSR either as I'd secretly set off behind Moodie on Wednesday race week's evening practice, catching him at Glen Vine. His two stroke was definitely slower than my RC45 and I knew it was never going to beat me unless I had a problem. Which is exactly what happened.

I edged further into the lead in the middle of the race and came into the pits at the end of lap four over eighteen seconds up on Moodie, but I lost much more than that at the stop. Our fuel nozzle had a slight leak which the crew had stopped by turning off the valve at the base of the overhead tank. They forgot to turn it on before I arrived.

The rear wheel change went beautifully well, but the fuel filler nozzle was in the tank for over twenty seconds before anyone realised nothing was coming out. This silly mistake cost me my lead and I went out again for the last two laps and I really let the RC45 go this time, completely flat to the top everywhere I could, praying I'd keep the last little bit of strength I had left in my arm. This RC45 was so quick I'd known it was going to be possible to break the 125mph barrier with it and this was just the situation I needed to go for it, similar to the Fogarty-Hislop showdown the last time the record had gone.

I pushed so hard on lap five from the standing start, I'd snatched back a 4.9 second lead and really got my head down for the final circuit. I came down Bray Hill through Douglas faster than I'd ever gone before in my life, deciding I was going to shatter the lap record, and shut my armchair critics up for good, one handed or not. I had the bike moving around on the slide beautifully, plenty of feel and I felt completely untouchable, putting in a scorching lap that I knew was going to sit in the record books for a long, long time until I got a huge moment at the Black Dub.

It was a big, big, uncontrolled slide sideways up the road coming around the right hander and it tried to highside me, feet off the pegs out of my seat, everything going wrong, but I caught it at the last second, the 750's front end slapping around and shaking its head for the rest of the corner, but I gassed her out of it, hung on, got it all under control and blasted on.

I'd saved it and the extra adrenalin rush made me feel more invincible until three comers or so later when I got a twenty second lead signal, I realised just how big a moment it was and asked myself whether I wanted to risk the win for the sake of the record. I also remembered that at the refuelling stop we'd cocked up, I'd watched the fuel just flood over the top of the safety foam block inside the tank and then subside a bit as the filler cap was rammed home and I was off and away.

We knew from all our calculations that the fuel had to cover the foam to be absolutely sure of the bike finishing. I'd lost a 250 TT like this before and decided there and then I was going to just try and get her home. I'd been revving the bike to fifteen thousand but I throttled her right back at Glen Helen, changing up at around twelve thousand revs after that, concentrating on saving fuel for the rest of the lap. It just shows how fast I'd been going up until then, because that lap was timed at 122.22mph; I reckon if I'd completed the lap at that early pace, the 125mph lap would have been completely blown to pieces.

I'd beaten Moodie by 8.7 seconds, the slide had been a big warning and made me cool it off, an excellent decision because at the end of the race, there wasn't enough fuel left in the tank to fill an egg cup, not even enough for the scrutineers to sample.

I'd given everything I'd got left physically and mentally for that win, but it was back to business the next weekend in the British 600 Super sport Championship at Brands Hatch, where I struggled with exhaustion and injury, part of the reality of a professional rider's life, finishing out of the points, but making up for it in the fifth round with a second place at Thruxton, a race led at one stage by an unknown teenager, one James Toseland.

Oulton Park's next round was halted early as I began my charge through the field to the front, the red flag rules dictating I got points for seventh place, even though I was further ahead on the stoppage lap, which I followed up with sixth place at Mallory Park and a crowd pleasing third at Knockhill, having fought through to the front from thirteenth place on the grid, to keep me in the Championship title race.

I knew my chances of repeating my clean sweep at the Ulster Grand Prix of the year before had gone when Michael Rutter destroyed the factory engine in his RC45 and took mine over for his British Championship campaign. The RC45 chassis I had now perfected was left without a motor, leaving me without a superbike for the Dundrod meeting. I was determined to make up for the disappointment of my lack of 250 results though and qualified in third place, managing second on my 600, which I qualified on in the superbike class too, ready to have a go in those races, knowing I'd have a chance particularly if it was wet.

The Ulster Grand Prix course is at quite a high altitude, which was affecting the sensitive 250, making it down a little bit on power. Carrying very high corner speed is the way to win races at Dundrod, with its series of fast 130 - 150mph corners and I was being held up by some other riders early on in the race.

I took the chance to pass several bikes at once coming up to Deer's Leap and came into the turn very quickly indeed, catching up to the back of a Belgian rider too fast and I pulled the bike over very hard at about 130mph in an effort to avoid him, the front tucked in and I was sliding down the road. I wasn't too worried scrubbing speed off like that, because there was nothing to hit and slides don't hurt you much but suddenly there was a terrific pain when another bike hit me from the rear, so hard it nipped the forks right off the front of it.

I'd chipped a bone in my elbow but much worse had a spinal injury, thought to be very serious at first and I had to lie flat and perfectly still in the hospital bed for quite a few days. It gave me plenty of time to try and work out how quickly I could get back to the British Supersport Championship, but it wasn't long before we worked out I'd stretched my knee ligaments quite badly too, enough to put me out for the rest of the season with a plaster cast on the leg for six weeks, ending my hopes of finally landing a British Championship.

It gave me time to reflect on a very successful year; I'd followed up my four Isle of Man wins in 1996 with a TT hat trick, equalling Steve Hislop's record of eleven TT wins, just three behind Mike Hailwood in the list of all time winners, while Joey was still adding to his, way out in front.

I'd been so near to that elusive 125mph record on the best bike Honda had ever given me too, but we were already planning our 1998 campaign as I'd now been given the most important job Honda had ever asked me to do. My price was a return to the British Superbike Championship on the ultimate racing motorcycle, a two wheeled missile that was to be hand built for me by HRC in Japan, to my exact specification.

The 1998 Isle of Man TT meeting was to be an important part of Honda's global fiftieth anniversary celebrations. With so many dignitaries from Japan and other parts of the world expected to fly in to the home of road racing for the occasion, victory in the Formula One and Senior TT had become absolutely mandatory. The ultimate responsibility for these wins, the absolute bare minimum acceptable fell on the shoulders of Honda Britain and me.

Our plans began many months before, regarding the equipment we were to receive from HRC. They were to build me a machine from the ground up, to my exact requirements, right down to the gear ratios which I specified myself. After so many years of riding lesser equipment, finally I was to receive the ultimate accolade from Japan.

Towards the end of 1997 I was back in the saddle, taking second place in the Macau Grand Prix on Joe Millar's V4 Yamaha, pleased to have done so well after such a lengthy lay off. Flying home to begin preparation for 1998, I was so excited at my chance of returning to the short circuit superbike scene. This was my opportunity to finally lay the ghost of the frustrating two years I'd spent battling superior superbike machinery in the British Supercup. Not only was this brand new factory RC45, a priceless jewel, being built just for me to take to victory on the Isle of Man in June, but Tadao Baba, creator of the Honda Fireblade was personally blueprinting a hand made engine, using parts individually selected from the production line, the motor being built to the finest tolerances for my Production TT machine. All this investment was being made to leave no doubt that I had the very best tool for the Formula One and Senior TT and to ensure I had the best possible chance of fighting off the threat of Yamaha's big bore 1,000cc R1 in the Production race.

But it quickly became apparent that HRC were not going to be able to deliver my RC45 in time to prepare for the start of the British Superbike Championship season, even though frustratingly, the team and facilities were all in place. I overcame my disappointment and concentrated on dialling myself in, ready for the critically important job I had to do on the roads that year, while aiming at winning the British 600 Supersport Championship that had continued to elude me.

An amazingly hot March opening round at Brands Hatch caught most of the field out and I only picked up a single Championship point because of the bike overheating in the mid-summer conditions, losing a huge amount of power. Trick oversized radiators I had manufactured in Austria solved that problem and we were back to form in the second round at Oulton Park with a cracking third place.

The Championship battle then moved to Thruxton during the May Bank Holiday weekend, where the abrasive Wiltshire track was as demanding on tyres as ever. We worked hard with Michelin to get the perfect combination for Saturday's practice sessions and we made good progress, taking pole position towards the end of Sunday's final qualifying. We experimented further with different compounds and lost first place in the dying moments, but I was happy, although still undecided as to rear race tyre choice.

I ended up choosing a very hard compound for the race and got away well from the front row, taking things steady in fourth place working to get enough heat into the tyre. My plan was to stay in touch with the front runners and then mount an assault in the second half of the race, when my rear tyre would be up to working temperature and coming into its own, whereas the leaders should be slowing their pace, having already had the best performance from their rubber.

Coming into the chicane on lap three I opened the throttle and the next thing I knew I was twenty foot up in the air, crashing back down onto the tarmac at around eighty miles an hour and the pain in my back was so intense I knew something was terribly wrong.

No specialists were on duty in Winchester General Hospital on that Bank Holiday Monday, but the expressions on everyone's face who'd seen the X-rays were enough to tell me it wasn't particularly good news. Three vertebrae at the base of my spine were damaged; one crushed, one broken and the most serious, one moved a lot sideways, an exacerbation of the damage I'd done at the Ulster Grand Prix the year before. I wasn't allowed to move before a specialist examined me. Very scary indeed. There's never a good time to get hurt, but this was a bad injury, just when I needed it least, with the North West 200 only two weeks away.

I didn't have a manager to take on the burden of running the team and there was nothing for it but to remain positive and keep moving forward. Manda took a week off her school teaching duties to be at my bedside; I picked up my mobile phone and tried to keep everything together, flat on my back. The very next day after the accident, the shipment from HRC Japan arrived at our Louth workshops, containing one absolute work of art - my priceless hand built RC45, another endurance RC45 rolling chassis from Honda France, plus four brand new full factory 'sprint' specification engines, which are only designed to run at race speeds for a maximum of two hours.

Technician Dennis Willey immediately set about building up the Elf France bike, being joined by the Japanese specialist who'd hand built the brand new one and followed it to England, flying halfway around the world to make sure everything was in perfect order for me to take it to the victory it deserved.

Meanwhile, my confidence in what the National Health Service could offer me on a busy Bank Holiday weekend wasn't improved by the fact that a specialist didn't turn up for three days. During this time I had no alternative than to lie flat on my back, worrying about what was wrong and whether I'd be able to ride at the North West.

My morale wasn't helped by the fact that the poor woman in the bed opposite me, who had come in for a hip replacement, had been in a coma for months. A young chap in the next ward who'd been in a bike accident hadn't been getting any attention for ten weeks and no one seemed to have a clue what was going on.

I plotted my escape with the collusion of an Irish physiotherapist, who strapped me up and in intense pain I managed to get to the back seats of my car outside and Manda drove me to the workshops in Louth. I remember every tiny bump of that four hour journey.

And there it was, surrounded by security, no photographers allowed. I couldn't believe I was seeing this exquisite equipment in the physical condition I was in. The superbike I had always wanted was now right there in front of me, even with the luxury of spare engines - I had a Japanese technician who knew the thing back to front, Dennis Willey and the rest of my team on hand, well ahead of our preparation and I could hardly stand up because of the pain I was in.

To make matters worse for Honda, my team was under instruction to prepare the French based bike for Joey Dunlop. The trouble was he'd also crashed (at the Tandragee 100) just a couple of weeks before, meaning Honda's two top road racers were amongst the walking wounded leading up to the TT, where the heavyweight top brass of Honda from around the world would be gathering in less than a month's time.

I travelled back to Northern Ireland, determined to do my very best to try and recover enough from the injury to race, knowing in my heart there was no way in the world I was going to be able to compete at the North West 200. I felt in much safer hands now I could seek the expert advice of my medical guru Fred McSorley. Working with Mr Fee and Mr Nicholas, two expert consultants, these doctors confirmed my worst fears; the vertebra that had been moved further sideways during my Thruxton crash was now endangering the safety of the spinal cord. While I was in no immediate danger, the consequences of one more crash could be extremely serious, but as luck would have it, a temporary solution presented itself at about the same time.

The V&M team had just parted company with Honda, leaving Michael Rutter and Ian Simpson without a 600 ride. It took a lot of organising, but we managed to get them, my race bikes and team to the North West 200 grid for the Supersport 600 race and Simpson won with Rutter in third place, both riders agreeing they were the best 600 machines they had ever ridden.

They're both superb riders, but we only had one Production bike and in the end it went to Rutter. I spent a long time working with Michael before the start, really firing him up for the win up to the very last minute on the grid itself, driving it into him how important it was for Honda and us to beat the big threat of the Yamaha R1. Michael did the job in the end and took a fighting win with an excellent move, squeezing out Yamaha man David Jeffries on the very last corner. Job done.

I stayed in Northern Ireland for the run up to the TT under the intensive care of my doctor, specialist and physiotherapists, but as the days ticked away to practice week it became clearer that I was out of time, the doctors' prognosis was that I needed at least six months to recover.

The TT is not something you take on carrying a mild injury, let alone a major spinal problem and the media speculation about my fitness really put the spotlight on me. The bottom line was I knew I wouldn't be able to pass the strict medical examination which was going to be tougher than usual because of the press reports. I knew deep down it was going to be a big struggle to race, but with so much at stake, I didn't want to give up until the last possible moment. It was with a heavy heart I finally withdrew my entry.

I explained the situation to Honda's Dave Hancock who was disappointed but said if I couldn't win the races myself, could I help the other riders perform to their best ability? I readily agreed and his orders were to do whatever I had to do to get the wins. My continuing management job began from the moment our team arrived on the island, to find the temporary garages in a complete mess and inhabited by other members of the Honda team who were occupying the whole of the huge amount of space available.

I didn't sleep for three days. The team and I worked non stop all through the night, reorganising the space allocation within the workshop area, painting the whole complex and finally getting our surroundings into some sort of order. My two winning CBR600s and the two priceless RC45 superbikes were allocated to Michael Rutter and Ian Simpson. Rutter couldn't believe how good the RC45 was after we'd fine tuned it during practice week and neither could Ian Simpson. They were so very lucky to have the chance to ride machinery of that excellence, the best superbikes they had ever ridden, or ever will for that matter.

The team prepared the bikes with meticulous detail under my direction and they didn't let us down. Simpson and Rutter did the job, coming home first and second in the Formula One race. To say I was devastated not to be able to take my bike to victory for myself and Honda is the

190

understatement of my life, but injuries are a fact of racing life and I took comfort in the fact that we'd orchestrated the win from behind the scenes.

I'd always managed a team of course - mine! - for my whole career, so the only really new thing for me was ensuring my riders had everything they needed and then motivating them to get the best result they were capable of achieving. These were factory superbikes designed for tracks and they weren't handling at all well in early practice. The technicians and I worked very hard with Simpson and Rutter and using all my experience and expertise, sent them out again and again in the practice sessions with new settings, until we got both riders very happy with their bikes.

Sitting in a television commentary box, airing my views to the world at large during the Junior TT was a totally new experience. I'd much rather have been out on the track on one of my Motorcycle City CBR600s and it was hard containing my excitement as 'my boys' brought them home first and second in the Junior TT, completely dominating a magnificent race.

I'm embarrassed to confess that I ignored Mr Baba's instructions for the Production TT and put far more Shell Advance engine oil in the Fire blade than he specified. He wanted to minimise the power sapping 'drag' that oil costs any engine. However, I wanted to be sure the motor got all the protection it needed over the jumps of the tough TT course, where I was afraid gravity and 'g' forces might lead to engine damage if the oil level wasn't high enough.

It was academic in the end as Mr Baba's second bike won the race and Honda's 100th TT in the hands of Jim Moodie as on this occasion, I failed to get Rutter's mind off the Senior TT he so desperately wanted to win in the afternoon. He had suffered some bad luck in losing the Formula One race to Ian Simpson a week before after leading it for so long and was terribly disappointed about it. I think he was determined to make up for it in the Senior and was saving his best effort for his second race of the day.

If it was me, I wouldn't have been thinking about the Senior until I'd got that race won; it's a long week on the Isle of Man and you have to discipline yourself to take each race one by one. If you concentrate on just one, particularly the later races and you don't succeed, then suddenly you're left with nothing. In fact Michael was terribly unlucky to pick up a puncture in the Senior that afternoon and lost out again.

Jim Moodie had only ridden at the North West 200 and the TT that year and as I had now decided to listen to my doctor's advice and not race for the rest of season, we agreed that he would ride my CBR600 Honda in the remaining rounds of the British 600 Supersport Championship. He did a terrific job for us, winning at Knockhill, plus a third at Silverstone being two highlights of a string of excellent results, ending the season fifth in the Championship. It was a really good performance from him and our team as he hadn't even ridden in the first half of the season.

As I was still injured, I arranged for him to ride for Joe Millar in the Macau Grand Prix at the end of the season as a reward for his hard work and it was on the roads and beaches of Thailand I removed the support corset I'd been wearing all summer and started light training and running with Jim, on the long road back to race fitness.

12

I didn't get my usual Honda invitation to England's International Motorcycle Show at the NEC at the end of 1998 which was worrying. There had been some senior personnel changes in the Company and when I finally got to speak to the decision makers, all they could commit to for 1999 was support for another 600 super sport campaign. Honda had appointed a new domestic racing manager who had some new ideas and I was told there was no 750 superbike for Michael Rutter or me to ride, because the only two available bikes had been allocated to Jim Moodie and Ian Simpson.

It was good to see Jim get the offer and I certainly didn't hold it against him; I was pleased to have helped him get back on the pace and reestablish his career, as he'd been out in the wilderness for a couple of seasons. I think they didn't actually believe I was going to be able to ride again, but I explained to Honda that I was going to be fit and ready for the season. The trouble was there just wasn't another superbike available by then so it left me in a difficult position. I was still fiercely loyal to Honda but couldn't consider just taking a 600 to the North West and the TT, I obviously had to have a superbike too.

For the first time in over a decade I found myself looking for a bike capable of beating a Honda. I was privileged to receive offers from so many individual sponsors, businesses and four major motorcycle manufacturers for equipment and funding to race in the British Championships, the North West 200 and the Isle of Man. I'd like to take this opportunity to thank all of them.

My sponsors Motorcycle City continued to support me and we quickly reached agreement together with Yamaha to assist me with equipment. I was disappointed but not worried at losing my job with Honda because I knew Yamaha's big 1,000cc R1 was a magnificent weapon which nobody had yet used to its full potential.

My sponsors took two of them and a pair of R6's out of their showroom stock and we set about preparing the two 600s for the British Championship, plus one R1 in Production trim and the second to develop as our superbike. We christened this awesome machine the 'F1R1' in anticipation of a successful 1999 Formula One TT. A budget was set and agreed to run the team until the end of TT fortnight, when I felt it was probable I'd announce my retirement and concentrate on developing and expanding the new avenues which had started to open up for me.

My whole professional life was undergoing quite a big change then as Motorcycle City wanted to open a specialist Performance Centre for their customers, but were struggling to find management with the right expertise. I'd always been disappointed with quality standards in the technical side of the retail industry and felt I could make a big difference in this area.

I thought long and hard about my future and worked out a deal with them, which involved me launching the new Performance Centre venture using my expertise and track knowledge for the benefit of the company's road going customers.

We nearly forgot about racing for a month or so as I focussed all my energies on developing the new operation for my employers, full of enthusiasm and ideas for this excellent new venture. Apart from the performance parts and tuning side of the business, I was quickly finding that so many customers were delighted to have someone to spend ten minutes with them, who was capable of actually explaining how their bikes worked and getting their chassis and suspension set up properly for them.

It was good for me too, I was really pleased to be giving something back to motorcyclists, whether they even knew me or not, but particularly pleased if I could help out one of my fans and really make a difference to their knowledge and enjoyment of their bike out on the road. The experience started to suck me into the motorcycle business; I was surprised to have found a job that was diverting my attention from the world I'd been in for so long.

My first competitive ride on a Yamaha R1 was on what felt like a winter's day at Cadwell Park in March, in the opening round of the British

Sports Production Championship. In the first few laps of practice I immediately felt the potential of this brilliant machine.

I started from the back of the grid and just eased myself into the wet race, gradually upping the pace and was very pleased to find myself in sixth place in no time at all after such a long lay off. Just down the road from the circuit in our race workshops at Louth, we were putting the finishing touches to our 'F1R1', which had received the full Tony Scott tuning treatment and, along with 41mm flat slide carburettors, remapped ignition, Micron exhaust, a specially made ram-air system and other development work was spitting out over 170bhp at the back wheel.

State of the art Brembos, Ohlins forks and suspension plus lots of carbon fibre, with an oversize fuel tank and quick release rear wheel system had produced an absolute missile of a bike that we took to the Tandragee 100 in May, my 'home' course, where I hadn't raced for seven years.

It was great to be back in front of an enthusiastic crowd and I led the first superbike race from James Courtney, who nipped through for the win after I overshot the final corner, but I made sure of the second superbike event. It was the first time I'd ridden a Yamaha to victory in twelve years.

Two days later the team arrived at Donington Park for round two of the Sports Production Championship, a race we were really using as a final shakedown test before the North West 200 meeting. All my life May Days have been bad luck for me. In 1987 I blew my 250 Rotax to pieces, wrote off my new 125 Honda and my car on the way home from the May Day meeting, nearly killing myself driving off the side of a road, rolling down some banking and ending up upside down.

I'd broken my back at Thruxton and destroyed my 1998 season on May Day again and now on this May Day, I fell at Donington's Goddards Bend at the end of a really fast qualifying lap. The idea had been to go out and take it easy but I'd got a bit excited from going so well on the Yamaha without really trying and went for a hot lap which was pole without a shadow of a doubt, then a slower rider cut right across me with only a few yards to go to the line and we both went flying.

I landed on my long abused left shoulder and pushed the blade backwards, stretching the muscles. I was sore but went out in the next day's face thinking it was one of those injuries that would go away and most unusually for me, pulled out of the race, something I can't ever remember having done before through injury. I was losing power and feeling in my left arm badly enough to prevent me riding the bike safely.

The North West was still two weeks away and in a repeat of the previous year I went home for intensive treatment and physiotherapy in an attempt to get the injury better for the major road races we were so keen to win. The x-rays showed I'd cracked two ribs at the back in addition to the ligament and soft tissue damage in my shoulder and the medical team did a terrific job with physiotherapy work and manipulation to get rid of the pain.

In practice for the North West though it was clear my left arm didn't have the strength to properly control the massive power of the new superbike, so I didn't worry too much about qualifying, finishing fourth on the grid with my Yamaha R6, starting the first superbike race in sixth place from the second row of the grid. I was in terrible pain on the big bike and in real trouble on the brakes, but even so I was catching the leading group of three riders on the final lap and I think if there'd been one more circuit to go I might have got amongst them, but I finished fourth which was an amazing effort under the circumstances.

I couldn't even turn the nimble R6 now like I wanted to in the 600 race, which was a three way duel between Jim Moodie, David Jeffries and me. I was really suffering on the coast road which is where you do all the winning at the North West, twisting and turning through that long section. The other places where you can get an advantage on the brakes are going into the Metropole and the last chicane. With my left arm just not working at all in the closing stages, I lost the race by a whisker at the chicane to David Jeffries who was now showing his full road racing potential.

I felt I was back to the top of my form and riding skills, but I was handicapped so badly by this injury and apart from the Tandragee 100 win, we hadn't won anything of substance all year, including the North West, with only one race to go. I had so much determination inside me to get a win for Yamaha and my team and all our sponsors who'd put so much faith and investment in me, that I started the final and main event of the day as hard as I could.

At the new, very fast section coming out of the roundabout at Portstewart you have to manhandle your bike a bit under acceleration to get the front end light going over the rise where the road twists a bit. It was here on the second lap that I hauled the big F1R1 over and something snapped in my back.

It felt like a carving knife had gone straight through me, I knew something big had snapped inside and the pain that washed over me was so intense I nearly fainted on the bike, knowing I was going to have to stop. I rested my head on the tank and just lay there on the straight, taking the power off the bike quite a bit, just watching the road rush underneath me, knowing I was badly hurt this time, wondering if one of the cracked ribs had broken in two.

Ian Duffus came past and I felt quite relaxed about it all, knowing I had to let him go and pull into the pits, but I realised Duffus didn't seem to be getting away much even though I'd knocked off my pace a lot. I sat behind him in agony for a couple of laps, letting him do all the work and somehow I got past him at the last chicane to snatch third in so much pain I didn't know what to do with myself. I had to be helped off the bike.

I was convinced there must have been a bone visibly displaced in my upper back and was amazed when the team told me there wasn't. It was just a culmination of so many years of abusing that shoulder, the Donington Park accident and the effort of controlling our wild Yamaha F1R1. The shoulder blade had finally torn itself completely away from the muscle group holding it in place; the doctors said the healing process would be very slow before it returned to full strength, but I only had two weeks before I was due to defend my TT titles.

I had faith and genuinely believed I could fix this injury in time and with the benefit of superb treatment back home again, got all the movement back in the shoulder and the arm. No one could believe how much progress we'd made and I arrived on the island believing I was in with a chance. It was all hopeless of course. I just didn't have anywhere near the strength to wrestle 170bhp of superbike around the mountain course, holding it over jumps as we flew through the air at 150mph, braking from 190mph into tight corners - there was just no way it was going to be possible, but I tried.

Practice week was wet - sessions were cancelled or shortened - and I knew I could only risk single laps in an attempt to protect the injury and it wasn't giving us enough time to get the superbike handling anything like I needed. We'd had three and a half inch wheels made for the bike, whereas I usually used a three and three quarter size which spread the front tyre a bit for road racing, giving me a bigger contact patch and more stability at high speed, and this was causing a problem.

There was nothing wrong with the Production bike or the 600, I was second quickest on the rocketship R6 at 118.82mph from a standing start and led Production qualifying with a 118.27mph lap. It was the superbike we were struggling to master, but the pain and lack of practice time was made worse by the fact that I was only able to ride the bike with one arm, so we weren't getting a true feel of things - it was impossible setting up a brand new bike for the TT course under such limitations. The frustrating thing was I knew the bike was more than capable of winning, it just needed perfecting that's all, but I wasn't physically capable of doing it.

We tried to make it more comfortable for me by setting the rear suspension soft on the spring and high on the damping to make it work more and take some of the hardness out of it and that was what let us down in the Formula One race. The setup overworked the damping in the first two laps and it burst a seal, losing all the gas out of the cylinder and I remained in the pits at the first stop.

I was so weak in the Junior race and terribly confused as to what was going on, why I couldn't work out what the problem was. We spent ages in the pit stop trying to make the suspension better for me and I went back out finally finishing seventh, but desperately depressed, knowing it was becoming too dangerous to carry on.

In the early evening open practice session following the Junior, I took the superbike out for a final practice before Friday's Senior TT and I just couldn't control the bike on the 195 mph corners. I confessed to the team about the amount of pain I was in and it didn't take much soul searching to decide discretion was going to be the better part of valour for our 1999 TT campaign and we decided to withdraw from Friday's Production and Senior races.

We were all so tired after such a tough fortnight; the team packed up on Thursday evening and caught the late ferry back to the mainland with most of the equipment on board, leaving technician Jim McMahon to clear the rest of the garage and follow on behind with the Production R1 and remaining spares the next day.

Usually I'd have an early night before a race so I took the opportunity for once to have a couple of beers with my wife and sponsors and got to bed about midnight. My sleep was troubled though and I woke up at about 3am, wondering if it really was my fault that I couldn't get the big F1R1 to work on the island - ok, I was thinking, my arm was totally useless and the rear shock had gone off in the Formula 1 race, but even so, usually I'd be able to ride through those sorts of problems for some sort of a result.

We'd been working so hard testing at Jurby (airfield) every night until dark; we'd tried '98 superbike forks, '99 Ohlins, standard, standard with modified internals - different head settings, different off-sets, every suspension setting, every single possible thing and still nothing worked. We ended up blaming me and the arm, but the Production bike had handled perfectly from the moment we arrived. We'd had hot laps of 118 and 119 mph from standing starts - it was basically the same bike - so what was wrong?

I couldn't sleep thinking about it all until around dawn, I finally worked out it had to be the profile of the superbike's front slick. I'd used the same tyre for three years but remembered it had been redesigned the year before. Dennis Willey and the team had arrived back in Louth by then and I rang him up at 5am to see if it was possible for us to race in the Production TT with what the team had left behind. I asked him to nip down to the workshop to check on some tyre profiles to see if I was right and got Jim McMahon out of bed, who rushed to the garage to prepare the Production R1 to race.

My sponsor's representative was very surprised when I woke him up so early to discuss the prospect of racing in the Production TT. I gave him five minutes to join me for a dawn lap of the course in my car to talk it all through, while checking the roads for damp patches, knowing I'd be in serious trouble trying to save a slide with my arm so useless. I was speaking to Dennis Willey on my mobile phone during the lap, who'd arrived at the workshop and confirmed my theory about the tyre profiles, using some cardboard templates.

It was so frustrating to work out at the end of race week that it wasn't just my arm but the superbike's tyre profile that was a big problem. Manda wasn't at all impressed with the idea of me racing, being very worried about my safety. I was shattered and tired and injured but she eventually agreed to support me and I decided to race, knowing I couldn't leave the island without a final attempt at a podium finish, no matter how slim the chances.

I have to thank Adrian, my Isle of Man physiotherapist who has done so much work with me during TT fortnight. He strapped up my shoulder again ready for the start and I decided to see how I felt at my first signal point at Glen Helen and pull out then or carry on, depending on my position.

With a hastily organised volunteer pit crew I blasted away down Bray Hill and into the race and was third at Glen Helen, so I hung in there and kept going, riding as safely as I could and the luck that had deserted our team all season turned on the final lap.

I was lying fourth just a few seconds behind Ian Duffus, who ran out of petrol less than a mile from the finish and I salvaged our pride with a one-armed third place, for me, one of the best rides and most satisfying results of my whole career.

After the race was all over I was helping to load the last truck to go home and I was holding the Yamaha with my injured arm and it just fell over; I hadn't felt it go at all. Further medical tests showed that I'd stretched all the nerves in the whole arm, meaning I hadn't been able to feel anything properly since the North West. The lack of sensation continued for some weeks after that; I noticed I was dropping lots of cups and other things from my left hand, which was numb for most of the time. That was why the toughest set up job on the F1R1 had been impossible; mentally I could see it all, but I just couldn't sense what the bike was doing through my left arm, and 'feel' is everything on a race bike.

Some people get a reward just from finishing, but I'd always raced to win and if you do that, second or third is only a consolation - beyond that you're nowhere. That feeling was growing inside me. I started my racing career on a Yamaha and was now beginning to wonder whether it had just ended on another. It was becoming so frustrating not being able to give of my best due to injury and not being able to achieve my goals.

I was definitely at a big crossroads in my life, wondering which way to go. I'd walked away a winner from the TT in 1997, but not like I planned to, so in 1998 I wanted to win all of the four races I was in and then go home, but that didn't happen because of injury.

In 1999 I went back again to try and make this final achievement, but didn't quite have the right preparation this time, plus I was injured big time again, before I even started. It still makes me want to go and finish the job off properly, but I don't think that will ever happen again now, I'm thinking far too sensibly.

I've got a wonderful wife, too good a job, a nice house and I don't want to lose all that. I've now realised there's only one way to go from winning four TTs in a week and that's down - in reality whatever you'd do after that, you wouldn't ever match such achievements.

I've still got the urge and the will to do it and I can still ride a bike, but getting switched into that mode, that place I have to get to when I'm winning, turns me into a totally different person to the man sitting here right now. That state of mind, the place I've been lucky enough to be able to get to, is the difference between winners and losers. That mental ability is what enabled me to come back from my 1990 Temple 100 crash to win a tough superbike race five weeks later, pain free once I was riding, purely with the power of my mind.

Even after that big crash, when I came round in hospital seriously hurt and temporarily blinded, I never thought about stopping - I'd survived hadn't I? And I just wanted to get back out there on the track with the bike and start winning again. I just couldn't walk away a loser and that's why I'm struggling now to stop.

You can't let a serious accident like that get to you. I just told myself to get on with the job and that if it happened, it happened, but really deep down I just blacked it out, convincing myself I was indestructible and that it never would. I was seriously smashed up in my accident in the Lightweight TT in 1997 on my 250 too, but came back in Wednesday's Junior to nearly win. I was just hurting too much then to overcome Ian Simpson who was riding really well, but just one day's preparation got me in good enough shape for Friday, when I beat everyone twice, fair and square.

A lot of people talk about preparing for days before a race, but I couldn't ever do that and the reason's very simple. When you start thinking and working like that, you use up energy because you're in a different zone; once you start doing that, you're burnt out even before the race has started. And also of course I was the rider, the manager, the motivator, the organiser, so if I started preparing to ride two hours before the race I might not have got everything done.

There were always sponsors to look after too, so I was keeping busy five minutes until I was due on the bike, the last to arrive and the last to get ready. When I finally put on my helmet, everything we'd set out to be done was done and only then was I ready to switch into race mode and think about nothing else.

The state of mind I get into when I'm winning is way beyond anything else, such a dangerous level of concentration you can do yourself harm thinking like that before you even got on the bike, it's something I have to reserve just for the motorcycle.

From early on in my career, in the build up to the start of a race I seemed to go into a sort of trance on the grid and focus on the other riders one by one with my eyes. I thought I was just weighing them up, looking at them, but I was doing more than that, beating a lot of them there and then, before the race had even started. I knew I was doing something but I didn't know what. That of course is what a boxer does when confronting an opponent in the ring before the fight. The riders who know me well can't believe it's the same person who's so friendly and helping them out in the paddock when they come across the mean man riding the motorbike - it isn't the same person they know.

I started to read as much as I could about psychology in 1992, so many books you wouldn't believe it and I started working with sports psychologists in 1996, the same group that helped Steve Collins win his fights with Chris Eubank. Even though we're the boss, very few people control their minds like they should. It is possible to control the mind and the mind controls the body.

The ability I've developed to do that has helped in so many ways. I've learnt how to totally relax and I mean totally, and I also have the ability to mend really quickly. I can recover from injuries, genuinely heal in remarkable time, by lying still for hours and hours, focussing all the power of my mind and body into the injury.

You can't do anything else because the power you need to fix the problem is so great, but I can tell you it works. You can use the same power in so many ways; in business, your personal life, anything. The sports psychology gave me a real boost just before my great successes of 1996 and 1997, but it did start to scare me too. My mind was completely set, nothing or nobody was going to beat me at the TT and that was it, I was going to win four out of four. Looking back, I now realise those two big 1997 crashes on my 250 were warnings.

I'd lost that time in the pits at the TT in 1997 and I crashed going overboard because the bike wasn't quite fast enough, it wasn't set up just right, but in my mind I was going to make up for it. I was up against some good people though - Joey Dunlop's a great rider and I paid the price, very nearly the ultimate price for being too confident. You don't realise it at the time, but my wife Manda could see what was happening long before I did and told me of her concerns.

I really wanted to get Bell and Howell, my new 250 sponsors a result but the bike just wasn't right, we hadn't had enough trick time to get the thing set up properly and I crashed heavily at the Ulster Grand Prix too, another warning and I started to tone it down a bit after that.

I really believe I helped talk Michael Rutter into winning that brilliant Production race on the Honda Fireblade at the North West 200 in 1998. With Yamaha having just launched the much faster R1, it was so important for us to win that race for the sponsors, but most importantly for Honda. I think I helped Michael a lot with psychology that day.

The level of concentration and discipline modern World Superbike and Grand Prix riders have to go to now is so high, you just cannot ride road races at that level and survive. Up until 1999, my last year of riding I've been in control of that, right to the very, very edge and then stopped it - that's why I did succeed over a lot of people - and I've been lucky.

In 1997 I'd been doing more and more track riding on the English short circuit scene and pushing things to the limit and I did go over that edge, I think. In many ways it made it easy going back to road racing because no one else was pushing it that hard.

A lot of riders have lost their lives in the sport, Simon Beck being one of them. I was only minutes behind him when he crashed in practice for the 1999 TT on the factory RC45 he'd taken over from an injured Ian Simpson.

I knew Simon was badly hurt as soon as I saw him at the thirty-third, which you take at about 150mph coming down into fifth gear on a big bike. It's difficult there, two corners you make into one and you have to judge where to get the gas on, because you're right over on the edge of the road at the exit and it's so easy to over do it at that point. The TT is a challenging place to go and compete, but I wouldn't stop anyone going because it's such a brilliant feeling to race there, particularly if you're lucky enough to do well.

Simon had just done a 120mph lap and I'd been chatting to him, giving him a little bit of advice about the RC45 in fact, just before he went out again on that fateful lap. I'd seen the thin black line get thicker and thicker as it went up the road and then Simon. His passing did affect me. I talked to a lot of people about it after the racing was over and started to think for the first time in my life about whether I should continue racing. For the first time in my life I realised I was becoming detached from the world I'd been a part of for so long.

He was a good friend, we'd been to Macau together and partied there; he'd really helped me out by lending me some wheels for my R1 at the TT and when I was stuck at the North West, even though I was going to be tough opposition. He was someone you could rely on if you needed help and that's the measure of a good man.

How lucky I've been to survive such big warnings. They've happened early enough for me to realise I've got too sensible to go to that level of racing now and recognise what the signals are, that it's time for me to get out - now. People talk about riding the TT at ninety or ninety five percent, but those riders don't win, it's a hundred percent or nothing and that's the only way I know how to ride, I can't adjust my style to suit particular situations like the amazing Joey Dunlop, it's all or nothing and that's it.

As technology advances, everything's getting so sensitive, machinery, suspension, countless production tyre compounds that let you choose one that will only last a certain distance and of course everything's more powerful. Race bikes used to be unusable below a certain number of revs, but it's different now with all the recent developments and you can ride them like road bikes, with power everywhere, from as low down as you like. In fact I never rode anything as powerful as my 1999 F1R1 Yamaha, lots of grunt from as low as two thousand revs.

The downside of that massive power is that the tiniest little flick of the throttle can send you off it in a flash - it's a really powerful bike - yet another reason for having to be at the absolute height of my powers to race it. It's a great shame I wasn't physically up to riding it to its full potential.

I'm constantly receiving offers from sponsors, teams and owners. We've actually still got our 1999 'F1R1' Yamaha and I have never stopped thinking about using it to finish the job properly and go out in style; maybe just race at the Tandragee 100, the North West and the TT, but that's just another recipe for disaster.

I can't get my mind to where it needs to be to survive and win on those courses and I've realised I'm kidding myself to think I can. The process of winning those races begins the year before, with meticulous preparation, physical and mental training over the winter and hard practice and racing in the early season, building and sharpening all the time.

Only then is it possible to enjoy the privilege of reaching that place in my mind, that highest level of all when the bike is just an extension of me, part of my body and I'm feeling every single bit of it moving around beneath me. So, if I can't go and do it properly, then we'll not be going. And that's the end of it.

Mine's a simple story and I hope you've enjoyed it; winning motorcycle races at the highest level, on the toughest courses in the world is just the greatest feeling there is not only afterwards but while you're doing it. And winning is the hardest thing in the world to do, that's why it's the ultimate thrill, why so much dedication, money and effort goes into it, from so many people all over the world.

I've had the privilege of working with the very best of those people with equipment good enough to get the job done and we've managed to conjure up that magical combination with the luck we needed too, in the right place, at the right time. I count myself one of the luckiest men alive to have had all that and that's how I'm going to stay.

Alive and happy and retired.

Phillip McCallen - Race Results Index

1986 - Road Races
(excluding Southern Ireland)
Tandragee 100
	TZ125 Yamaha	4th
	(1st in Group B)	

Killinchy 150
	TZ125 Yamaha	7th
	(1st in Group B)	

Temple 100
	TZ125 Yamaha	DNF

Mid-Antrim 150
	TZ125 Yamaha	8th

Carrowdore 100
	TZ125 Yamaha	8th

1986 - Short Circuits
(excluding Southern Ireland)
Aghadowey
In Heat	TZ125 Yamaha	11th
In Final	TZ125 Yamaha	9th

Kirkistown
In Heat	TZ125 Yamaha	8th
In Final	TZ125 Yamaha	14th

Nutts Corner
In Heat	TZ125 Yamaha	3rd
In Final	TZ125 Yamaha	9th

Nutts Corner
In Heat	TZ125 Yamaha	11th

Nutts Corner
In Heat	TZ125 Yamaha	5th
In Final	TZ125 Yamaha	8th

Nutts Corner
In Heat	RS125 Honda	5th

Kirkistown
In Heat	RS125 Honda	7th
In Final	RS125 Honda	10th

Kirkistown
In Heat	250 Rotax	11th

1987 - Road Races
Tandragee 100
	RS125 Honda	2nd
	250 Rotax	5th

Cookstown 100
	RS125 Honda	2nd
	250 Rotax	1st

Killinchy 150
	RS125 Honda	2nd
	250 Rotax	5th

Skerries	RS125 Honda	3rd
	250 Rotax	7th

Temple 100	RS125 Honda	1st
	250 Rotax	6th

Fore	RS125 Honda	1st
	250 Rotax	4th

Ulster Grand Prix 250/350
	250 Rotax	18th

Mid-Antrim 150
	RS125 Honda	3rd
	250 Rotax	DNF

Carrowdore 100
	RS125 Honda	1st
	250 Rotax	2nd

Killalane	RS125 Honda	1st
	250 Rotax	4th

1987 - Road Racing Championship Results

Irish 125 Championship	Joint 1st
Irish 250 Championship	1st
Ulster Championship	2nd
Ulster Championship	2nd
Road Racing Ireland Top Ten	6th

1987 - Short Circuits

Aghadowey	250 Rotax	8th
	250 Rotax	5th
Kirkistown	RS125 Honda	7th
	250 Rotax	10th
- Stock Cup		
	250 Rotax	16th
Aghadowey		
In Heat	RS125 Honda	5th
In Final	RS125 Honda	2nd
	250 Rotax	
- Embassy Final		
	250 Rotax	7th
Kirkistown	RS125 Honda	9th
	250 Rotax	11th
Nutts Comer		
	RS125 Honda	6th
	250 Rotax	9th
Aghadowey	RS125 Honda	1st
	250 Rotax	5th
- Race of Year		
	250 Rotax	10th
Kirkistown	RS125 Honda	2nd
	250 Rotax	8th
- King of Kirkistown		
	250 Rotax	10th
Nutts Comer		
	RS125 Honda	5th
Knockhill		
- Round 1	RS125 Honda	1st
- Round 2	RS125 Honda	1st
	250 Rotax	4th
Kirkistown (Sunflower Meeting)		
	RS125 Honda	11th
	250 Rotax	
- Embassy Final		
	250 Rotax	17th

- Sunflower Trophy

250 Rotax	13th

1988 - Road Races

Cookstown 100		
	RS125 Honda	2nd
	RS250 Honda	1st
	TZ350 Yamaha	1st
Tandragee 100		
	RS125 Honda	1st
	RS250 Honda	1st
- Invitation Race		
	RS250 Honda	2nd
	TZ350 Yamaha	3rd
	North West 200	DNF
Skerries	RS125 Honda	1st
	RS250 Honda	1st
- Grand Final		
	RS250 Honda	3rd
Southern 100		
	RS250 Honda	2nd
- Solo Founders Race		
	RS125 Honda	2nd
- 1st Match Race		
	TZ350 Yamaha	4th
- 2nd Match Race		
	TZ350 Yamaha	6th
Temple 100	RS125 Honda	1st
	RS250 Honda	2nd
	TZ350 Yamaha	
Ulster Grand Prix		
	RS250 Honda	6th
	TZ350 Yamaha	6th
Mid-Antrim 150		
	RS125 Honda	1st
	RS250 Honda	1st
	TZ350 Yamaha	3rd
Carrowdore 100		
	RS125 Honda	1st
	RS250 Honda	5th
	TZ350 Yamaha	4th
Killalane	RS125 Honda	1st
	RS250 Honda	1st
- Grand Final		
	TZ350 Yamaha	4th

Manx GP
- Lightweight Race
      RS125 Honda   1st
- Newcomers Race
      RS250 Honda   1st

1988 - Road Racing Championship Results

Irish 125 Championship	1st
Irish 250 Championship	1st
Irish 350 Championship	1st
Ulster 125 Championship	1st
Ulster 250 Championship	1st
Ulster 350 Championship	1st

1988 - Short Circuit Races

Aghadowey	RS125 Honda	DNF
	RS250 Honda	7th
- Enkalon Trophy		
	TZ350 Yamaha	5th
Kirkistown		
- In Heat	RS125 Honda	2nd
- In Final	RS125 Honda	4th
	RS250 Honda	13th
- Embassy Round		
	TZ350 Yamaha	14th
Nutts Corner		
	RS125 Honda	2nd
	RS250 Honda	6th
- Embassy Round		
	TZ350 Yamaha	14th
Kirkistown	RS125 Honda	2nd
	RS250 Honda	2nd
	TZ350 Yamaha	6th
Aghadowey		
	RS250 Honda	1st
Kirkistown		
	RS125 Honda	3rd
	RS250 Honda	1st
- Embassy Round		
	TZ350 Yamaha	4th
Nutts Corner		
	RS250 Honda	4th
- King of the Corner		

	TZ350 Yamaha	7th
Kirkistown		
- Round 1	RS125 Honda	3rd
- Round 2	RS125 Honda	3rd
	RS250 Honda	2nd
- Embassy Final		
	TZ350 Yamaha	2nd
Kirkistown	RS125 Honda	
- Round 1	RS250 Honda	5th
- Round 2	RS250 Honda	2nd
Aghadowey	RS125 Honda	2nd
	RS250 Honda	2nd
Brands Hatch		
	RS125 Honda	5th
	RS250 Honda	10th

1988 - Short Circuit Championship Results

Irish 125 Championship	4th
Irish 250 Championship	5th
Ulster 250 Championship	1st

1989 - Road Races

Cookstown 100		
- Regal 600	600 Kawasaki	DNF
Tandragee 100		
	RS250 Honda	7th
	600 Kawasaki	2nd
Skerries	CBR600 Honda	3rd
	RC30 Honda	2nd
- Grand Final		
	RC30 Honda	2nd
Munster 100		
- Round 1	RS250 Honda	1st
- Round 2	RS250 Honda	1st
	CBR600 Honda	4th
	RC30 Honda	2nd
- Grand Final		
	RC30 Honda	2nd
Fore		
- Round 1	RS250 Honda	1st
- Round 2	RS250 Honda	1st
	CBR600 Honda	3rd
	RC30 Honda	1st

Temple 100	CBR600 Honda	3rd
	RC30 Honda	3rd
Ulster Grand Prix		
	CBR600 Honda	2nd
- F1	RC30 Honda	8th
- King of the Road		
	RC30 Honda	5th
Mid-Antrim 150		
- Regal 600	CBR600 Honda	1st
	RC30 Honda	DNF
Carrowdore 100		
	RC30 Honda	2nd
Killalane	CBR600 Honda	1st
	RC30 Honda	1st
- Grand Final		
	RC30 Honda	1st
Macau Grand Prix		
	RC30 Honda	2nd

1989 - Road Racing Championship Results

Regal 600 Championship	3rd

1989 - Short Circuit Races

Kirkistown		
- Regal 600	600 Kawasaki	8th
Kirkistown		
- Regal 600	600 Kawasaki	4th
- Invitation	600 Kawasaki	3rd
Aghadowey	600 Kawasaki	1st
Kirkistown		
- Regal 600	600 Kawasaki	2nd
- 250 Production		
	KR-1S Kawasaki	1st
- 750 Production		
	750 Kawasaki	5th
Kirkistown		
- In Heat	600 Kawasaki	1st
- In Final	600 Kawasaki	3rd
Aghadowey	RC30 Honda	2nd
- Ace of Aghadowey		
	RC30 Honda	3rd
Nutts Corner	RC30 Honda	2nd
- Invitation	RC30 Honda	2nd

Aghadowey	RS250 Honda	2nd
- Regal 600	CBR600 Honda	1st
	RC30 Honda	1st
- Invitation	RC30 Honda	1st
Aghadowey		
- Regal 600	CBR600 Honda	4th
	RC30 Honda	1st
- John Wallis Trophy		
	RC30 Honda	3rd
Mallory Park	RC30 Honda	1st
	CBR600 Honda	3rd
- Invitation	RC30 Honda	2nd
Kirkistown	RS250 Honda	4th
	CBR600 Honda	3rd
- King of Kirkistown		
	RC30 Honda	5th
Sunflower	RS250 Honda	7th
	CBR600 Honda	6th
- Round 1	RC30 Honda	8th
- Round 2	RC30 Honda	6th
- Sunflower Trophy		
	RC30 Honda	5th
Pembrey		
- Round 1	RC30 Honda	1st
- Round 2	RC30 Honda	1st
	RC30 Honda	1st

1989 - Short Circuit Championship Results

Ulster Short Circuit 1000cc Championship	1st
Ulster Short Circuit 600cc Championship	3rd
The Regal 600cc Championship	3rd

1990 - Road Races

Cookstown 100		
	RC30 Honda	1st
Tandragee 100		
	CBR600 Honda	5th
	RC30 Honda	1st
North West 200		
	RS250 Honda	3rd
- Junior	RS250 Honda	5th

- Supersport		
	CBR600 Honda	7th
- Superbike	RC30 Honda	4th
- NW200	RC30 Honda	2nd
Killinchy 150		
	RS250 Honda	5th
	CBR600 Honda	5th
	RC30 Honda	2nd
Skerries		
- Round 1	RS250 Honda	1st
- Round 2	RS250 Honda	1st
	RC30 Honda	
- Grand Final		
	RC30 Honda	1st
Munster 100		
- Round 1	RS250 Honda	1st
- Round 2	RS250 Honda	2nd
	RC30 Honda	
- Munster 100		
	RC30 Honda	1st
Temple 100	RS250 Honda	2nd
Carrowdore 100		
	RS250 Honda	2nd
	RC30 Honda	1st
Killalane		
- Round 1	RS250 Honda	1st
- Round 2	RS250 Honda	1st
- Grand Final		
	RC30 Honda	2nd
Vila Real - (Portugal) Formula 1		
	RC30 Honda	4th
Kouvla - (Finland) Formula 1		
	RC30 Honda	DNF
Macau Grand Prix		
- 1st leg	RC30 Honda	5th
- 2nd leg	RC30 Honda	5th

1990 - Road Racing Championship Results

Irish 750 Championship	1st
McBrides 250	
Irish Championship	2nd
The Regal 600 Championship	8th
The Gene McDonnell Trophy Winner	

1990 - Short Circuit Races

Kirkistown	RS250 Honda	1st
- Regal 600	CBR600 Honda	4th
	RC30 Honda	1st
- Stock Cup		
	RC30 Honda	1st
Aghadowey		
- Regal 600	CBR600 Honda	3rd
	RC30 Honda	1st
Kirkistown	RS250 Honda	2nd
- Regal 600	CBR600 Honda	3rd
Kirkistown	RS250 Honda	3rd
- Norman Brown Memorial		
	RS250 Honda	3rd
	RC30 Honda	1st
Aghadowey	RS250 Honda	2nd
	RC30 Honda	3rd
Mallory Park	RS 250 Honda	5th
- Round 1	RC30 Honda	2nd
- Round 2	RC30 Honda	3rd
- Round 3	RC30 Honda	3rd
Aghadowey	RS 250 Honda	4th
	RC30 Honda	1st
- Invitation	RC30 Honda	2nd
Aghadowey		
- Celtic Match 1		
	RC30 Honda	2nd
- Celtic Match 2		
	RC30 Honda	2nd
	RS250 Honda	3rd
	CBR600 Honda	3rd
Nutts Corner		
	RS250 Honda	3rd
- King of the Comer		
	RC30 Honda	2nd
Kirkistown (Sunflower Meeting)		
- Round 1	RS250 Honda	5th
- Round 2	RS250 Honda	7th
	CBR600 Honda	7th
- Round 1	RC30 Honda	8th
- Round 2	RC30 Honda	7th
- Sunflower Trophy		
	RC30 Honda	8th

1990 - Short Circuit Championship Results

Irish 250cc Championship		1st
Irish 750cc Championship		2nd

1991 - Road Races

Cookstown 100		
- Regal 600	CBR600 Honda	3rd
	RC30 Honda	1st
Tandragee 100		
	RS250 Honda	1st
- Regal 600	CBR600 Honda	2nd
- Tandragee 100		
	RC30 Honda	1st
North West 200		
- Round 1	RS250 Honda	2nd
- Round 2	RS250 Honda	9th
- Regal 600	CBR600 Honda	1st
Killinchy 150	RS250 Honda	1st
- Regal 600	CBR600 Honda	1st
	RC30 Honda	2nd
Skerries		
- Round 1	RS250 Honda	1st
- Round 2	RS250 Honda	1st
	CBR600 Honda	2nd
- Grand Final		
	RC30 Honda	1st
Fore		
- Round 1	RS250 Honda	2nd
- Round 2	RS250 Honda	2nd
	CBR600 Honda	1st
Munster 100		
- Round 1	RS250 Honda	1st
- Round 2	RS250 Honda	1st
	CBR600 Honda	3rd
- Grand Final		
	RC30 Honda	1st
Dundalk	RS250 Honda	1st
Ulster Grand Prix		
- Round 1	RS250 Honda	1st
- Round 2	RS250 Honda	1st
	CBR400 Honda	1st
	CBR600 Honda	2nd
- Round 1	RC30 Honda	2nd
- Round 2	RC30 Honda	2nd

Mid-Antrim 150		
	RS250 Honda	1st
- Regal 600	CBR600 Honda	1st
	RC30 Honda	1st
Carrowdore 100		
	RS250 Honda	1st
- Regal 600	CBR600 Honda	1st
	RC30 Honda	1st
Killalane		
- Round 1	RS250 Honda	1st
- Round 2	RS250 Honda	1st
	CBR600 Honda	2nd
- Grand Final		
	RC30 Honda	1st
Macau Grand Prix		
- 1st leg	RC30 Honda	4th
- 2nd leg	RC30 Honda	3rd

1991 - Road Racing Championship Results

Irish 250cc Championship		1st
Irish 600cc Championship		1st
Irish 750cc Championship		1st
The Stanley Woods Trophy Winner		
The Walter Rusk Trophy Winner		
The Gene McDonnell Trophy Winner		

1991 - Short Circuit Races

Nutts Corner		
- Regal 600	CBR600 Honda	4th
	RC30 Honda	3rd
- Stock Cup		
	RC30 Honda	3rd
Aghadowey	CBR600 Honda	3rd
	RC30 Honda	2nd
- Enkalon Trophy		
	RC30 Honda	1st
Kirkistown	CBR600 Honda	4th
- Round 1	RC30 Honda	1st
- Round 2	RC30 Honda	1st
- King of Kirkistown		
	RC30 Honda	1st
Nutts Comer		
- Regal 600		

	CBR600 Honda	3rd
	RC30 Honda	1st
Kirkistown	RS250 Honda	1st
	RC30 Honda	2nd
- Norman Brown Memorial		
	RS250 Honda	3rd
Aghadowey	CBR600 Honda	1st
	RC30 Honda	2nd
- John Wallis Trophy		
	RC30 Honda	1st
Mondello Park		
	CBR600 Honda	5th
	RC30 Honda	1st
- Leinster 200		
	RC30 Honda	3rd
Nutts Corner		
- Regal 600	CBR600 Honda	2nd
	RC30 Honda	2nd
- Invitation	RC30 Honda	1st
Aghadowey		
- Regal 600	CBR600 Honda	1st
	RC30 Honda	1st
- Ace of Aghadowey		
	RC30 Honda	2nd
Nutts Corner		
	CBR600 Honda	2nd
	RC30 Honda	1st
- King of the Corner		
	RC30 Honda	1st
Nutts Comer		
	CBR600 Honda	1st
	RC30 Honda	1st
- Race of the Day		
	RC30 Honda	2nd
Kirkistown (Sunflower Meeting)		
- Round 1	RS250 Honda	3rd
- Round 2	RS250 Honda	3rd
- Round 1	RC30 Honda	5th
- Round 2	RC30 Honda	7th
- Sunflower Trophy		
	RC30 Honda	4th

1991 - Short Circuit Championship Results

Irish 600cc Championship	1st
Irish 750cc Championship	1st
Regal 600cc Championship	1st

1992 - Road Races

Cookstown 100		
	RS250 Honda	1st
- Regal 600	CBR600 Honda	1st
- Cookstown 100		
	RC30 Honda	1st
Tandragee 100		
	RS250 Honda	1st
- Regal 600	CBR600 Honda	1st
	RC30 Honda	1st
North West 200		
	RS250 Honda	1st
	CBR400 Honda	1st
- Regal 600	CBR600 Honda	1st
- Superbike	RC30 Honda	1st
- NW 200	RC30 Honda	1st
Temple 100	RS250 Honda	1st
- Regal 600	CBR600 Honda	1st
	RC30 Honda	2nd
Dundalk		
- Round 1	RS250 Honda	1st
- Round 2	RS250 Honda	1st
- Grand Final		
	RC30 Honda	1st
Mid-Antrim 100		
	RS250 Honda	2nd
- Regal 600	CBR600 Honda	6th
	RC30 Honda	1st
Killalane	RS250 Honda	1st
	CBR600 Honda	1st
- Grand Final		
	RC30 Honda	1st
Southern 100		
- Round 1	CBR400 Honda	1st
- Round 2	CBR400 Honda	1st
- Regal 600	CBR600 Honda	1st
	RC30 Honda	1st
- Solo Championship		
	RC30 Honda	1st
Steam Packet Races		
	RS250 Honda	2nd
	RC30 Honda	2nd

1992 - Road Racing Championship Results

Irish McBrides 250cc Championship	1st
Irish Road Race 600cc Championship	1st
Irish Road Racing 750CC Championship	2nd
Gene McDonnell Trophy Winner	

1992 - Short Circuit Races

Daytona 200

- In Heat	RC30 Honda	7th
- Daytona 200	RC30 Honda	DNF
Aghadowey	CBR400 Honda	2nd
- Regal 600	CBR600 Honda	2nd
	RC30 Honda	2nd
Kirkistown	CBR400 Honda	3rd
- 1st Regal 600	CBR600 Honda	1st
- 2nd Regal 600	CBR600 Honda	1st
- Round 1	RC30 Honda	1st
- Round 2	RC30 Honda	2nd
Bishopscourt	CBR400 Honda	1st
- Regal 600	CBR600 Honda	2nd
	RC30 Honda	1st
Nutts Corner		
- Regal 600	CBR600 Honda	2nd

Kirkistown (Sunflower Meeting)

	CBR400 Honda	3rd
- Senior 1	RC30 Honda	5th
- Senior 2	RC30 Honda	6th
	CBR600 Honda	4th
- Sunflower Trophy	RC30 Honda	7th
Cadwell Park	CBR600 Honda	6th
Oulton Park	CBR600 Honda	6th
Brands Hatch	CBR600 Honda	5th

1992 - Short Circuit Championship Results

Regal 600cc Championships	3rd

1993 - Road Races

North West 200

- Junior	RS250 Honda	2nd
- 400 Supersport	CBR400 Honda	5th
- 600 Supersport	CBR600 Honda	7th
- NW 200	RVF750 Honda	3rd
Ulster Grand Prix	RS250 Honda	1st
	CBR600 Honda	1st
	RVF750 Honda	1st
Killalane	RS250 Honda	1st
	CBR600 Honda	1st
	RC30 Honda	1st
- Grand Final	RC30 Honda	1st
Macau Grand Prix		
- 1st leg	RVF750 Honda	DNF
- 2nd leg		4th

1993 - Short Circuit Races

Brands Hatch	RC30 Honda	1st
Knockhill	RC30 Honda	8th
Oulton Park	RC30 Honda	6th
Snetterton		
- Round 1	RC30 Honda	11th
- Round 2	RC30 Honda	11th
Cadwell Park		
- Round 1	RC30 Honda	7th
- Round 2	RC30 Honda	15th
British Grand Prix		
- Superbike	RC30 Honda	7th
Mallory Park		
- Round 1	RC30 Honda	11th
- Round 2	RC30 Honda	9th
Kirkistown (Sunflower Meeting)		
- Round 1	RS250 Honda	4th
- Round 2	RS250 Honda	5th

	CBR600 Honda	5th
- Senior	RC30 Honda	7th
- Sunflower Trophy		
	RC30 Honda	10th

1993 - Short Circuit Championship Results

British Supercup Championship 12th

1994 - Road Races

North West 200

- 1st Junior	RS250 Honda	3rd
- 2nd Junior	RS250 Honda	3rd
- 600 Supersport		
	CBR600 Honda	4th
- Superbike Race 1		
	RC45 Honda	3rd
-NW 200	RC45 Honda	2nd

Ulster Grand Prix

- Round 1	RS250 Honda	1st
- Round 2	RS250 Honda	1st
	CBR600 Honda	1st
- Round 1	RC45 Honda	1st
- Round 2	RC45 Honda	1st
Scarborough	CBR600 Honda	1st
	CBR600 Honda	3rd
	RC45 Honda	2nd
	RC45 Honda	4th
- Gold Cup	RC45 Honda	2nd

Macau Grand Prix

| - 1st leg | 500 V4 Yamaha | 2nd |
| - 2nd leg | | 3rd |

1994 - Short Circuit Races

Kirkistown Euro Championships

| | RCA5 Honda | 1st |
| - Race 2 | RC45 Honda | 1st |

Donington Park

- Supercup	RC45 Honda	14th
	RC45 Honda	14th
Mallory Park	RC45 Honda	9th
	RC45 Honda	9th
Snetterton	RC45 Honda	DNF

	RC45 Honda	8th
Donigton Park		
	RC45 Honda	8th
	RC45 Honda	14th
Oulton Park	RC45 Honda	12th
	RC45 Honda	12th
Brands Hatch		
	RC45 Honda	9th
	RC45 Honda	8th
Pembrey	RC45 Honda	11th
	RC45 Honda	9th
Brands Hatch		
	RCA5 Honda	12th
	RC45 Honda	10th

1994 - Other Short Circuit Races

Kirkistown (Sunflower Meeting)

	CBR600 Honda	2nd
	RC45 Honda	6th
	RC45 Honda	6th
- Sunflower Trophy		
	RC45 Honda	4th

1995 - Road Races

North West 200

- Round 1	RS250 Honda	1st
- Round 2	RS250 Honda	4th
	CBR600 Honda	1st
	RC45 Honda	3rd

North West 200 Race

	RC45 Honda	2nd
Scarborough	CBR600 Honda	1st
	CBR600 Honda	1st
	RS250 Honda	1st
	RS250 Honda	2nd
	RC45 Honda	2nd
	RC45 Honda	2nd
- Gold Cup	RC45 Honda	2nd

Macau Grand Prix

| | 500V4 Yamaha | 2nd |

1995 - Short Circuit Races
Mallory Park
- Supercup CBR600 Honda   6th
Cadwell Park CBR600 Honda   2nd
Donington Park
             CBR600 Honda   3rd
Jerez - Span. GP Thunderbikes
             CBR600 Honda   10th
Nurburgring - German GP
             CBR600 Honda   18th
Monza - Italian GP
             CBR600 Honda   12th
Donington Park - British GP
             CBR600 Honda   8th
Le Mans - French GP
             CBR600 Honda   DNF
Brno - Czech GP
             CBR600 Honda   8th

1996 - Road Races
Cookstown 100
             CBR600 Honda   1st
- Cookstown 100
             RC45 Honda   1st
North West 200
- 1st Junior RS250 Honda   2nd
- 2nd Junior RS250 Honda   DNF
- 600 Supersport
             CBR600 Honda   1st
- Superbike RC45 Honda   2nd
-NW200   RC45 Honda   1st
Scarb'gh Cock 'o' the North
             CBR600 Honda   1st
             RC45 Honda   1st
             RC45 Honda   1st
Ulster Grand Prix
             RS250 Honda   1st
             RS250 Honda   1st
             CBR600 Honda   1st
             RC45 Honda   1st
             RC45 Honda   1st
Macau Grand Prix
             500V4 Yamaha   1st

1996 - Short Circuit Races
Donington Pk. - Thunderbikes
             CBR600 Honda   1st
Thruxton   CBR600 Honda   9th
Oulton Park CBR600 Honda   DNF
Snetterton   CBR600 Honda   1st
Brands Hatch CBR600 Honda   10th
Knock Hill   CBR600 Honda   5th
Cadwell Park CBR600 Honda   5th
Mallory Park CBR600 Honda   DNF
Brands Hatch CBR600 Honda   DNF
Donington Park
             CBR600 Honda   7th

1996 - Short Circuit Racing Championships
British Thunderbike Supercup
Championship   6th

1997 - Road Races
North West 200
- Superbike RC45 Honda   1st
- 600 Supersport
             CBR600 Honda   2nd
- Production CBR900 Honda   2nd
- NW200   RC45 Honda   5th
Macau Grand Prix
             500V4 Yamaha   2nd

1997 - Short Circuit Races
Donington Pk. - 600 Supersport
             CBR600 Honda   1st
Oulton Park CBR900 Honda   DNF
Snetterton   CBR900 Honda   DNF
Brands Hatch CBR600 Honda   16th
Thruxton   CBR600 Honda   2nd
Oulton Park CBR600 Honda   7th
Mallory Park CBR600 Honda   6th
Knockhill   CBR600 Honda   3rd
Thruxton
- Sports Production
             CBR900 Honda   10th
- 2nd leg   CBR900 Honda   10th

1997 - Short Circuit Championship Results
British 600 Supersport
  Championship   8th

1998 - Short Circuit Championship Results
Brands Hatch - 600 Supersport
              CBR600 Honda   15th
Oulton Park CBR600 Honda   3rd
Thruxton   CBR600 Honda   DNF

1999 - Road Races
Tandragee 100
 - Open Event
        F1R1 Yamaha -   2nd
Tandragee 100
        F1R1 Yamaha   1st

North West 200
 - 600 Sup'sport
              R6 Yamaha   2nd
 - 1st Superbike
              F1R1 Yamaha   5th
 - NW200   F1R1 Yamaha   3rd

1999 - Short Circuit Races
Cadwell Park
 - Sports Prod.
              R1 Yamaha   6th
Brands Hatch
 - 600 Supersport
              CBR600 Honda   13th
Thruxton   R6 Yamaha   15th
Oulton Park   R6 Yamaha   7th
 - Sports Prod.
              R1 Yamaha   7th
Mallory Park R1 Yamaha   9th
Donington Park
              R1 Yamaha   DNF

ISLE OF MAN TT RESULTS

	Place	Avg Speed (mph)	Fastest Lap (mph)
1989 TT			
Formula 1	15th	112.01	114.64
750 Production	15th	106.90	109.06
600 Supersport	28th	102.01	107.45
125	7th	98.80	99.81
Senior	17th	110.52	112.51
1990 TT			
Formula 1	39th	101.60	117.74
600 Supersport	14th	105.87	107.80
250 Junior	6th	111.61	113.39
Senior	DNF		107.54
1991 TT			
Formula 1	4th	117.46	120.37
600 Supersport	14th	112.37	113.64
125	4th	104.44	104.32
250 Junior	2nd	114.77	116.75
Senior	3rd	118.35	121.66
1992 TT			
Formula 1	1st	119.80	122.68
600 Supersport	1st	115.04	116.25
400 Supersport	2nd	109.28	111.42
250 Junior	DNF	113.83	
Senior	DNF		121.60
1993 TT			
Formula 1	2nd	117.89	119.73
600 Supersport	7th	113.58	115.24
250 Junior	DNF		114.89
Senior	1st	118.32	120.65
1994 TT			
Formula 1	2nd	118.08	122.08
600 Supersport	4th	114.80	115.53
250 Junior	DNF		115.79
Senior	2nd	117.96	120.39
1995 TT			
Formula 1	1st	117.84	120.85
600 Junior	DNF		116.76
250 Lightweight	4th	114.32	116.37
1996 TT			
Formula 1	1st	116.18	119.41
Production	1st	117.32	118.93
600 Junior	1st	117.65	118.94
250 Lightweight	4th	112.70	116.94
Senior	1st	119.76	122.14
1997 TT			
Formula 1	1st	119.90	122.98
Production	1st	117.12	117.53
600 Junior	2nd	117.65	118.64
250 Lightweight	DNF		116.71
Senior	1st	119.55	122.22
1999 TT			
Formula 1	DNF		
Production	3rd	118.30	116.56
600 Junior	7th	119.50	117.60

Laps at 120mph plus: In Practice

Year	mph
1992	120.48
1994	120.71
1994	120.44
1994	121.15
1995	120.84
1995	120.33
1997	120.90
1997	121.52

Laps at 120mph plus: In Races

Year	mph
1991	120.37
1991	121.66
1992	120.43
1992	120.97
1992	120.90
1992	122.68
1992	120.26
1992	121.60
1993	120.65
1993	120.56
1993	120.11
1994	120.18
1994	122.08
1994	120.39
1994	120.10
1994	120.01
1995	120.85
1995	120.41
1996	121.69
1996	122.14
1996	121.59
1996	120.03
1997	122.98
1997	122.40
1997	121.43
1997	121.19
1997	121.45
1997	121.18
1997	121.39
1997	122.22

Printed in Great Britain
by Amazon